JOURNAL FOR THE STUDY OF THE NEW TESTAMENT SUPPLEMENT SERIES

42

Executive Editor, Supplement Series
David Hill

Publishing Editor
David E. Orton

JSOT Press
Sheffield

MATTHEW'S INCLUSIVE STORY

A Study in the Narrative Rhetoric of the First Gospel

David B. Howell

Journal for the Study of the New Testament
Supplement Series 42

To
Glo Howell

Published by JSOT Press
JSOT Press is an imprint of
Sheffield Academic Press Ltd
The University of Sheffield
343 Fulwood Road
Sheffield S10 3BP
England

Typeset by Sheffield Academic Press
and
Printed in Great Britain
by Billing & Sons Ltd
Worcester

British Library Cataloguing in Publication Data
Howell, David B.
    Matthew's inclusive story
    1. Bible. N.T. Matthew—Critical studies
    I. Title   II. Series

ISSN 0143-5108
ISBN 1-85075-236-2

CONTENTS

Chapter 6
CONCLUSION: JESUS AS EXEMPLARY

ACKNOWLEDGMENTS

This book is a revision of my 1988 doctoral thesis which was presented to the Theology Faculty of Oxford University. I am indebted to a number of people who have helped me reach this point. I hope that my footnotes in the book give adequate credit to the tradition of scholarship which preceded this work. It remains for me to give personal acknowledgment to some in particular who have aided me in this project. First of all, to my parents, Dr and Mrs James Howell, and my wife's parents, Mr and Mrs Richard Osborn, for their encouragement and financial support during our stay in England. To staff and fellow graduate students of Regent's Park College, Oxford, for providing an atmosphere and fellowship congenial to study. To Canon John C. Fenton, who initially guided my research and shared his infectious enthusiasm for Gospel studies. To Rev. Robert C. Morgan, who introduced me to literary criticism and supervised this thesis to its conclusion. His critical acumen and patient counsel saved me from many errors and enabled me to make a clearer presentation than would otherwise have been the case.

Gratitude must also be expressed to those who assisted in the revision of the thesis. To Gary Phelps of William Jewell College, Liberty, Missouri, who has allowed me time away from my administrative duties at the college to teach some and revise the thesis. To David Hill, David Orton, and the editorial staff at JSOT Press for editorial assistance in transforming a doctoral thesis into a book.

Finally, I must express thanks to my family. To my parents again, Dr and Mrs James Howell, who not only inculcated in their son the value of learning, but who also first taught him, at an early age, how to read the stories of the Bible. To my son Andrew, who has endured his father's divided attention these past three years. And to my wife, Glo, who has not only shared in my dream but whose love, encouragement, and support has helped more than anyone else turn it into reality. This book is dedicated to her.

ABBREVIATIONS

AnaBib	Analecta Biblica
ATR	*Anglican Theological Review*
Bib	*Biblica*
BJRL	*Bulletin of the John Rylands Library*
BThB	*Biblical Theology Bulletin*
BZ	*Biblische Zeitschrift*
CBQ	*Catholic Biblical Quarterly*
CBQMS	Catholic Biblical Quarterly Monograph Series
EKK	Evangelisch-Katholischer Kommentar zum Neuen Testament
ETL	*Ephemerides Theologicae Lovanienses*
ExpT	*Expository Times*
FRLANT	Forschungen zur Religion und Literatur des Alten und Neuen Testaments
Int	*Interpretation*
JAAR	*Journal of the American Academy of Religion*
JBL	*Journal of Biblical Literature*
JR	*Journal of Religion*
JSNT	*Journal for the Study of the New Testament*
JTS	*Journal of Theological Studies*
KuD	*Kerygma und Dogma*
NovT	*Novum Testamentum*
NovTSup	Supplements to Novum Testamentum
NTAbh	Neutestamentliche Abhandlungen
NTS	*New Testament Studies*
PTMS	Pittsburgh Theological Monograph Series
SANT	Studien zum Alten und Neuen Testament
SBLDS	Society of Biblical Literature Dissertation Series
SBS	Stuttgarter Bibelstudien
SBT	Studies in Biblical Theology
SJT	*Scottish Journal of Theology*

SNTSMS	Society for New Testament Studies Monograph Series
ST	*Studia Theologica*
TDNT	*Theological Dictionary of the New Testament*
ThSt	*Theological Studies*
TIM	*Tradition and Interpretation in Matthew*
WUNT	Wissenschaftliche Untersuchungen zum Neuen Testament
ZNW	*Zeitschrift für die Neutestamentliche Wissenschaft*
ZThK	*Zeitschrift für Theologie und Kirche*

Chapter 1

INTRODUCTION

A. *The Problem*

The Gospels can be read and used in a variety of different ways: they can be used as sources for historical information about either Jesus or the communities for which they were written; they can function as the basis for theological propositions or ethical guidelines; they can be read devotionally; or they can serve liturgical purposes in the prayers and worship of the church.[1] While Matthew can be read for these purposes, it is not a historical account, a theological tract, a rule of discipline, or a liturgical formulary. The text type of the Gospel is narrative, and it can be read as a story with its own integrity rather than as a collection of traditional units and pericopae.[2]

1 Cf. Anthony C. Thiselton, 'Reader-Response Hermeneutics, Action Models, and the Parables of Jesus', in *The Responsibility of Hermeneutics*, Roger Lundin, Anthony C. Thiselton, and Clarence Walhout (Exeter: Paternoster, 1985), p. 112. He has written in the context of discussing an action model for hermeneutics that 'the Bible may be understood on different levels. In other words, its text performs a variety of actions on the reader, and the reader's repertoire of interpretive responses themselves constitute a varied range of actions'. See also Christopher Tuckett, *Reading the New Testament: Methods of Interpretation* (London: SPCK, 1987), p. 1.

2 An emphasis upon the narrative character of the Gospels is not limited to scholars who are interested in using literary criticism to interpret the Gospels. Others operating within the parameters of the more traditional historical critical paradigm also recognize the importance of the narrative text type of the Gospels. For example, see Ulrich Luz, *Das Evangelium nach Matthäus (Mt. 1-7)* (EKK I/1; Neukirchen: Neukirchener Verlag, 1985), pp. 24ff.; Robert Guelich, 'The Gospel Genre', in *Das Evangelium und die Evangelien*, ed. Peter Stuhlmacher (WUNT 28; Tübingen: J.C.B. Mohr, 1983), p. 219.

Telling a story involves what Robert Tannehill calls 'narrative rhetoric' because 'the story is constructed in order to influence its readers and particular literary techniques are used for this purpose'.[1] A narrative world is constructed or projected by the Gospel within which the narrative events occur. It is populated by the story's characters, structured according to a particular system of values, and the reader is invited to inhabit imaginatively this world. An important part of the narrative rhetoric of Matthew is that the Gospel does not simply tell the past story of Jesus' life. A recent commentator has labelled the narrative an 'inclusive story' because of the double horizon visible in the Gospel.[2] On the one hand Matthew operates within a linear-temporal framework that is concerned with the story of the earthly Jesus and his disciples. On the other hand the evangelist appears to address the members of his community throughout the Gospel, telling a story and interpreting discourses for a later audience without exhibiting any apparent concern to establish the sense the story had for earlier audiences.[3] The so-called mission dis-

Both men contend that Matthew must be read as a narrative whole. Guelich writes that 'the exegetical atomization of the Gospels leads to the distortion of the literary products' (p. 219).

1 Robert C. Tannehill, *The Narrative Unity of Luke-Acts: A Literary Interpretation*. Vol. 1: *The Gospel According to Luke* (Philadelphia: Fortress, 1986), p. 8, cf. p. 4.

2 Luz, *Matthäus*, p. 58. Cf. Ulrich Luz and Peter Lampe ('Diskussionsüberblick', in *Das Evangelium und die Evangelien*, p. 424), who have written that Matthew 'erzählt eine "inclusive story", eine Geschichte in der die Gegenwart in Gestalt der Jünger in das Geschick des irdischen Jesu eingeschlossen ist'. In this respect Matthew is similar to Mark, whereas Luke has written an 'incomplete story' in his Gospel which is followed by another volume (Acts) where the ministry and mission of Jesus is linked up with the history of the early church. See. I. Howard Marshall, 'Luke and his "Gospel"', *Das Evangelium*, pp. 293ff., 299 for a defense of this characterization of the synoptic Gospels.

3 This feature is not unique to Matthew but appears as a characteristic of the other Gospels as well as religious literature in general. Cf. W.A. Beardslee (*Literary Criticism of the New Testament* [Philadelphia: Fortress, 1970], p. 21), who writes that 'one characteristic of the Gospel form is thus its combination of two distinct functions of

course in ch. 10 provides us with a clear example of the tension between these two horizons in the Gospel. Instructions which are ostensibly given to the disciples for a pre-Easter mission to Israel also seem directed to the post-Easter Matthean community since they reflect the experiences of the post-Easter mission (10.17ff.). The disciples in the Gospel thus appear as historical persons, companions of the earthly Jesus in one reading, while being transparent for the Matthean community when seen from a different perspective.[1]

Traditional biblical scholarship has usually discussed these two perspectives in the Gospels on the basis of historical and theological rather than literary categories. The issues are debated in terms of a historical reconstruction of the evangelist's theology and placed in the historical context of his community.[2] In Matthean studies, for example, the theological concept of salvation history has often been used as the interpretive category which attempts to encapsulate the two horizons in the Gospel. Georg Strecker's thesis emphasizes the

---

religious narrative: the reenactment of the past and the leading into the future'; cf. also Robert A. Polzin's comments about Deuteronomy in 'Literary and Historical Criticism of the Bible: A Crisis in Scholarship'. in *Orientation by Disorientation. Studies in Literary Criticism and Biblical Literary Criticism*, ed. Richard A. Spencer (PTMS 35; Pittsburgh: Pickwick, 1980), pp. 108-11.

1 In recent years scholars have debated whether the disciples function in a 'historicizing' or a 'transparent' manner in Matthew. See Georg Strecker, *Der Weg der Gerechtigkeit* (FRLANT 82. Göttingen: Vandenhoeck & Ruprecht, 1962), who is a leading proponent of the historicizing interpretation, while Ulrich Luz, 'The Disciples in the Gospel according to Matthew', in *The Interpretation of Matthew*, ed., G.N. Stanton, Issues in Religion and Theology 3 (London: SPCK, 1983), pp. 98-128, criticizes Strecker's position and argues for a transparency interpretation. Matthew can still be seen as an inclusive story in either interpretation. Even with Strecker's historicizing reading of the Gospel, the time of the church is included in the Gospel narrative.

2 See. J.D. Kingsbury, 'Reflections on "The Reader" of Matthew's Gospel', *NTS* 34 (1988), pp. 445-54, for a discussion of this tendency in redaction criticism to equate Matthew's primary reader with his intended reader (i.e. a member of the evangelist's church living at the end of the first century).

historicizing perspective in the Gospel narrative.[1] He proposes that the problem of the delay of the parousia was resolved by the evangelist with a salvation history theology in which the time of Jesus is treated as a past epoch. Others such as J.D. Kingsbury emphasize the element of transparency in the narrative by constructing a two-fold scheme of Matthean salvation history theology in which the time of the church is included in the time of Jesus. The disciples are thus representative of Christians in the evangelist's church, and Matthew is able to assert 'the unbroken continuity and legitimacy of the tradition of doctrine and practice observed by his own community'.[2]

In neither interpretation is the historicizing or transparency element in the narrative considered absolute, but the different narrative perspectives are discussed within parameters defined by the reconstructed historical situation of a Christian community and the theology of an evangelist at the end of the first century CE.[3] There seems to be an underlying assumption that the message of the Gospel is a set of theological propositions, and that its inclusive nature should be interpreted in static categories which have been mined from the text.[4] The issues at stake in the debate can, however, be recast

1 See Strecker, *Weg*, pp. 45-47, 184ff.
2 Kingsbury, *Jesus Christ in Matthew, Mark, and Luke* (Philadelphia: Fortress, 1981), p. 87. Cf. Kingsbury, *Matthew, Structure, Christology, Kingdom* (London: SPCK, 1976), pp. 31-37.
3 For Strecker, Peter functions as a typological or transparent portrayal of the Christian life of individuals in Matthew's church. He thus bursts the constraints of the historical 'Einmaligkeit' of the life of Jesus (*Weg*, p. 205). Peter also has a 'salvation-historical' primacy in Kingsbury's interpretation as well as a representative role ('The Figure of Peter in Matthew's Gospel as a Theological Problem', *JBL* 98 [1979], p. 71). With respect to miraculous activity, Kingsbury believes Matthew posits 'something of a disjuncture between ministry of the earthly Jesus and of pre-Easter disciples and ministry of the post-Easter Church ('The Verb *Akolouthein* ('To Follow') as an Index of Matthew's View of His Community', *JBL* 97 [1978], p. 70). The empowering of the disciples by Jesus in the mission to Israel (10.1, 8) is thus exceptional (p. 72).
4 Richard A. Edwards, 'Uncertain Faith: Matthew's Portrayal of the Disciples', in *Discipleship in the New Testament*, ed. Fernando F.

in literary categories which are more sensitive to the movement and dynamism of the story. That is to say, questions about the 'inclusive' nature of Matthew's narrative could be formulated as questions concerning how readers of the gospel are to appropriate and involve themselves in the story and teaching of the Gospel.[1] Who is 'included' in Matthew's story and how are they 'included'? Are literary techniques used which help structure a reader's response to the story and its message? If so, how do they function?

This book is an attempt, with the help of selected aspects of narrative criticism and a type of reader-response criticism, to describe the narrative rhetoric of Matthew in order to understand better the inclusive nature of the narrative. Our approach to the question of a reader's response to Matthew will be bifocal: it will examine the narrative structure to be realized and the structured act of realization.[2] It is hoped that a literary approach to the Gospel rather than the use of a more

Segovia (Philadelphia: Fortress, 1985), p. 47, describes this approach in the following way: 'the Gospel of Matthew is viewed as an essay in story form—that is, as a static construction in which each statement and incident are given equal weight'.

1 In this respect, traditional methods of biblical interpretation have also been concerned with the role of the reader even if it has not been recognized. That is to say, the realization of a text has always been the concern of a reader. Cf. Luz, 'Disciples', p. 111, where he writes that for Matthew 'transparency in the disciple concept means becoming contemporary with a figure of the past'. Luz applies the concept of transparency to the situation of a historical community at the end of the first century CE, but the concern of how to appropriate the Gospel material is also relevant to modern readers, and can thus be explored by literary methods. In fact, the only way a reader can become 'contemporary with a figure of the past' is through imaginative participation in the story, and this process can be described most easily with literary critical categories. Cf. Tannehill (*Narrative Unity*, p. 8), who describes Luke–Acts as 'a system of influence which may be analyzed in literary terms'.

2 Wolfgang Iser's definition of the 'implied reader' describes this dual focus: 'This term incorporates both the prestructuring of the potential meaning by the text, and the reader's actualization of this potential through the reading process' (*The Implied Reader. Patterns of Communication in Prose Fiction from Bunyan to Beckett* [London: Johns Hopkins University Press, 1974], p. xii.

traditional historical or theological paradigm will provide the critic with a different repertoire of interpretive devices and categories which can shed light both on the mechanisms used by the evangelist to communicate his message and on the ways a reader responds to and appropriates that message when the gospel is read. Since there are no basic facts of reading which are independent of interpretation,[1] our description of Matthew's narrative rhetoric will also develop the thesis that the disciples are not to be equated with the readers included or implied in the story. Discipleship is not membership in a character group but acceptance of the value system espoused by Jesus. Since he embodies these values and virtues in his life, he functions as a model for discipleship in Matthew.

B. *Narrative Criticism and the Literary Paradigm*

The use of narrative criticism to interpret Matthew involves a shift in critical assumptions and strategies from those used in the prevailing historical critical paradigm of biblical studies. We will thus outline some of the limitations of the historical critical paradigm in providing a theoretical framework for explicating how readers appropriate the Gospel and create meaning in their involvement with the narrative, before going on to delineate the critical presuppositions of our literary paradigm. The designation 'historical critical paradigm' is used in an inclusive sense with the awareness that it is dubious to speak of *the* historical critical paradigm when there is actually a plurality of historical methods.[2] W.S. Vorster's definition of 'historical paradigm' as 'a broad and general term for presuppositions, values, beliefs, techniques and historical methods which are used to provide perspectives on and to manipulate the data of the New Testament and primitive Christianity' is adequate for our purpose.[3] A similar inclusive

1 See Steven Mailloux, *Interpretive Conventions: The Reader in the Study of American Fiction* (London: Cornell University Press, 1982), p. 206.
2 Cf. Martin Hengel, 'Historische Methoden und theologische Auslegung des Neuen Testaments', *KuD* 19 (1973), p. 85.
3 W.S. Vorster, 'The Historical Paradigm—Its Possibilities and Limitations', *Neotestamentica* 18 (1984), p. 105.

sense is intended by the use of the term literary or reader-response paradigm, for it too comprehends a variety of different literary methods and presuppositions.

1. *Limitations of the Historical Critical Paradigm and the Move to a Literary Paradigm in Gospel Studies*

Biblical texts exhibit three closely related and interdependent features: a historical, a structural, and a theological dimension.[1] In the synoptic Gospels the historical dimension is two-fold. First, it is represented in their reference to past historical events such as the life and crucifixion of Jesus. Second, it is present in the existence of the text as a historical phenomenon with its own history; that is, the Gospels reflect the process of transmission of material as well as the time and communities in which they were written. The structural dimension of the synoptic Gospels refers to the fact that we encounter the Gospels in the form of a specific literary structure. Not only does the text exhibit certain grammatical and semantic features; equally, the various parts of the Gospel are related to each other in the text as a literary whole. Finally, the theological dimension of the Gospels means that the texts contain statements about God and humankind with specific theological and soteriological import.

Traditional historical critical methods used in the interpretation of the Gospels have focused primarily on the historical and theological dimensions of the text. The Gospels are read for the information they contain either about the historical Jesus or about the theology of the evangelist and the historical situation of the community for which he wrote.[2] Even when

---

1 Bernard C. Lategan, 'Some Unresolved Methodological Issues in New Testament Studies', in *Text and Reality*: *Aspects of Reference in Biblical Texts*, Bernard C. Lategan and Willem S. Vorster (SBL Semeia Studies; Philadelphia, Fortress, 1985), p. 5.

2 Hans W. Frei, *The Eclipse of Biblical Narrative* (London: Yale University Press, 1974), pp. 151ff., 179f., and John Barton, *Reading the Old Testament*, *Method in Biblical Study* (London: Darton, Longman & Todd, 1984), pp. 161ff., have observed that English scholarship and German scholarship have been predominantly characterized by different approaches to the information conveyed in the biblical texts: English scholarship is more concerned with the historical factuality

the structural dimension of the Gospels has been examined, as in form criticism for example, the studies have usually been restricted to historical concerns.[1] Form critics conceived their task to be the reconstruction of the origin and history of the small units of tradition in the Gospels. Once the originally independent traditional units had been identified, the different forms were related to specific sociological or institutionalized activities of the early Christian communities which transmitted the traditions.[2] In this way literary and aesthetic considerations of the Gospels as whole narrative texts were avoided in much traditional historical critical exegesis. Form criticism was concerned with the small units of tradition, and redaction criticism focused on the editorial seams as indicators of an evangelist's theology.

In recent years, however, some scholars have become dissatisfied with the historical critical paradigm which tended to operate by dissection, cutting up the biblical narrative texts into their smallest component parts. While it is acknowledged that historical critical methods illumine some of the dimensions of the biblical text, certain limitations in providing an overall perspective for understanding narrative texts are also recognized.[3] Perhaps the most fundamental limitation in the

of the events narrated, and German scholarship is more concerned with the ideas communicated.

1 In recent years two exceptions can be found in the work of Erhardt Güttgemanns, *Candid Questions Concerning Gospel Form Criticism. A Methodological Sketch of the Fundamental Problematics of Form and Redaction Criticism*, transl. W.G. Doty (PTMS 26; Pittsburgh: Pickwick, 1979); and Gerd Theissen, *Miracle Stories of the Early Christian Tradition*, transl. F. McDonagh (Edinburgh: T & T Clark, 1983).

2 See Rudolf Bultmann, *The History of the Synoptic Tradition*, transl. J. Marsh (Oxford: Basil Blackwell, 1963), pp. 3-4, for example. Edgar V. McKnight (*The Bible and the Reader. An Introduction to Literary Criticism* [Philadelphia: Fortress, 1985], p. xv) has observed that form criticism 'emphasized the historical situation of the community as the matrix for the development of the forms of the Gospel narratives'.

3 See Norman Petersen, *Literary Criticism for New Testament Critics* (Philadelphia: Fortress, 1978), pp. 9-28, and 'Literary Criticism in Biblical Studies', in *Orientation by Disorientation*, pp. 25-50; Vorster,

traditional historical critical paradigm is its disregard for the narrative integrity of the Gospel stories. Because of the historical paradigm's interest in the development of the Gospel traditions, the tendency is to disintegrate the narrative text as it now stands. Form criticism sought to get behind the Gospels in order to study the transmission of the small units of tradition about Jesus. Literary criticism in this paradigm has become source criticism, as is seen when Klaus Koch writes:

> Properly understood, literary criticism can now only be considered as a branch, along with many others, of form criticism. It is that aspect of form criticism which is concerned with the transmission of books, tracing their development right back to their many written sources.[1]

Redaction criticism may be seen as a movement towards the reintegration of the narrative, but even it is still concerned with the separation of tradition from redaction. The redaction critic is interested in the theology expressed in the finished Gospel, but it is assumed that this can best be found in the editorial activity of the evangelist.[2] The effect of focusing on the

'Historical Paradigm'; Archie L. Nations, 'Historical Criticism and the Current Methodological Crisis', *SJT* 36 (1983), pp. 59-71; and O.C. Edwards, 'Historical-Critical Method's Failure of Nerve and a Prescription for a Tonic: A Review of Some Recent Literature', *ATR* 59 (1977), pp. 115-34, for general discussions of recent dissatisfaction with and critiques of historical critical methods for interpreting the New Testament.

1 Klaus Koch, *The Growth of the Biblical Tradition. The Form-Critical Method*, transl. S.M. Cupitt (New York: Scribner's, 1969), p. 77. Cf. K. Grobel's essay 'Biblical Criticism', *Interpreter's Dictionary of the Bible*, Vol. 1, p. 412, where he defines biblical literary criticism as the process in which 'the critic must ask himself whether the writing before him is integral or composite'. Norman Petersen, 'Literary Criticism', p. 27, argues that literary criticism so conceptualized is concerned with 'textually-*dis*integrative features' rather than 'textually-integrative features'.

2 Cf. the description of the redaction critic's activity and assumptions by B. Van Iersel and A. Linmans, "The story on the lake" Mk iv 35-41 and Mt viii 18-27 in the light of Form Criticism, '"Redaktionsgeschichte" and Structural Analysis', in *Supplement to Novum Testamentum 48, Miscellanea Neotestamentica*, vol. 2, ed. T. Baarda, A.F.J. Klijn, and W.C. Van Unnik (Leiden: Brill, 1978), pp. 44ff.

preliterary parts of the Gospel narrative in the historical critical paradigm, however, has been to dissolve the sense of a narrative whole.[1] The traditional historical critical paradigm has
not been able to explore adequately the narrative dimension of
the Gospels, because it simply has not always appreciated the
Gospels as texts with their own integrity. Although the final
narrative text may in some ways resemble a mosaic, it was
intended to be read as a homogeneous whole.

This tendency of the historical critical paradigm to disintegrate the Gospel narratives can be seen as part of a more general historicist approach to literary texts. Scholars working
with the traditional paradigm are concerned with the genesis
of a text: with the original author's meaning and intention,
and with the immediate historical and cultural context which
called forth the Gospel and in which it received.[2] The primary

They write that the redaction critic 'attaches the most value to what
the author revised in his source. Generally that which the author
added or changed is considered more important than what he
adopts. One can ask oneself what the reason for this is. One will
receive nowhere an explicit answer, but one can surmise that this
sort of active operations on a given text are assumed to require more
attention from the author than the more passive acceptance'.

1   Cf. Robert Tannehill, 'Tension in Synoptic Sayings and Stories', *Int*
    34 (1980), p. 148, who has written of Mark that 'preoccupation with
    the pre-Gospel units of tradition and with the editorial modification
    of those units obscured the fact that Mark is a continuous narrative
    presenting a meaningful development to a climax and that each
    episode should be understood in light of its relation to the story as a
    whole'.

2   John Barton has astutely pointed out that it has not been the case
    that the concerns of biblical scholars operating within the historical
    critical paradigm were not literary, but that their concerns were
    essentially historical interests shared with secular literary critics
    before the rise of New Criticism: 'the quest for the original author's
    meaning and intention; to studying texts in their historical context;
    and to aproaching them as vehicles through which ideas were con-
    veyed, rather than as art objects in their own right'. The biblical
    scholar has thus not been so much 'out of *touch*' with literary criti-
    cism as 'out of *date*' (*Reading the OT*, pp. 155). Cf. also Terry Eagle-
    ton, *Literary Theory: An Introduction* (Oxford: Basil Blackwell,
    1983), p. 74, who argues that the history of modern literary theory
    could be periodized in roughly 3 stages: 'a preoccupation with the

task of the biblical critic thus conceptualized is determining what the text 'meant' in the mind of the author and in its reception by its first readers.[1] With this approach, however, what one ends up examining in order to understand the Gospel is not the narrative text but something external to the text. George Stroup describes the historical critical *modus operandi* in biblical studies in the following way:

> Understanding the text means looking behind or outside of the text at its development or formation, historical setting, the theological intentions of the author, and at parallels in other religious or cultural traditions.[2]

The starting point of exegesis is therefore often not the texts as they have actually come down to us but some hypothetical historical situation or hypothetical 'text' within the extant document.[3]

author (Romanticism and the nineteenth century); an exclusive concern with the text (New Criticism); and a marked shift of attention to the reader over recent years'. The concerns of traditional historical biblical criticism would be those shared with the first period in Eagleton's scheme.

1 Krister Stendahl gives expression to this historicist concern in his article, 'Biblical Theology, Contemporary', *Interpreter's Dictionary of the Bible*, Vol. 1, pp. 418-31, where he draws a distinction between the descriptive task ('what it meant') and the hermeneutical task ('what it means') in biblical theology. The former task consists of an objective, historical description of the theology in the biblical texts. Cf. I. Howard Marshall's remarks in his introductory essay in the collection of essays he edited (*New Testament Interpretation: Essays on Principles and Methods* [Exeter: Paternoster, 1977], p. 15), where the aim 'to discover what the text meant in the mind of its original author for his intended audience' is distinguished from 'reaching a meaning for ourselves'.

2 George Stroup, *The Promise of Narrative Theology* (London: SCM, 1984), p. 141.

3 Cf. Schuyler Brown, 'Biblical Philology, Linguistics and the Problem of Method', *Heythrop Journal* 20 (1979), p. 297, who has written that 'even those scholars using the same discipline often come to diametrically opposed conclusions because they start with different unverifiable assumptions concerning the historical situation out of which the books were written. All too often the exegete takes as his starting point a hypothetical reconstruction of earliest Christianity,

The limitations of a textually disintegrative and historicist approach in the historical critical paradigm resulted in a failure by biblical critics to appreciate the narrative character of the Gospel texts. The Gospels came to be read for the information they contain, and the story simply seemed to be considered as a vehicle for this information. Using an image first proposed by Murray Krieger, the historical critical paradigm treated the narrative of the Gospels as 'windows' through which the critic looked at historical events or theological ideas.[1] Reading the Gospels merely for the historical or theological information they contain, however, involves a reduction of the richness of the narrative at best, and may at worst make the story form in which the information is communicated irrelevant and dispensable, once the informational content is extracted.[2] The adequacy of the traditional historical critical paradigm is thus limited in providing an overall perspective for reading the Gospels, because it overlooks the ways narrative can involve readers and disclose new possibilities for understanding and existence.[3]

rather than the texts which have actually come down to us'.

1 Murray Krieger, *A Window to Criticism: Shakespeare's Sonnets and Modern Poetics* (Princeton University, 1964), p. 34. Krieger's images of the 'window' and the 'mirror' are used by both Petersen, *Literary Criticism*, pp. 19, 24ff. and R. Alan Culpepper, *Anatomy of the Fourth Gospel: A Study in Literary Design* (Fortress, 1984), pp. 3ff. Cf. the remarks by Anthony Thiselton, 'Reader-Response Hermeneutics', p. 100. Thiselton contrasts this type of historical inquiry 'which uses texts merely as tools for the reconstruction of ideas or events by the religious historian with the kind of historical inquiry which proceeds in order to do full justice to the texts themselves'. In the case of the Gospels, 'to do full justice to the text' means to take the narrative character of the Gospel seriously.

2 Cf. Werner H. Kelber, 'Apostolic Tradition and the Form of the Gospel', in *Discipleship in the New Testament*, pp. 32ff., who offers two principal causes for the disregard of the narrative character of the Gospels in the traditional historical critical paradigm: (1) a difficulty in appreciating 'the story about Jesus apart from reference to historical actuality', and (2) a hidden assumption that 'a Gospel functions as carrier of ideational content'.

3 Bernard C. Lategan ('Reference: Reception, Redescription, and Reality', in *Text and Reality*, p. 92), describes the mediating and

For biblical scholars who have moved toward a literary paradigm in their studies,[1] the meaning of biblical narratives such as the Gospels is not something which could be detached from the text and stated independently of the narrative. The stories are considered valuable for more than just the information which can be extracted from them.[2] Special attention is given by this new breed of biblical literary critical not only to the way a narrative's component parts interrelate as part of the narrative, but also to its effects upon the reader and to the way it achieves these effects.[3]

transforming role of narrative in the following way: 'It is precisely because of the persuasive powers of the narrative to depict a world which is familiar enough to recognize, but different enough to be inviting, that the evangelists use the narrative form'. Cf. Robert Tannehill's remark that 'biblical scholars ought to have a greater awareness of how stories are told and how they communicate' ('The Disciples in Mark: The Function of a Narrative Role', *JR* 57 [1977], p. 387).

1 Recent examples in Gospel studies of such an approach, to name just a few, are found in Petersen, *Literary Criticism*; J.D. Kingsbury, *Matthew as Story* (Philadelphia: Fortress, 1986); David Rhoads and Donald Michie, *Mark as Story. An Introduction to the Narrative of the Gospel* (Philadelpha: Fortress, 1982); Culpepper, *Anatomy of the Fourth Gospel*; Robert J. Karris, *Luke: Artist and Theologian. Luke's Passion Account as Literature* (New York: Paulist Press, 1985); and the essays in *Neotestamentica* 18 (1984) and *Semeia 31* (1985), which are primarily devoted to reader-response interpretations. See Robert C. Tannehill, *The Sword of His Mouth: Forceful and Imaginative Language in Synoptic Sayings* (SBL Semeia Studies 1; Philadephia: Fortress, 1975), for an example of a literary approach to the sayings material.

2 Cf. James Barr, 'The Bible as Literature', in *The Bible in the Modern World* (London: SCM, 1973), p. 70, who argues that 'in so far as a work is really literary and not merely informational in its scope and character,... it does not have a detachable meaning which can be stated in some other way'. Barton, *Reading the OT*, pp. 163ff., cites the creation accounts in Gen. 1-2 as examples of Biblical narrative which are often construed as conveying either historical information about the creation of the world, or theological propositions such as 'God made the world'. Both interpretations replace the narrative with discursive informational statements.

3 Cf. W.S. Vorster, 'Kerygma/History and the Gospel Genre', *NTS* 29 (1983), pp. 91-93, where he contends that the narrative nature of the

Such critics consider the primary reference in the text or story to be the narrative world of the Gospel rather than some historical event or theological idea which lies behind the text. This narrative world is a reality which is a creation of the author of the Gospel who presents to his readers a world of 'characters, actions, settings, and events which constitute the narrative'.[1] Literary critics are convinced that even if an author remains as true as possible to the 'real world' when he or she composes a narrative, 'the resemblance between narrative world and real world cannot be seen as a one to one relationship'.[2] The interpreter of the Gospel must therefore

text is more important to understanding the Gospel genre than either the kerygmatic or historical model. The Gospels should be read as story and not as sermon or history. See Barton, *Reading the OT*, pp. 16ff. and 199ff., who argues that the goal of any literary criticism is 'literary competence' which he defines with the concept of 'genre-recognition'. An interpreter is literarily competent who knows '*what sorts of questions it makes sense to ask*' of a particular work (p. 17); that is, what the text should be 'read as' (p. 199). Literary critical methods recognize the primacy of the narrative nature of the Gospel texts when they help the interpreter to read the Gospels as narrative. See Gerald L. Bruns, 'Intention, Authority, and Meaning', *Critical Inquiry* 7 (1980), pp. 300, n. 5, 303, for a discussion of the 'reading-as' nature of interpretations.

1 M.H. Abrams, *A Glossary of Literary Terms* (4th edn; New York: Holt, Rinehart and Winston, 1981), p. 143.

2 W.S. Vorster, 'Meaning and Reference: The Parables of Jesus in Mark 4'. In *Text and Reality*, p. 61. The reason such a one to one correspondence between the two works is impossible is because narrative is always 'the remaking of reality' (ibid., pp. 60ff.). In a similar vein Nicholas Wolterstorff (*Art in Action: Toward a Christian Aesthetic* [Grand Rapids: Eerdmans, 1980], p. 125) writes that even when the world of a work of art 'is not incompatible with the actual world, that is, even when everything constituting the world of the work actually occurs, still the world of the work is only a *segment* of the actual world, never the whole of it. Thus the world of a work of art is always distinct from the actual world'. Cf. also the remarks of R. Alan Culpepper, who uses the image of a 'window' to describe the Gospels as 'stained glass windows': 'Light shines through from the other side, but the figures are on the surface of the window, fashioned there by the literary artist' ('Story and History in the Gospel', *Review and Expositor* 81 (1984), p. 471). Hans Frei (*Eclipse of Biblical Narrative*, p. 16) thus describes the biblical story as

guard against committing the 'referential fallacy' which consists of 'construing the signifier alone as the sign and as referring directly to the real world object, without regard to the
signified as the conceptual aspect of the sign'.[1] When the conceptual autonomy of the narrative world of the Gospel is recognized and respected, historical questions concerning the
events or theology refered to in the Gospel can be seen to be of a
secondary sort, because the scholar must reconstruct them
from the narrative world.[2]

The movement to a literary paradigm in Gospel studies
should not, however, be construed as invalidating or illegit-
imizing historical and theological questions which may be
asked of the narrative. The interrelatedness of the three
dimensions of the Gospel text must be emphasized, for they
never function in isolation, but as part of a 'dynamic process of

---

'history-like'. Problems have arisen, however, because this history-
like material has been evaluated for its quality as history; 'the realistic or history-like quality of biblical narratives, acknowledged by
all, instead of being examined for the bearing it had in its own right
on meaning and interpretation was immediately transposed into the
quite different issue of whether or not the realistic narrative was
historical'.

1 Lategan, 'Unresolved Methodological Issues', p. 22, and Petersen,
Literary Criticism, pp. 39ff. Petersen argues that to overlook the
conceptual autonomy of the narrative world is 'fallacious literarily
because it mistakenly posits a real world where there is only a narrative world, and it is fallacious historically because it assumes
what the historian must demonstrate, namely, the evidential value
of the narrative world for reconstructing the real world of events to
which it refers' (p. 40).

2 See Culpepper, 'Story and History', p. 472, who has written that 'the
narrative world of a gospel is not an exact reflection of either the
world of Jesus or that of the evangelist. Undoubtedly the narrative
worlds of the gospels are related in various ways ... to both the
world of Jesus and the social world of the evangelist. Primarily,
though, the narrative world of a gospel is the literary world created
by the author'. Cf. Kingsbury, 'Reflections on "The Reader"',
pp. 458-59, and Petersen, *Rediscovering Paul*, p. 7. Petersen has
observed that critics already consider the Gospels as 'secondary
sources from which history has to be reconstructed'. This is apparent from even a cursory comparison of the synoptic Gospels with
their different representations of the same events.

communication'.[1] A responsible biblical literary criticism cannot be ahistorical, and at least one prominent biblical literary
critic has warned New Testament scholarship to avoid the
mistake of secular literary criticism, which moved from absolutizing narrative texts as windows behind which meaning lay
to absolutizing texts as mirrors in which meaning was locked
up.[2]

Two reasons are cited most frequently as to why critical
historical inquiry should remain indispensable for interpreting the Gospels.[3] First, communication always takes place
within a specific context, and in the case of the gospels, this
context is first-century Palestine.[4] The evangelists used realistic, if not real, people, places, customs and events to tell their
stories, and the common or shared experiences of their readers enabled communication to take place.[5] Twentieth century
readers do not, however, share this same world. This means
that a cultural and linguistic gap exists between us and the
Bible which must be bridged, at least in part, for successful
communication to occur.[6] Historical criticism which expli-

---

1 Lategan, 'Unresolved Methodological Issues', p. 6.
2 Petersen is referring to the Anglo-American New Criticism, and
  calls for a 'bifocal' approach to the Gospel narrative (*Literary Criticism*, pp. 24-25).
3 See Leander E. Keck, 'Will the Historical Method Survive? Some
  Observations', in *Orientation by Disorientation*, pp. 123ff.; Tuckett,
  Reading the NT, pp. 174-87; Lategan, 'Unresolved Methodological
  Issues', pp. 24ff., for a defense of the place of historical reference
  and inquiry in the interpretation of narrative.
4 See Vorster, 'Meaning and Reference', p. 57, who has written that
  'the whole text is embedded in first-century Palestine'. Cf. also
  Lategan, 'Unresolved Methodological Issues', pp. 23ff.
5 Cf. Bernard C. Lategan, 'Reference: Reception, Redescription, and
  Reality', in *Text and Reality*, p. 74, who observes that 'although the
  world of the text enjoys a relatively autonomous existence, this may
  be deceptive, because its very existence is made possible by and
  depends on the accompanying context from which it arose, which
  forms a link with the context of the reader in terms of shared codes
  and shared experience'.
6 Cf. Peter Rabinowitz, 'Truth in Fiction: A Reexamination of Audiences', *Critical Inquiry* 4 (1977), pp. 126ff., who has argued that
  authors always presuppose that their readers will know or not know

cates the historical moorings of the text is essential for this task.

Secondly, historical criticism remains indispensable for responsible literary interpretation of biblical narratives because of the way in which it reminds readers of the 'otherness' of the Gospel text. Historical criticism contributes to a 'distantiation' between reader and text which prevents an easy domestication of the text, and instead helps the interpreter 'hear it on its own terms'.[1] Without respecting the historical dimension of the Gospel narrative, the text may soon become a mirror which merely repeats what the critic already knows and believes. Historical criticism can thus function in helping the biblical literary critic rule out fanciful interpretations.[2]

The issue is therefore not whether the biblical critic must choose between historical criticism or a literary interpretation of the Gospel narrative, but how the methods peculiar to each perspective may both contribute to a fuller understanding of Matthew's Gospel.[3] Because the structured form we

---

certain things when they write a work. He concludes that 'if historically or culturally distant texts are hard to understand, it is often because we do not possess the knowledge required to join the authorial audience' for whom the author has designed the narrative. The Gospels fit the description of such texts, and it is historical criticism which provides the scholar with the historical information that helps the twentieth century readers to bridge the gap between themselves and the first century authorial audience. Vorster, 'Historical Paradigm', pp. 108-11, points out, however that this original historical context of author and readers is only one aspect of the question of context. Traditional historical critical interpretations of the Gospel have tended to limit too narrowly the situational context within which communication occurs.

1 Walter Wink, *The Bible in Human Transformation* (Philadelphia: Fortress, 1973), pp. 24ff. Cf. Stroup, *Narrative Theology*, pp. 143ff., and Anthony C. Thiselton, 'The New Hermeneutic', in *New Testament Interpretation*, pp. 315-17.
2 Vorster ('Historical Paradigm', p. 104) writes that the historical paradigm provides 'information for setting the parameters of valid reading of the New Testament'. Cf. pp. 118ff.
3 Thiselton, 'Reader-Response Hermeneutics', pp. 82ff., 106, thus warns against making any hermeneutical paradigm an 'over-

encounter in the Gospels is that of narrative, however, a literary approach which is sensitive to the way narrative functions appears to be essential in Gospel interpretation. It is at this point that many biblical literary critics see a literary approach serving as a corrective to a deficiency in the traditional historical critical paradigm. When looked at from a broadly based understanding of method in biblical study, the use of literary criticism on the Gospels needs no further justification. John Barton has argued that each of the different methods used in biblical criticism should be seen as a 'codification of intuitions about the text which may occur to intelligent readers'.[1] Literary criticism thus comprises that set of questions which properly may be asked of literary and narrative texts such as the Gospels.

A literary approach to the interpretation of the Gospels serves to highlight the ways that readers respond to them. They can be read for historical and theological information, but to read them solely for history or theology appears to be an unnecessary narrowing of the scholar's task, and may mean that the critic and text are working at cross purposes. The Gospels can also be read as stories which invite the reader to enter into a narrative world. Robert Karris's description of Luke as a 'kerygmatic story' which is 'meant to preach to the reader in narrative form and to elicit from the reader an act of Christian faith' could be applied to any of the Gospels.[2] A literary approach to the Gospels which seeks to understand their message by examining both the interplay between the constitutive elements of the narrative and the way the text engages the reader may be more true to this message than methods which encourage an impersonal uninvolved objectivity on the part of the interpreter.[3]

---

arching solution to *all* hermeneutical problems regardless of the kind of text in view or of the particular purpose for which the text is being read'. He quotes with approval the dictum that 'a text does not have a single door nor a single key' (from *Exegesis: Problems of Method and Exercises in Reading*, ed. F. Bovan and G. Rouiller [Pittsburgh: Pickwick, 1978], p. 1).

1 Barton, *Reading the OT*, p. 5.
2 Karris, *Luke: Artist and Theologian*, p. 8.
3 This is the essence of Walter Wink's indictment of the historical

Finally, given the uncertainties surrounding competing source hypotheses in gospel studies today, a literary approach which operates on the basis of the wholeness or integrity of the narrative may prove more fruitful for delineating the shape of Matthean theology than methods which seek to isolate Matthean redaction.[1] It is reasonable to presume that many

critical paradigm. Its emphasis on the uninvolved objectivity of the interpreter made one incapable of so interpreting 'the Scriptures that the past becomes alive and illumines our present with new possibilities for personal and social transformation' (*The Bible in Human Transformation*, pp. 2-15). Wink was not the first to argue that the historical critical method was inherently inappropriate for the subject matter of the Bible, but others have correctly pointed out that literary critics are still critics, and thus exhibit the same impersonal objectivity that expresses itself in judgments about the text. Cf. Robert M. Polzin, 'Literary and Historical Criticism', pp. 106-11; Robert M. Fowler, 'Who is "The Reader" in Reader Response Criticism?', *Semeia* 31 (1985), pp. 5-10; George Steiner, ' "Critic"/"Reader" ', *New Literary History* 10 (1979), pp. 432-52. While such a caveat puts the claims of some literary critics in a proper perspective, it does not negate the usefulness of literary criticism to explicate how narratives engage the reader and disclose new horizons to the reader. The emphasis in traditional historical criticism on history and theology has not always fully appreciated this capacity of narrative to reveal new understandings or possibilities of existence. Cf. Lynn M. Poland, *Literary Criticism and Biblical Hermeneutics: A Critique of Formalist Approaches* (AAR Academy Series 48; Chico, CA: Scholars Press, 1985), pp. 66ff., who sees this as one of the valuable contributions that literary criticism can make to biblical studies, although she argues that the formalist New Critical literary model must be modified.

1 Jack D. Kingsbury, 'The Figure of Jesus in Matthew's Story: A Rejoinder to David Hill', *JSNT* 25 (1985), p. 62. The question of whether recent arguments against Markan priority and the existence of Q provide a better solution to the Synoptic problem than the two source hypothesis lies outside the scope of the present book. We merely point out that the relationship between the Synoptic gospels is far from a settled issue in many quarters of New Testament scholarship today. Cf. E. Earl Ellis's remarks on the assumptions of tradition and redaction criticism as they are currently practiced in 'Gospels Criticism: a Perspective on the State of the Art', in *Das Evangelium*, pp. 32ff. As methods of research, they are no stronger than their underlying pillars—one of which is made up of classical

people read one Gospel through as a whole literary story. To such an audience it is probably immaterial which evangelist wrote first, or what sources were used by the different evangelists. The dissection of a Gospel which is so much a part of the traditional historical critical paradigm is thus absent.[1]

The biblical scholar who chooses to utilize a literary paradigm in Gospel studies, however, faces a chaotic field of competing literary theories in contemporary literary criticism. There is no scholarly consensus or established method of literary study. Furthermore, the biblical scholar must decide whether the normative claims of biblical literature place any constraints upon the use of literary theories which have been developed primarily through the study of fiction.[2] The theoretical underpinnings and methods which will be followed in this literary study of Matthew must therefore be specified and delineated at the outset.

form criticism and the two source hypothesis. Even if it was possible to prove a particular source hypothesis, numerous scholars who practice literary or narrative criticism have agreed with Norman Perrin's questioning of the adequacy of redaction criticism because it 'defines the literary activity of the Evangelist too narrowly' ('The Interpretation of the Gospel of Mark', *Int* 30 [1976], p. 120). Cf. J.D. Kingsbury, 'The Theology of St. Matthew's Gospel according to the Griesbach Hypothesis', in *New Synoptic Studies*, ed. W.R. Farmer (Macon, GA: Mercer University Press, 1983), p. 332, who has written that 'separating tradition from redaction, the watchword of redaction-criticism in its infancy, tends to overlook the important truth that traditional units Matthew may have appropriated could, in any particular instance, have given adequate expression to his own point of view'.

1 David Hill, 'The Figure of Jesus in Matthew's Story: A Response to Professor Kingsbury's Literary Critical Probe', *JSNT* 21 (1984), pp. 37-38. Another kind of piecemeal approach to reading the Gospels which must be guarded against is the tendency to read Scripture in short sections. Both preaching and liturgy encourage this approach.

2 See William Kurz, 'Narrative Approaches to Luke-Acts', *Bib* 68 (1987), pp. 195-200, for a brief discussion of the suitability of some modern literary theories and presuppositions for interpreting biblical texts.

2. *Literary Presuppositions*

a. The integrity rather than the fragmentation of the Gospel narrative is assumed. This presupposition has almost become axiomatic in literary studies of the Gospels,[1] and has at least two important corollaries. First, it means that an interpreter considers the Gospels as a narrative whole without recourse to source theories which tended to dissect the narrative into its various component parts. Second, the assumption of narrative wholeness means that the Gospel is in some way treated as a self-contained and 'closed' narrative world; that is, it is conceptualized as a complex structured entity in which partial meanings are dependent upon their relationship to the whole. Certain formalist literary theories have absolutized the second corollary with the result that the autonomy, self-sufficiency, and objectivity of a literary work of art is stressed.[2] The principles of this approach to literature were enshrined by New Criticism in analyses of numerous heresies and fallacies of literary criticism.

1 Joanna Dewey, *Markan Public Debate: Literary Technique, Concentric Structure, and Theology in Mark 2.1--3.6* (SBLDS 48; Chico, CA: Scholars, 1980), p. 5, gives a succinct statement of this axiom when she writes that the 'text may be treated as a legitimate literary entity, even if it does contain layers of tradition and redaction. The final text is considered to have a validity of its own, independent of its prehistory'. Cf. however Stephen D. Moore's comments ('Are the Gospels Unified Narratives?', *SBL 1987 Seminar Papers*, ed. K.H. Richards [Atlanta: Scholars, 1987], pp. 443-58). Moore questions the viability of asserting the narrative unity of the Gospels and Acts on the basis of one's use of literary/narrative criticism.

2 See Poland, *Literary Criticism and Biblical Hermeneutics*, for her critique of the way this kind of criticism eliminates the historical dimension from both the text and its interpretation: 'By severing the literary work's ties to its origins in human experience, and by suppressing a text's claim to disclose something about the world, formalist criticism de-historicizes and de-contextualizes the works it studies' (p. 4). The problem with this program is that it 'tends to prevent literature from exercising those cognitive and thus transformative powers which this theory also wishes to claim for it' (p. 159). Poland is primarily concerned with New Criticism in her study, although the same criticisms can be made of structuralism since it can be seen as a 'radicalizing extension' of the basic formalist tendencies of new Criticism.

In New Critical theory a consideration of the author was ruled out by the intentional fallacy. This fallacy confused the intention of the author who wrote the poem as the cause of the poem with the use of that intention as a standard to judge the poem's meaning and worth.[1] For the New Critics, however, the meaning of a literary text must be public and objective—something which inheres in the text—since the literary text is an autonomous object. The views of Wellek and Warren are representative of the type of anti-intentionalism found in formalist theory:

> The whole idea that the 'intention' of the author is the proper subject of literary history seems, however, quite mistaken. The meaning of a work of art is not exhausted by or even equivalent to, its intention. As a system of values, it leads an independent life. The total meaning of a work of art cannot be defined merely in terms of its meaning for the author and his contemporaries.[2]

1 See William K. Wimsatt and Monroe C. Beardsley, *The Verbal Icon* (Lexington, KY: University of Kentucky Press, 1954), p. 21. In short, the intentional fallacy 'begins by trying to derive the standard of criticism from the psychological cause of the poem, and ends in biography and relativism' (p. 21). Cf. Frei, *Eclipse*, p. 301, who defines the intentional fallacy as the illusion that the author's purpose can be reconstructed 'indirectly from the text and from other evidence, rather than being expressed directly in the text'. Poland, *Literary Criticism and Biblical Hermeneutics*, p. 79, sees the intentional fallacy as a subspecies of the genetic fallacy, which the New Critics saw as an overvaluing of the relevance of historical and social influences on the author's shaping of a text. Robert Weimann, *Structure and Society in Literary History. Studies in the History and Theory of Historical Criticism* (London: Lawrence & Wishart, 1977), p. 6, believes that New Critics wrongly interpreted the genesis of texts solely in terms of individualism and biography.

2 Rene Wellek and Austin Warren, *Theory of Literature* (2nd edn; London: Jonathan Cape, 1961), p. 34. See also p. 157, where they write: 'the work of art, then, appears an object of knowledge *sui generis* which has a special ontological status'. Frank Lentricchia, *After the New Criticism* (London: Athlone, 1980), p. 257, labels this major tenet of New Criticism 'the organic fallacy'. John Barton, *Reading the OT*, pp. 148ff., has pointed out, however, that the anti-intentionalism of the New Critics is often misunderstood and exaggerated. They were primarily concerned with outlawing 'certain

In a similar way, consideration of the reader in interpretation was ruled out by the affective fallacy. This fallacy is the 'confusion between the poem and its *results* (what it *is* and what is *does*), a special case of epistemological skepticism'.[1] In analyzing the affective fallacy, New Critics were reacting against literary criticism which was 'concerned with the emotive effect that literature had on the reader'.[2] As with the intentional fallacy and the bracketing of questions about the author from literary criticism, New Criticism hoped that by sealing off questions about the reader it could protect critical literary evaluation from relativism.

The result of formalist literary theory postulating the literary text as an autonomous object for study, however, is that it developed a non-referential theory of literature. Cleanth Brooks's essay 'The Heresy of Paraphrase' illustrates this perspective when he attacks the idea that the meaning of a poem can be summed up by a paraphrase of its content. He writes that this heresy results from

> yielding to the temptation to mistake certain remarks which we make *about* the poem—statements about what it says or about what truth it gives or about what formulations it illustrates—for the essential core of the poem itself.[3]

Content cannot be separated from the form of the poem. For the New Critics, a poem cannot be reduced to the information it conveys, but simply exists as a poem. John Barton has summarized the formalists' non-referential view of literature with the dictum that if 'literature is about something after all, it is about literature itself'.[4] As with the other fallacies, New Criticism's warnings about paraphrase were intended to protect the integrity of the poem. The critic was not allowed to

---

illicit ways of *establishing*' an author's meaning in a literary work of art. That meaning can only be discovered in the work itself and not some kind of 'extrinsic' evidence.

1 Wimsatt and Beardsley, *Verbal Icon*, pp. 21, 59.
2 Barton, *Reading the OT*, p. 143.
3 Cleanth Brooks, *The Well Wrought Urn* (New York: Reynal and Hitchcock, 1947), p. 182, from Poland, *Literary Criticism and Biblical Hermeneutics*, p. 82.
4 Barton, *Reading the OT*, p. 159.

abstract a set of ideas from it.

It is not surprising that New Criticism concentrated on poetry, using the poem as the paradigm of a literary text from which general pronouncements about literary theory were made. This particular literary genre is most suited to the text being sealed off from author and reader, and so being treated as a literary artifact. The theory of literature which results is both anti-intentionalist and non-referential.[1] Problems may arise, however, in trying to apply this theory to other types of literature or narrative. Biblical scholars who appropriate New Critical models for interpreting the Bible must be wary of these difficulties. John Barton pinpoints this difficulty for Gospel studies when he poses the question, 'Is it true that the Gospels are narrative whose value lies in its narrativity, rather than attempts to tell the reader what he needs to know about Jesus?'.[2] Furthermore, the Gospel narratives are unable to exercise their transforming powers if they are completely cut off from the reader and the world. There is a referential aspect to the narrative world of the Gospels, a 'subject matter' with theological and soteriological implications, with which a reader must interact existentially, in order for the Gospel narratives to have their transformative effect.[3]

The assumption of the narrative integrity of the Gospels must not therefore necessarily drive us to the extremes of New Criticism, which sealed off the literary work of art as an aesthetic object from both author and reader. However, the insight of formalist literary theory that the text itself is the proper focus of literary study should be retained by the biblical literary critic. The importance of such an approach is brought into sharp focus by Werner Kelber when he argues that

> it is inadmissible, and hardly even possible, to grasp a gospel's place in the ongoing hermeneutical discourse

1 See Eagleton, *Literary Theory*, pp. 50ff.
2 Barton, *Reading the OT*, p. 164.
3 See Poland, *Literary Criticism and Biblical Hermeneutics*, pp. 4ff., 95ff., and 181, for her critique of formalist theory's inability to account for the historical dimension of interpretation by relating the meaning of a poem or a piece of literature to 'other arenas of meaning outside' the literary work.

unless one has first come to terms with its rhetorical and imagistic inner landscape.[1]

b. Point of view is an indispensable element in narrative. The narrative world which is projected by a Gospel contains characters who act within particular societal, geographical, temporal, and spatial boundaries and relationships. To construct this world in the act of narration always involves selective communication, however, since it is impossible to be exhaustive when telling a story. Some information is included and other information is omitted, and that which is selected is told in a particular manner which has been chosen out of numerous possible ways. A story may be told in different ways by different witnesses without it becoming an essentially different story, for example. A specific point of view governs this selective and evaluative process, and is thus always present in narrative.[2]

There has been a tendency in literary criticism, perhaps under the influence of New Criticism with its neglect of the author, to limit discussion about point of view to the narrative voice in the story. While it has been pointed out that the issue here is partly one of preferred usage of the term, this formalist usage of the concept tends to hide the fact that the judgment of the author is always present in a narrative text. It is ultimately the author who decides what sort of 'persona' and evaluative perspective will be utilized in telling the story.[3] Point of view will thus be used to include all the numerous narrative strategies used by an author to communicate a story. It also reveals the author's own interpretation of the projected narrative world, what he or she considers important

1 Kelber, 'Apostolic Tradition', p. 33.
2 Cf. the judgment of Robert Weimann, *Structure and Society*, p. 246, who writes that point of view is 'indeed the absolute prerequisite of all narrative activity'. W.S. Vorster considers point of view to be 'the most strking characteristic of the gospel genre' ('Kerygma/History', p. 91).
3 Wolterstorff, *Art in Action*, p. 136; Clarence Walhout, 'Text and Actions', in *The Responsibility of Hermeneutics*, p. 64. Cf. Wayne C. Booth, *The Rhetoric of Fiction* (2nd edn; Chicago: University of Chicago Press, 1983), pp. 20, 149 who also emphasizes the role of the author.

and significant in this world.

The element of point of view is indispensable to narrative, however, in other ways than just a consideration of the author's methods of selecting, controlling, and shaping material. For the reader of a narrative, point of view is the 'mode of perception' by which the reader is dependent for his or her experience of the narrative world. Perceptions of the characters and events in the story are filtered through the point of view of the author who has shaped the narrative.[1] Authorial point of view is one of the major determining factors in how a reader appropriates and actualizes a story.

c. The reader of the narrative has a role in the production of textual meaning. Formalist literary theory such as New Criticism, with its emphasis on the objectivity of the literary text, tended to devalue the reading experience and obscure the dialogical nature of communication. Some literary theorists have come to recognize, however, that communication is not complete until the 'message' of a text has reached its destination; that is, until it is comprehended by a reader. From this perspective, meaning is not something which merely inheres in the text or is produced in an author's mind, but it is found in the interaction between author, text, and reader. Reading thus comes to be viewed as an essentially creative or 'productive activity' in which the reader is an active, not passive, participant.[2] According to Wolfgang Iser's model of reading, the reader contributes to the production of meaning by supplying the portions in the narrative which are not written but implied—the areas of 'indeterminacy' or 'gaps'.[3] It is in this

---

1 Robert Scholes and Robert Kellogg, *The Nature of Narrative* (New York: OUP, 1966), p. 275.
2 Lategan, 'Reception, Redescription, Reality', pp. 68ff. Cf. the remarks of Thiselton, 'Reader-Response Hermeneutics', p. 94, who writes that meaning for reader-response critics is 'always potential in terms of the text, but actual in relation to the reader'; McKnight, *The Bible and the Reader*, p. 12, who states that the thesis of his book is 'readers make sense'.
3 Wolfgang Iser, 'Indeterminacy and the Reader's Response in Prose Fiction', in *Aspects of Narrative*, ed. J. Hillis Miller, (New York: Columbia University Press, 1971), pp. 1-45; *Implied Reader*, pp. 38-

sense that a narrative text is 'open'. A reader must participate
in the narrative world projected by the text if it is to be read
and appropriated.[1] In contrast to New Criticism and its
polemic against the affective fallacy, this new type of criticism
would argue that a poem cannot be understood apart from its
results!

Criticism's newfound interest in the reader, without whom
literature would not exist, has resulted in a proliferation of
different types of readers.[2] The real author and the real reader
are the actual persons who produce and read the text. In
reading a narrative text, however, one encounters not this
actual author but his or her image in the text; and this author
is related not to the actual reader but to an image of the reader
which the text invites one to become. These textual persona
are defined by the paired concepts of 'implied author' and
'implied reader'. As Wayne Booth writes,

40. Cf. Meir Sternberg, *Expositional Modes and Temporal Ordering
in Fiction* (London: Johns Hopkins University Press, 1978), p. 50,
who writes that 'the literary text may be conceived of as a dynamic
series of gaps'. Sternberg is primarily concerned with those 'gaps'
which the *author* creates in the ordering of the narrative, and
which are to be filled in later in the work, whereas Iser is primarily
concerned with describing the *reader's* actions in filling a gaps in
the narrative. Both men, however, show how the idea of indeterminacy is linked to point of view; that is, it is the author's choice which
decides where and what kind of gaps should occur in the narrative.

1 See Poland, *Literary Criticism and Biblical Hermeneutics*, pp. 181f.,
and her discussion of Paul Ricoeur's work in interpretation theory.

2 See Wolfgang Iser, *The Act of Reading. A Theory of Aesthetic
Response* (Baltimore: Johns Hopkins University Press, 1978), pp.
30ff., for a brief discussion of a few of these 'readers'. Cf. also Rabinowitz, 'Truth in Fiction', pp. 121-41, who identifies at least four different audiences in every narrative literary text. The terminology of
Seymour Chatman, *Story and Discourse. Narrative Structure in
Fiction and Film* (Ithaca, NY: Cornell University Press, 1978),
pp. 147-51, explicates the basic concepts and will be followed here. It
should be noted that the textually encoded authors and readers are
theoretical concepts and as such are not gender-linked. When mas-
culine pronouns are used in the book to refer to these textual interlocutors, it is purely a stylistic matter and their usage is not
intended to be exclusive.

> The author creates, in short, an image of himself and
> another image of his reader; he makes his reader, as he
> makes his second self, and the most successful reading is
> one in which the created selves, author and reader, can find
> complete agreement.[1]

Finally, narrator and narratee are terms which refer to the
voice telling and the person listening to the story. They may be
obliquely present, or they may be overtly portrayed as characters in the story.

In general literary theory, criticism which focuses on the
reader is usually subsumed under the critical category of
'audience-oriented' or 'reader-response' criticism. Reader-
response critics recognize that a literary work is composed of
two poles, which Wolfgang Iser has labeled the 'artistic' and
the 'aesthetic'. The artistic refers to the text as it is created by
the author and the aesthetic to the reader's actualization of
the text through the reading process. Iser concludes that

> from this polarity follows that the literary work cannot be
> completely identical with the text, or with the realization of
> the text, but in fact must lie halfway between the two.[2]

However, this common critical category actually disguises a
wide variety of critical assumptions and approaches.[3] The

---

1 Booth, *Rhetoric of Fiction*, p. 138. Cf. also pp. 397-98.
2 Iser, *The Implied Reader*, p. 274.
3 For a general introduction and orientation to the various interpretive assumptions and approaches subsumed under this broad category, see Susan Suleiman, 'Varieties of Audience-Oriented Criticism', in *The Reader in the Text*, ed. S.R. Suleiman and I. Crosman. (Princeton: Princeton University Press, 1980), pp. 3-45; Jane
   Tompkins, 'Introduction to Reader-Response Criticism', in *Reader-
   Response Criticism. From Formalist to Post-Structuralism*, ed. J.P.
   Tompkins (London: Johns Hopkins University Press, 1980), pp. ix-
   xxvi; Steven Mailloux, 'Reader-Response Criticism?', *Genre* 10
   (1977), pp. 413-31; *idem* 'Learning to Read: Interpretation and
   Reader-Response Criticism', *Studies in the Literary Imagination* 12
   (1979), pp. 93-108; Fowler, 'Who is "The Reader"', pp. 5-23;
   McKnight, *The Bible and the Reader*; idem, *Post-Modern Use of the
   Bible* (Nashville: Abingdon, 1988). For examples of biblical scholars
   who have applied reader-response criticism to the study of biblical
   narratives, see James L. Resseguie, 'Reader-Response Criticism
   and the Synoptic Gospels', *JAAR* 52 (1984), pp. 307-24, and the essays

specific relationship between text and reader is defined differently by different reader-response critics. Some focus on the hypothetical reader '*in the text*' (Gerald Prince), others on the actual reader's dominance '*over the text*' (Norman Holland and David Bleich), and others on the interaction of the implied reader '*with the text*' (Wolfgang Iser, Wayne Booth, and Stanley Fish).[1] Reader-response critics further debate over who is the dominant figure in the reading process; that is 'does the text control the reader or does the reader control the text?'.[2]

In whatever way this question is answered—and different reader-response theories place the emphasis on the co-ordinates differently—-the biblical literary critic who adopts some of the critical assumptions of reader-response criticism must take care not to focus too much attention on the act of reception by the reader. Bernard Lategan warns that the critic who makes the reader 'the almost exclusive arbiter, or creater of, the meaning of the text' repeats the problems of the intentional fallacy 'in the form of a "receptor's fallacy"'.[3] In this case, however, it is not authorial intention which exclusively prescribes a single valid interpretation but the criteria of an undeterminable reader. As Lategan argues, 'just as the intention of the author can only be determined in terms of his text, so the text constitutes the basis for analyzing the anticipated reception by the reader'.[4] The text thus contains restraints which limit the range of possible meanings and interpretations. Not only is the text interpreted by the reader, but the reader is in turn challenged and interpreted by the text.[5]

in *Semeia* 31 (1985).

1 Mailloux, 'Learning to Read', p. 94.
2 Fowler, 'Who is the "Reader"', p. 13.
3 Lategan, 'Unresolved Methodological Issues', p. 15.
4 Idem, 'Reception, Redescription, Reality', p. 69.
5 Cf. Bernard Brandon Scott, *The Word of God in Words: Reading and Preaching the Gospels* (Philadelphia: Fortress, 1985), pp. 45-46, who uses the analogy of music to describe the reading process. The reader is the musician and the text is his musical score. Reading thus conceptualized is a performance and the text is the score which provides the directions for that performance. The reader must be careful not to play false notes; that is to say, does one's reading per-

Conclusions reached about the reader in the literary paradigm for which we are arguing are therefore based upon a textually centered approach. By starting with the text, the biblical literary critic focuses attention on the 'implied reader'. Iser has defined this hypothetical reader as a 'sort of fictional inhabitant of the text' who 'embodies all the predispositions necessary for a literary work to exercise its effect'.[1] The implied reader is thus on the receiving end of all the various textual strategies and rhetorical devices used to communicate, representing the response which the author may have been aiming at for his audience. In this sense the implied reader 'functions as a heuristic device to uncover the meaning of the text'.[2] By reconstructing the hypothetical responses of this hypothetical reader in the text, the biblical literary critic can identify some of the possible effects the Gospel narrative might have on an actual reader—effects and meanings which the evangelist may have been trying to achieve in writing the Gospel.[3] In a sense, the implied reader becomes the route by which the evangelist reaches the hearts of real readers.[4] A study of the implied reader by the biblical scholar can therefore help underline the normative dimension of the Gospel narratives, because it suggests possible effects and meanings

form the text or ignore it?

1 Iser, *Act of Reading*, pp. 33-34. Cf. Menakhem Perry, 'Literary Dynamics: How the Order of a Text Creates its Meanings', *Poetics Today* 1 (1979), p. 43, who defines this reader as 'a "maximal" concretization of the text that can be justified from the text itself while taking into account the norms (social, lingusitic, literary, etc.) relevant for its period and the possible intentions of the author'.

2 Lategan, 'Reception, Redescription, and Reality', p. 70. Many reader-response critics intensify this sense of the implied reader by talking about the 'ideal reader'. Cf. Rabinowitz, 'Truth in Fiction', pp. 133ff., for example, who talks about the 'ideal narrative audience' as that audience which accepts the narrator's ideological point of view.

3 See Rhoads and Michie, *Mark as Story*, p. 137, for an example of this practical use of reader-response criticism in biblical interpretation.

4 See Edgar V. McKnight, 'The Contours and Methods of Literary Criticism', in *Orientation by Disorientation*, p. 57, who argues that 'the rhetorical axis of communication includes the implied author and reader who are not unrelated to the actual author and reader'.

intended by the evangelist.

d. The most important aspect of the interaction between reader and text is its temporal, sequential dimension. This represents an important modification of formalist literary theory which operated with a static spatial model that had been brought about by its objectification of the text.[1] Instead of concentrating on the end product of reading, reader-response critics use of dynamic temporal model which is concerned with the reading process as it occurs. Although reading is treated as a sequential encounter with words and ideas, it is not simply an irreversible, or what Menakhem Perry has termed 'uni-directional', linear experience.[2] The readers not only anticipate and form hypotheses about what lies ahead in a story, but they may also be required to revise hypotheses and repattern earlier parts of the text through retrospection and review as they read. The sequential nature of reading, however, does require one to take seriously the ordering of material in a text if the text is to be understood properly.[3] The biblical literary critic should therefore be sensitive to the rhetorical models and patterning in the text, and to the effects these have on the way readers actualize the story when interpreting biblical narratives such as the Gospels.

Interpretations based upon the static and spatial model of readings, found in formalist literary theories (and often used in the history of ideas approach of traditional biblical criticism) can ultimately give only a holistic interpretation of the text. The meanings specified are thus retrospective ones which the reader might have constructed *after* his or her temporal reading experience, and ultimately they can only describe the author's attempt to communicate a thematic message. It cannot be denied that the sequential acts by a reader include a final interpretive synthesis of the reading (what one might call the 'theology' of an evangelist in Gospel studies), and this is not

1 Mailloux, 'Learning to Read', pp. 95ff.; Fowler, 'Who is "the Reader"', pp. 19ff.
2 Perry, 'Literary Dynamics', p. 58.
3 Cf. *ibid.*, p. 356. Perry writes that 'the linearity of language entails that not each meaning can be made clear at once'.

to be rejected by a temporally based model of interpretation; such a model simply takes the final synthesis as part of the total response, and grants significance to the series of interpretations and effects which led up to this synthesis.[1] A temporally based reader-response model of interpretation is thus able to provide a more comprehensive account both of an author's rhetorical and communicative techniques, and of a reader's appropriation of a narrative.

Steven Mailloux has argued, however, that a reading model remains inadequate if it is based solely on the account of a reader's temporal and sequential activities of reading: a reading model must also account for what constrains these activities.[2] Although there can be no absolute guarantees, what is it that ensures that a reader will have the experience and reaction which the author intends at any given place in the time flow of reading? The temporal element of reading suggests one answer to this question, for the cumulative effects of narrative ordering and plot pressure a reader to react in certain ways to later passages. A second element is also present and represents the final literary presupposition in our reader-response literary paradigm.

e. Reading has a social dimension in which authorial intention and communicative conventions produce and constrain a reader's response in the midst of the temporal flow of reading. To understand a narrative, readers must come to the literary text with certain abilities which will be used throughout the reading experience. Without these abilities, or 'literary competence', the reader would find it difficult to make sense out of the narrative.[3] Communicative conventions, however, are not merely something which the *reader* uses. The *author* also

---

1 See Mailloux, *Interpretive Conventions*, pp. 70ff.
2 *Ibid.*, p. 90.
3 Jonathan Culler, *Structuralist Poetics: Structuralism, Lingusitics and the Study of Literature* (London: Routledge & Kegan Paul, 1975), p. 118, defines literary competence as 'a set of conventions for reading literary texts'. John Barton, *Reading the OT*, p. 16, uses the concept of genre recognition to define literary competence. When one recognizes what type of writing a narrative text belongs to, one knows what this narrative text should be 'read as'.

makes use of this shared system of reading conventions when writing, just as the reader uses them to understand the text.[1] It is by the literary conventions which are utilized that the author of a narrative text may be able to anticipate, and in some sense control, a reader's response to the work.[2] The strategies in the text in turn orient the reader's search for the intentions underlying the author's selection and combination of conventions.[3]

The use of different conventions, literary forms and genres by both author and reader thus plays an important role in the act of communication. The different forms utilized condition the response of the reader. That is to say, they serve an interpretive function which helps create meaning.[4] The author of a narrative creates content or thought in the process of creating the form of a text, and the reader must recognize this form to understand and appropriate the text. For example, a newspaper is composed of different forms or genres. Articles on the front page will be reported in as objective and factual a manner as possible, whereas the form of the 'editorial page' conditions the reader to expect opinions. On such a page one might find a satirical political columnist. If one failed to recognize the conventions utilized in such a column, however, one would completely misread the article.

The interaction between author, reader, and text thus takes

---

1 Culler, *Structuralist Poetics*, p. 116, thus writes that literary conventions can be thought of 'not simply as the implicit knowledge of the reader but also as the implicit knowledge of authors. To write a poem or a novel is immediately to engage with a literary tradition or at the very least with a certain idea of the poem or the novel'.
2 Cf. *ibid.*, p. 30 who has written that for an author 'to intend a meaning is to postulate reactions of an imagined reader who has assimilated the relevant conventions'.
3 Cf. Iser, *Act of Reading*, pp. 25, 61.
4 See Frank Kermode, *The Genesis of Secrecy: On the Interpretation of Narrative* (Cambridge: Harvard University Press, 1979), pp. 162-63, n. 20, who discusses this function of literary form when he describes genre as a 'context of expectation, an "internal probability system"'. Cf. also Poland's discussion of Paul Ricoeur's interpretation theory which emphasizes the 'generative rather than the taxonomic function' of literary genres (*Literary Criticism and Biblical Hermeneutics*, pp. 171ff.).

place within the context of an interpretive community which helps define how one should read a narrative text. The function of interpretive communities in (some) reader-response critical theories is aptly summarized by Jane Tompkins when she writes that the phrase is

> shorthand for the notion that since all sign systems are social constructs that individuals assimilate more or less automatically (or, more accurately, that pervade and constitute individual consciousness), an individual's perceptions and judgements are a function of the assumptions shared by the groups he belongs to.[1]

The evangelist and his community can be seen as one interpretive community, but when we read Matthew today we also read it within the context of a modern interpretive community. This bears on our use of a reader-response literary paradigm in Gospel studies in at least two ways. First, it helps explain the predominance of the historical critical paradigm in the current state of biblical research. As members of a 'professional guild', biblical critics have learned to ask the questions of biblical narrative texts which are formulated by historical critical methods. The church, however, forms a second and wider interpretive community in which the biblical narrative texts are read. Within this community, the stories of the Gospels serve as the church's 'foundation story',[2] and the Bible continues to offer guidance and exercise a normative claim of some type in the life of this community.[3]

This normative aspect of the Bible's function in the ongoing

---

1 Jane P. Tompkins, 'A Introduction to Reader-Response Criticism', in *Reader-Response Criticism*, p. xxi.
2 See James Barr, 'Some Thoughts on Narrative, Myth and Incarnation', in *God Incarnate: Story and Belief*, ed. A.E. Harvey (London: SPCK, 1981), p. 15.
3 See Krister Stendahl, 'The Bible as a Classic and the Bible as Holy Scripture', *JBL* 103 (1984), pp. 8ff., where he argues that the Bible has a type of intrinsic normative claim to it since it is recognized as 'belonging to the genre of Holy Scripture'. Cf. Keck, 'Will the Historical Method Survive?', in *Orientation by Disorientation*, pp. 123ff., who argues that 'the survival of the historical-critical method and the survival of the Bible as the canon of the community appear to go hand in hand'.

life of the church places restraints on the plurality of acceptable interpretations of biblical narrative. In contrast to the radical indeterminacy of some structuralists and deconstructionists who use the notion of an interpretive community to postulate a seemingly infinite number of possible interpretations and meanings of a text,[1] the biblical literary critic stands in the tradition of the church which has recognized the authority of the Bible and accepted its normative claims. To be responsible to this tradition, the biblical literary critic must believe that interpretations can be validated.[2] A consideration of at least two elements will help the biblical critic in this task.

First, questions about authorial intention cannot be completely bracketed from literary criticism. The limits placed on questions of authorial intention by some types of literary theories have no doubt been helpful to biblical critics, because they highlight the fact that texts can have meaning which exceeds that which the original author intended.[3] Yet as E.D. Hirsch has argued in his book *Validity in Interpretation*, a text 'does not exist even as a sequence of words until it is construed: until then, it is merely a sequence of signs'.[4] Hirsch is arguing against the New Critical idea that meaning inheres in the text apart from any construing mind. He successfully shows that a narrative text can have meaning only when it is fitted into some larger context. Because of his assumption that a text can only have one meaning, however, Hirsch specifies that it is the construing mind, the intention, of the author which places a narrative within its wider context and thereby gives it mean-

---

1 It is this tendency against which E.D. Hirsch (*Validity in Interpretation* [London: Yale University Press, 1967], p. viii) and Helen Gardner (*In Defence of the Imagination* [Oxford: Clarendon, 1982], p. 133) are fighting.

2 Cf. Thiselton, 'Reader-Response Hermeneutics', pp. 103ff.

3 Barton, *Reading the OT*, p. 169. Hirsch, *Validity in Interpretation*, p. 8, recognizes this phenomenon and explains it by making a distinction between 'meaning' and 'significance'. The former is that 'which is represented by a text', and the latter 'names a relationship between that meaning and a person, or a conception, or a situation, or indeed anything imaginable'. Hirsch thus argues that a work's significance, and not its meaning, changes.

4 Hirsch, *Validity*, p. 13.

ing. While this is one possible context in which a text can be fitted, it is not necessarily the only one. Readers also supply the context in which narratives are fitted—so it can be *their* mind which construes meaning.[1] The reader's action in supplying a wider context for a narrative does not negate the fact that narrative texts need authors, however, and the intentions and actions of an author in forming a text can also serve as a guide to its meaning.

Our appeal for a consideration of authorial intentions should not be construed as a psychological appeal to examine the subjective intentions of an author's mind. The difficulties of such an enterprise have been exposed by New Criticism, but the extreme of the New Critics' position—which ignored the authors—should also be avoided. Authorial intention as conceived in our reader-response paradigm refers to those intentions which can be inferred from the communicative conventions utilized in the narrative.[2] These are relevant for interpreting texts because the choice of conventions utilized in the text may reveal something about what the author is trying to accomplish and communicate when writing. Questions about authorial intention thus serve as a way of exploring the convention network in which narrative texts are embedded. If we know what the texts were 'written as', it may help us to know what they are to be 'read as'.[3]

A second restraint on the possibilities of valid interpretations of biblical narrative is brought about by the recognition that the literary conventions utilized in the text are not limited to the linguistic and narrative world of the text. Literary conventions are part of a wider shared system of ways of making sense of reality. The author uses shared historical, social and cultural norms to communicate to the reader, and these

---

1 See Robert Crossan, 'Do Readers Make Meaning?', in *The Reader in the Text*, pp. 151, 154-64.

2 See Mailloux, *Interpretive Conventions*, p. 152, who has argued that 'intention in literary acts can be recovered only through communicative conventions: insofar as intention (as a state of mind) is not expressed or manifested conventionally, it is to that extent not recoverable'.

3 Cf. Barton, *Reading the OT*, p. 164, and Walhout, 'Text and Actions', pp. 48ff.

should be taken into consideration in a modern reading and interpretation of the narrative. As Anthony Thiselton has argued,

> the very grammar of the concepts involved is embedded in a history of events and behavior. It is part of the grammar of the concept of 'God' that he is the God of Abraham, of Isaac, and of Jacob (Exod. 3.6).[1]

A reader can still read the biblical narrative without the literary competence which recognizes this shared set of interpretive conventions, but the reading may in some sense be defective and unable to account responsibly for the normative dimension of the biblical narrative.[2]

Authorial intentions and communicative conventions should therefore combine with the temporal reading process to constrain a reader's actualization and interpretation of the biblical narratives. Since the historical situation of interpretive communities differs in different times and places, the actual ways in which the story and communicative conventions are realized and interpreted by readers will also differ. There is thus an acceptable critical plurality of interpretation within our reader-response paradigm, but in every case it is the textual structures which function as guides and set the limitations for valid or acceptable interpretation.[3] For biblical literary critics standing in the tradition of the church, interpretation of the story in the Gospel will include the response of the church

1 Anthony C. Thiselton, *The Two Horizons* (Exeter: Paternoster, 1980), p. 385. Cf. Lategan, 'Unresolved Methodological Issues', p. 24.
2 Mailloux, *Interpretive Conventions*. pp. 144ff., defines interpretation as 'acceptable and approximating translation'. When we interpret a narrative, we 'try to approximate the speaker's meaning as we create it for ourselves'. He argues that it is interpretive conventions which provide the 'mechanisms for the acceptable and approximating translation in the interpretative process' (p. 149).
3 Barton, *Reading the OT*, p. 169. Cf. Barr, 'The Bible as Literature', p. 72, who argues for an intermediate position between a literary text having one possible meaning (i.e. authorial intended meaning) and it having all possible meanings. The author's original meaning of biblical narrative, in as much as it can be established from the textual structures, could help delineate the 'fence of possible meanings drawn around the text' for which Barr is arguing.

throughout the ages.[1]

3. *Summary*

The reader-response literary paradigm which we have
described is an eclectic paradigm that has borrowed theories,
terminology and critical strategies from rhetorical, structuralist and phenomenological varieties of reader-response
literary theories.[2] It is felt that such an eclectic approach is
able to account more adequately for the normative aspect of
the Bible's use in the life of the church; especially in the way in
which it allows a place for the author in the literary paradigm.
Textual meaning arises out of the diverse and interrelated
actions of producing and using a narrative, actions which are
performed both by authors and by readers. Indeed, if the
action of an author in construing a text is ruled out in principle—as it is in some structuralist theories—there becomes no
reason why a reader cannot interpret the text in any way he
or she likes.[3] The intention of the author and the historical situation in which the text was produced are thus not a matter of
indifference for the biblical literary critic. These must be primarily inferred, however, on the basis of the literary genre
and the conventions utilized in the text.[4]

---

1   Cf. Harvey, 'Christian Propositions and Christian Stories', in *God
    Incarnate*, p. 5, and Thiselton, *Two Horizons*, p. 439. Thiselton,
    drawing upon the work of Gadamer, argues that tradition can affect
    the understanding of literary texts in a positive way; it is not only 'a
    bridge betwen the past and the present, but also a filter which
    passes on interpretations and insights which have stood the test of
    time'.
2   See Suleiman, 'Varieties of Audience-Oriented Criticism', in *The
    Reader in the Text*, pp. 3-45, for a discussion of the various
    approaches.
3   See Barton, *Reading the OT*, pp. 187ff., and his criticism of an ideo-
    logical use of structuralist methods.
4   In structuralism, these questions are addressed in a study of the
    surface structures of a text. Structuralists differentiate between
    three different types of structures or 'structural levels' in a narra-
    tive text: 'structures of enunciation, cultural structures, and deep
    structures' (Daniel Patte, *What is Structural Exegesis?* [Philadel-
    phia: Fortress, 1976], pp. 22-25). The first two surface structural
    levels, which are concerned with the constraints imposed upon the

Our reader-response literary paradigm is therefore based on a 'text-immanent' approach, and this appears to be one of its strengths, for it focuses the interpreter's attention on the *text* rather than something external to the narrative. It presupposes the wholeness and integrity of Matthew and approaches the Gospel as a story that possesses an inherently dramatic structure. No attempt will be made to distinguish Matthean redaction from tradition, for all material in Matthew is relevant for a literary analysis, whether or not it originated in the tradition. Our reader-response paradigm differs from the objectivism of a formalist literary paradigm because it considers the role of both the author and the reader in interpreting a literary work. Unlike the traditional historical critical paradigm, however, our approach does not limit the situational context in which communication occurs to the historical context of the evangelist and his community. The readers of the Goespel have a role in the production of meaning, but they are constrained by the communicative conventions utilized by the author in the text. The act of literary communication is conceived of as a dynamic event occurring in the temporal unfolding of the story.

C. *The Proposed Study*

It may be helpful to anticipate the following chapters by outlining how the literary paradigm will be used and by summarizing some of the results of our study. Chapters 3, 4, and 5 form the center of the book. They describe the narrative

text by the author's creativity and the situation one is addressing in the first instance, and the cultural conventions in the second, appear to be the most appropriate and helpful to the biblical literary critic. The third level of 'deep structures', the structural level which is the primary concern of most structuralists, we believe to be limited in its usefulness because it tends to overlook the normative dimension of biblical narrative. Furthermore, it is reductive as it neglects the way surface structure of a text enriches the meaning and experience of reading a narrative. John Barton (*Reading the OT*, p. 187) has argued that structuralism is really a 'theory of reading' since it does not allow the existence of meaning behind the text—a text is its own meaning.

rhetoric of Matthew's inclusive story by means of a narrative and reader-response criticism that examines respectively the Gospel story, story-teller, and audience.[1] These chapters are preceded by a chapter which relates the literary methods used here to more traditional methods of biblical interpretation, in this case represented by redaction criticism. In this chapter the reader-response literary paradigm functions as a type of 'meta-criticism' to see what in the experience of the reading Matthew produced both the similarities and differences in some previous redaction-critical interpretations of Matthew's inclusive story.[2] A short conclusion summarizes the study and suggests some ways in which Jesus functions as a model for discipleship for the implied reader.

Some previous redaction-critical studies of Matthew have atempted to encompass the double time horizon of the Gospel (the time of Jesus' ministry and the time of the church) by means of the theological category of salvation history. This concept is closely tied to the narrative form of Matthew, however, because it is based upon the chronological and configurational dimensions of narrative which are constitutive of its plot. Since the Gospel's narrator intrusively tells his story retrospectively, there are two different senses of the present moment in the Gospel; the present of the events unfolding in the story, and the present of the time of narration. It is these two different senses of the present moment that salvation history interpretations of Matthew are trying to account for.

---

1 In describing Matthew's narrative rhetoric, our literary paradigm will offer a 'story of reading' which narrates how a reader experiences and appropriates the story of Jesus' life and ministry narrated in the Gospel. See Stephen D. Moore, 'Stories of Reading: Doing Gospel Criticism As/With a "Reader"', *SBL 1988 Seminar Papers*, ed. David J. Lull (Atlanta: Scholars Press, 1988), p. 144.

2 See Stanley Fish, 'Interpreting the *Variorum*', in *Reader-Response Criticism*, p. 166, who uses this method to show how a common reading experience lies at the base of many critical disagreements in literature and poetry. Cf. Moore, 'Stories of Reading', p. 159, who sees the potential of reader-oriented research in biblical research as 'making the implicit features of our critical reading explicit by narrativizing our standard moves and reflecting them back to us in a mirror'.

A literary paradigm, however, provides perspectives and interpretive devices which enable one to explore more adequately the different present moments in the inclusive nature of Matthew. As the narrator's encoded interlocutor, the implied reader is present throughout the narration of Jesus' ministry, creating the impression that the implied reader is included in the story. Because the narrative world extends into the indefinite future, the implied reader also shares this temporally extended world. By means of the plot themes of promise/fulfillment and acceptance/rejection, Jesus' ultimate significance is highlighted and readers are encouraged to accept him and his teaching. The mode of narration which is used aligns Jesus so closely with the narrator that Jesus becomes a reliable spokesman and the medium for the implied author's system of values.

The readers implied or 'included' in the story, however, are not to be equated with the disciples or any other character group. They are the recipients of the narrator's exposition and commentary, and thus they know more than any character group in the Gospel. With this knowledge they are called to stand with Jesus and the narrator/implied author and judge every character according to whether he or she accepts or rejects Jesus and his teaching. Discipleship does not mean membership in a character group, but acceptance of the norms and values voiced by Jesus and the implied author.[1] The disciples provide the link between the implied reader and Jesus' teaching which is to be obeyed, but they at times fail to live up to the standards in Jesus' teaching. Jesus, however, embodies these values in his own life, so he can be seen to be a model for the demands of discipleship.

---

1 See Janice Capel Anderson, 'Matthew: Gender and Reader', *Semeia* 28 (1983), pp. 3-27, who also develops this thesis.

Chapter 2

THE USE OF 'SALVATION HISTORY' IN THE INTERPRETATION OF MATTHEW: A READER-RESPONSE CRITIQUE

A. *Introduction*

We have seen that point of view is an indispensable element in narrative. Its importance to narrative is not limited, however, to 'fictional' works. When an author is writing 'history', or constructing a realistic or 'history-like' narrative as in the case of the gospels, the narrative world which is projected still reflects the judgement of the author.[1] The author simply cannot be exhaustive in detail when telling a story, for the act of narration involves selective communication.[2] This phe-

---

1 See Ricoeur, 'Narrative Function', pp. 177-202; W.B. Gallie, *Philosophy and Historical Understanding* (New York: Schocken, 1964); Hayden White, *Metahistory: The Historical Imagination in Nineteenth-Century Europe* (London: Johns Hopkins University Press, 1973); *idem*, 'The Value of Narrativity in the Representation of Reality', *Critical Inquiry* 7 (1980), pp. 5-27, for discussions of the structuring element in the writing of history. The following comment by White is representative of the emphasis on narrative and point of view in these scholars' philosophies of history: 'the historian confronts a veritable chaos of events *already constituted*, out of which he must choose the elements of the story he would tell. He makes his story by including some events and excluding others. This process of exclusion, stress, and subordination is carried out in the interest of constituting a *story of a particular kind*. That is to say, he "emplots" his story' (*Metahistory*, p. 6, n. 5).

2 Cf. Susan Snaider Lanser, *The Narrative Act: Point of View in Prose Fiction* (Princeton, NJ: Princeton University Press, 1981), p. 60, who has observed that 'language functions to carry ideology... Every technical choice a writer makes betrays values and judgment of which the speaker him—or herself may be unaware...'.

nomenon of point of view in a literary work can be studied from many different perspectives. Boris Uspensky, for example, has identified the ideological, spatio-temporal, phraseological, and psychological planes or aspects of point of view.[1] Some of these different aspects of point of view merely reflect the manner chosen by an author to tell his story. The most basic of all the planes of point of view according to Uspensky, however, is the ideological plane; it is interested in the problem of how an author 'evaluates and perceives ideologically' the world which he describes in his narrative work. He defines it as a 'general system of viewing the world conceptually'.[2]

There appears, however, to be an ambiguity in the definition and use of the category of ideological or evaluative point of view by many literary critics. When it is used to designate a 'general system of viewing the world conceptually', ideological point of view seems to function as little more than an author's or narrator's *Weltanschauung* which, in Lotman's words, is central to 'the overall task of constructing a picture of the world'.[3] On the other hand, the category is also used more specifically to designate the system of values and beliefs that are operative in a narrative world. When ideological point of view is used in this way, the idea of evaluation is dominant, the concept denoting a way of looking at things which involves rendering a judgment of whether they are 'good' or 'bad' 'right' or 'wrong'.

When we turn to examine the narrative structure and reception of Matthew's inclusive story, we are confronted with the question of the evangelist's point of view in a way that

1 Boris Uspensky, *A Poetics of Composition: The Structure of the Artistic Text and Typology of a Compositional Form*, transl. V. Zavarin and S. Wittig (Berkeley: University of California Press, 1973), p. 6. Cf. also Lanser, *Narrative Act*, especially pp. 184-225, who builds upon and expands Uspensky's work.

2 *Ibid.*, p. 8. Cf. Lanser, *Narrative Act*, pp. 184, 222. 'Ideology' is used in this context as a technical literary-critical category without any positive or negative connotations.

3 J.M. Lotman, 'Point of view in a Text', *New Literary History* 6 (1975), p. 341. Cf. Weimann, *Structure and Society*, p. 235, who describes this as the 'representational' function of point of view that 'relates the novel to the objective nature of the world'.

reflects the two different aspects of ideological point of view in a narrative. The question is raised not only in terms of the manner in which Matthew tells his story (that is, how he tells an inclusive story), but also in terms of the content and value system of his inclusive story. That is, to what elements does the evangelist give significance in his narrative world, such that the experiences of his community become reflected in the story of Jesus and his earthly disciples?

Although literary categories have not been used by biblical critics working within the traditional historical critical paradigm, many have treated the theological concept of salvation history as the ideological point of view of Matthew in their interpretation of the Gospel.[1] With such a conceptual system, it is argued that Matthew was able to 'include' in his story of Jesus the prior history of Israel as well as the subsequent experiences of the Christian community so that this theological concept has become the chief principle used by the evangelist to organize the disparate material in his Gospel. John Meier is representative of this approach when he uses the concept as the hermeneutical key for understanding Matthew's theology; salvation history provided Matthew with the means 'to order his various traditions according to a divine economy'.[2] For the readers of the Gospel, the theological con-

---

1 Cf. Theissen, *Miracle Stories*, p. 197, n. 4, who has devised four categories to explicate the different ways individual motifs are combined in a narrative framework. The label 'overarching category' is the name given to 'the technique of composition which creates arches going beyond an immediate context to hold together the whole gospel' (pp. 211ff.). This technique explains or gives the narrative a sort of spherical completeness and unitary form, and thus has a role similar to the function of an ideological point of view in narrative. In Theissen's terms, salvation history functions as the 'overarching category of composition' in these interpretations of Matthew. Cf. also David R. Bauer, *The Structure of Matthew's Gospel. A Study in Literary Design*, (JSNT Supplement Series 31; Sheffield: Almond, 1988), pp. 44-54, who discusses the use of salvation history as a 'conceptual structure' to define the structure of the Gospel.

2 J.P. Meier, *Law and History in Matthew's Gospel*, AnaBib 71 (Rome: Biblical Institute Press, 1976), p. 163. Cf. also J.P. Meier, *The Vision of Matthew: Christ, and Morality in the First Gospel* (New

cept is equally important, for it provides an interpretive frame of reference that allows them to make sense of the narrative. The use of the salvation history concept in these interpretations represents a final interpretive synthesis of a thematic message of the Gospel, a synthesis which attempts to encapsulate the meaning of the narrative in a 'quasi-philosophical concept'.[1]

The question which must be raised, however, is whether the category of salvation history does justice to the inclusive nature of the Gospel. As a final interpretive synthesis of a thematic message in Matthew, does the use of this theological concept neglect or ignore part of the evangelist's rhetoric of entanglement which includes and involves a reader in the story? Is it able to provide a means to describe the way in which a reader participates in the story in order to appropriate it? Does it give expression to the system of beliefs and values which are operative in the Gospel? Some recent redaction-critical interpretations of Matthew which have used the concept of salvation history will be examined in this chapter, and an attempt will be made both to answer these questions and to demonstrate that a literary approach to the Gospels can provide interpretive categories better suited to addressing certain concerns about how narrative communicates. By using a reader-response literary paradigm in our look at redaction-critical approaches, we hope to demonstrate that salvation history has in fact been treated as the evangelist's ideological point of view. Attention will be given to those aspects of the narrative which have been used by critics to construct their formulations of the concept, for this may indirectly provide us with clues about the narrative structures pertinent for our examination of the inclusive nature of Matthew's story.

It should be remembered that the use of salvation history as an interpretive category for understanding Matthew represents a 'modern' reading of the Gospel. Because these scholars have operated within the historical critical paradigm, however, their concern has been with the genesis of the text; that is, they have been concerned with the original author's inten-

York: Paulist, 1979), pp. 29ff.
1 Barton, *Reading the OT*, p. 161.

tion and meaning, and with the historical context which both called forth the Gospel and determined its reception. The concept of salvation history is thus ascribed to the first century evangelist and his original audience, and is seen as the means by which Matthew appropriated the world in his Gospel, and by which his community appropriated the narrative world of the Gospel.

Each salvation history interpretation in our discussion will be examined in three parts. First, the use of salvation history as a heuristic device to explain the way Matthew organized his Gospel will be explored. Secondly, the role ascribed to salvation history in the reader's appropriation of the Gospel will be examined. Finally, the different aspects of narrative which are used and emphasized in the formulations of the theological concept of salvation history will be outlined.

Recent attempts to use salvation history as an overarching category in the interpretation of Matthew can be divided into formulations based on a tripartite schema and those based on a two-fold division. Those who delineated a tripartite schematization will be examined first, not only because they were chronologically the first in recent years to employ salvation history when interpreting Matthew, but also because of the similarity between their definitions of salvation history and the classic definitions of Oscar Cullmann and Hans Conzelmann. At the conclusion of each section, we will summarize the results of our survey and seek to delineate the common reading experience that lies at the base of the different salvation history interpretations of Matthew.

B. *Tripartite Schemes of Salvation History in Matthew*

1. *Georg Strecker*

One of the first, and perhaps one of the most influential, attempts in the twentieth century to utilize salvation history as a category to interpret Matthew is found in Georg Strecker's book *Der Weg der Gerechtigkeit*. Strecker, sharing an assumption made by Conzelmann in his study of Luke-Acts, thinks that the delay of the parousia posed the most significant problem for the second Christian generation. Consequently for Strecker (as in Conzelmann's view of Luke), the primary theological question in Matthew concerns the precise relationship between the historical and eschatological.[1] According to Strecker, Matthew solved this problem by 'historicizing' the synoptic traditions.[2] The evangelist used Mark to develop a continuous historical line shaped in the form of a 'Bios Jesu', a line which separates the time of Jesus from the preceding time of the Old Testament and the subsequent time of the church.[3] The time preceding the time of Jesus is a 'time of preparation', since it points forward to the life of Jesus.[4] The time of the church which follows is the time of world mission. The church's function in Matthew's scheme of history appears 'als legitime und zuverlässige Repräsentanz der eschatologischen Forderung in der Welt'.[5] Strecker contends that the historical significance of the time of Jesus is eschatologically qualified by Jesus' life and the ethical demands he proclaims, with the result that Matthew orders Jesus' life as 'the way of righteousness'. According to Strecker, the eschatological significance of salvation history is interpreted in an ethical sense by the evangelist.[6]

In formal terms, the scheme of salvation history in Matthew which results from Strecker's interpretation is not unlike that which Conzelmann finds in Luke. Matthew divides salvation history into three separate and distinct periods, 'the centre of which is the time of Jesus as the time of

1 Strecker, *Weg*, pp. 45-47. Cf. *idem*, 'The Concept of History in Matthew', in *The Interpretation of Matthew*, ed. G.N. Stanton (London: SPCK, 1983), pp. 69ff. This article is a brief summary of the main theses in Strecker's monograph. Strecker writes 'Das bedeutet, daß die Frage nach der theologischen Konzeption des Matthäus die Frage nach dem Verhältnis des Historischen und Eschatologischen in der Redaktion des ersten Evangeliums ist' (*Weg*, p. 47).
2 Strecker, 'Concept of History', p. 70.
3 Strecker, *Weg*, pp. 184-85.
4 Strecker, 'Concept of History', p. 73.
5 Strecker, *Weg*, p. 219. Cf. 'Concept of History', p. 79.
6 *Ibid*, pp. 185-86. Cf. 'Concept of History', pp. 74ff., where Strecker speaks of 'an *"ethicization"*' of the traditional material. He writes that 'the real mission of Jesus within history according to Mathew's understanding is the proclamation of the ethical demand in which the still-awaited Reign of God has become present' (p. 77).

revelation'.[1] Materially, Strecker claims that the difference between this and the Lukan concept—which was primarily concerned to show the 'fact' of the sequence of periods—is found in Matthew's ethical interests of working out the tasks of the different periods.[2] In the time of Jesus the ethical demands of the eschatological reign of God are proclaimed in Jesus' words and deeds, and these are to be obeyed in the climactic age of the church which extends to the consummation of all history.

In Strecker's salvation history interpretation of Matthew, this theological concept thus becomes the evangelist's response to the delay of the parousia. Salvation history functions as the ideological point of view for Matthew because it allows him to give an account not only of the future—in the development of the time of the church—but also of the past—in the 'historicizing' of the Jesus tradition. The 'historicizing' of the synoptic tradition by Matthew allows him to place Jesus in a unique and unrepeatable past time. The narrative world projected in Matthew is thus controlled by the salvation historical point of view, and contains a 'life of Jesus' that is bounded by the Old Testament time of preparation and by the church's time of fulfillment.

Although Strecker does not explicitly mention the role of the reader in his discussion of salvation history in Matthew, he appears to view the concept of salvation history as playing an important role in the appropriation of the Gospel by its audience. The concept of salvation history shows the readers that the significance of the time of Jesus lies in its function as a time of revelation and of the proclamation of God's ethical demand. They can see that Israel's rejection of the will of God as proclaimed by the Old Testament prophets has culminated in their rejection of Jesus and his proclamation of God's ethical demand.[3] This ethical demand of the Kingdom of God is now represented in time by the church. By proclaiming this demand, the church guarantees continuity between the different epochs in history. During the epoch of the church,

1 Strecker, 'Concept of History', p. 74.
2 *Ibid.*
3 Strecker, *Weg*, pp. 187ff.; 'Concept of History', pp. 74, 77.

which is the epoch in which the readers of the Gospel find themselves, they are confronted as individuals with the responsibility of obeying the ethical demand. For this task they have the exemplary obedience of Jesus to follow, for Jesus himself ideally realized the eschatological demand of God in the 'middle of time'.[1]

Strecker bases his schema of salvation history on what he perceives to be a 'historicizing' tendency in the Matthean narrative, and he appeals to a number of different aspects of the narrative to support his thesis. According to Strecker, the historicizing of salvation history is present through the increased use of temporal and geographical references in the traditional material. Even the Old Testament fulfillment quotations highlight the temporal and geographical elements in such a way as to interpret the history of Jesus as an event temporally and geographically distinct from the situation of the evangelist and his community. The use of the fulfillment quotations in this way is construed by Strecker as evidence that Matthew has 'historicized' what was originally an eschatological kerygma. It is in the life of Jesus, as a 'historisch-biographische Faktizität', that the Old Testament promises have found their fulfillment.[2] Finally, Strecker sees in Matthew an idealized picture of the disciples and with Jesus, a picture which evinces the idea that the time of Jesus is an unrepeatable holy past distinct from Matthew's own age.[3]

2. *Rolf Walker*
A similar tripartite division of salvation history is developed from a slightly different perspective by Rolf Walker in his book *Die Heilsgeschichte im ersten Evangelium*. For Walker, Matthew's salvation historical 'periodizing' centers around the different missions in the first Gospel. The evangelist writes from the perspective of the period of the universal Gentile mission. This is sharply distinguished from the mission to Israel which has rejected God's repeated offer of grace.[4]

1 Strecker, *Weg*, pp. 177ff., 186; 'Concept of History', p. 79.
2 Strecker, *Weg*, pp. 49-85; 'Concept of History', pp. 70-73.
3 Strecker, *Weg*, pp. 194ff.
4 Walker, *Heilsgeschichte* (FRLANT 91; Göttingen: Vandenhoeck &

According to Walker, Matthew works out his tripartite scheme of salvation history within the parameters of a *'vita Jesu'*. Walker delineates three periods in Matthew's time line: (1) the 'pre-history of the Messiah' which is visible in the genealogy, (2) the 'history of the call of Israel', and (3) the 'call of the Gentiles'. Walker isolates a further tripartite division even within the middle period.[1] The decisive break between the middle time of the mission to Israel and the time of the Gentile mission is placed at 70 CE. The church's mission had been directed to Israel prior to this time, but after the fall of Jerusalem, the Jewish mission was terminated and the Gentile mission began.[2] For Walker, Matthew's Gospel therefore contains both a *'vita Jesu'* and an *'Apostelgeschichte'* in one.[3]

According to Walker, the drama of the Gospel is a representation of salvation history: (1) Jesus' earthly ministry, which confirms that he is the Messiah, is restricted in principle to Israel; (2) Israel rejects the repeated offer of grace in Jesus; (3) Israel is in turn rejected by God and loses its place in salvation history as a result of its rejection of Jesus; (4) Israel is replaced in salvation history by the church which is drawn from the Gentile world.[4] The portrayal of Judaism in Matthew is thus historicized and projected back into the time of Jesus, so that the hostility between Jesus and the Jewish leaders in the Gospel does not appear in terms of the contemporary enmity between Matthew's church and Judaism, but rather in terms of Israel's rejection of their Messiah. This rejection sets the

Ruprecht, 1967), pp. 9, 114-15. Cf. p. 117, where Walker sums up his perspective with the dictum 'Heilsgeschichte ist Berufungsgeschichte' in Matthew.

1 *Ibid.*, pp. 114ff. The middle epoch is subdivided into the time of John the Baptist, the time of Jesus, and the time of the disiples until AD 70.

2 *Ibid.*, pp. 115, 117, 120, 126.

3 *Ibid.*, p. 114. According to Walker, this is one of the primary differences between Matthew and Luke. For both evangelists the mission to Israel was completed and replaced by the Gentile mission. The replacement of Israel by the Gentiles happened within the context of the 'vita Jesu' in Matthew, however, whereas in Luke it is moved to the setting of an apostolic church history. See *Heilsgeschichte*, pp. 125-26.

4 *Ibid.*, pp. 9ff.

stage for the Gentile mission, the time of Matthew's community.[1] The tripartite conceptualization of salvation history arises from Matthew's portrayal of Jesus' life as the 'Mitte der Zeit' (in Conzelmann's sense) between the time of the Messiah's pre-history and the time of the Gentile mission.

The concept of salvation history functions as Matthew's ideological point of view in Walker's interpretation of the Gospel because of the way it allows the evangelist to distinguish between the different missions. According to Walker, the narrative world portrayed in the Gospel is ultimately a 'Berufungsgeschichte' which narrates God's offer of grace through his Messiah; it comes first to Israel and then to the Gentiles.[2] As the evangelist's ideological point of view, the concept of salvation history encompasses the whole of this narrative world and enables the evangelist to narrate the temporally successive missions.[3] Since the Gospel is written in the form of a *'vita Jesu'*, salvation history is used to build the church on the sole foundation of the earthly Jesus. The Gentile mission and the entire life of the post-Easter church are thus linked to the commands of the earthly Jesus.[4]

As with Strecker's study, the focus in Walker's monograph is on the use of salvation history by the evangelist to construct his narrative world. Inasmuch as salvation history is examined by Walker in terms of its role in the reader's appropriation of the Gospel, its function seems to be to assist the readers in recognizing the Gospel's historical character.[5] When Matthew is correctly read in this manner, the earthly Jesus and the past are absolutized. Those sayings of the resurrected and exalted Lord which point to a universal mission thus

---

1 *Ibid.*, pp. 37-74. According to Walker (p. 55, n. 45), with the concept of Israel, 'Matthäus hält sich streng an seinen historischen Entwurf; er beschreibt die Situation von damals', that is, of the time of Jesus.

2 *Ibid.*, p. 117.

3 The Matthean church is thus not portrayed as the faithful remnant of Israel (contra Trilling, *Das wahre Israel*) according to Walker, but finds its place in the three-fold temporal sending to Israel (*Heilsgeschichte*, pp. 79-83).

4 *Ibid.*, pp. 116, 149.

5 Walker describes the Gospel as the foundational 'Kerygma-Geschichtsbuch' for Matthew's community (*ibid.*, p. 149).

merely confirm the spoken word of the earthly Jesus, whose sayings are normative for the ongoing life of the Matthean community. Israel's rejection of the Gospel and its subsequent rejection by God are also traced back to the time of the earthly Jesus. The readers can therefore see that Israel is a thing of the past in salvation history, and that the new period, of which they are a part, is the time of the calling of the Gentiles. In this way the fate of Israel, which is still 'offensive' to Matthew's readers, can be accounted for.[1]

Walker's salvation history interpretation of Matthew is based upon those aspects of the narrative which give the Gospel a linear temporal character, and in this respect it is similar to Strecker's study. According to Walker, salvation history is based upon the temporal succession of different mission commands; that is, Matthew writes a history of the 'Basileia-Predigt'.[2] The fulfillment quotations contribute to the sense of a linear concept of time in the Gospel. They show how from Matthew's perspective the life of Jesus was the middle of time, which stood between the time of Israel and its promise of a Messiah on the one hand, and the subsequent mission to the Gentile nations after Israel's rejection on the other.[3] Finally, the theme of rejection figures prominently in Walker's formulation of Matthean salvation history. The historicizing tendency of the evangelist is evident from the way Israel is treated as a complete unity, a 'massa perditionis', whose rejection and judgment has been definitively completed.[4]

3. *John P. Meier*

The final tripartite salvation history interpretation of Matthew we will examine is offered by J.P. Meier. Meier is very explicit in his use of salvation history as a concept

1   *Ibid.*, pp. 116, 145ff.
2   *Ibid.*, p. 146. Walker thus diasgrees with Leonhard Goppelt's interpretation that Matthew used the logion in 10.5b-6 as an 'apologetic proof of Jesus' Messiahship' (*Judentum und Christentum im ersten und zweiten Jahrhundert* [Gütersloh, 1954], p. 181). Rather, this saying serves as a 'historical marker of the great historical mosaic of Jesus' time' (*Heilsgeschichte*, pp. 62ff.).
3   *Ibid.*, pp. 132ff.
4   *Ibid.*, pp. 10, 145ff.

through which the modern interpreter gains a hermeneutical key for understanding Matthew's theology. He believes that salvation history provided Matthew with the means 'to order his various traditions according to a divine economy'.[1] Meier conjectures that the Matthean community was in a period of transition when Matthew wrote his Gospel; a Jewish-Christian church was becoming increasingly Gentile in composition. In this transitional period the evangelist wanted to 'remodel' the gospel to fit the new situation of his community. To accomplish this, Matthew needed to fit the older Jewish-Christian traditions of his church into a 'higher synthesis' with a wider, more universal outlook. According to Meier, salvation history provided the evangelist with a theological framework within which he could formulate his view.[2] Meier defines salvation history as 'a schematic understanding of God's dealings with men that emphasizes continuity-yet-difference'.[3] He conjectures that with this schema Matthew was able to include different traditions in his Gospel under the rubric of 'difference'. The evangelist was also able to affirm older Jewish traditions under the rubric of 'continuity', because he could show that the same God is working in the different periods and is now superseding those old traditions with newer traditions—traditions which are more congenial to the evangelist's outlook and to the new situation of his community.

Meier's method for uncovering Matthew's scheme of salvation history is to examine the different mission instructions in 10.5b-6; 15.24, and 28.16-20—texts which are all peculiar to Matthew. On the basis of these texts Meier postulates that the Matthean scheme is based upon the geographical and national limitations of a mission to Israel being widened to include the universal mission to all nations.[4] The death-resurrection of Christ is the turning point for Matthew at which the

1 Meier, *Law and History*, p. 163. Cf. *idem*, *Vision of Matthew*, pp. 29f., 'Salvation-History in Matthew: In Search of a Starting Point', *CBQ* 37 (1975), pp. 203-15, which is virtually identical to the second chapter in *Law and History*.
2 Meier, *Vision of Matthew*, pp. 28-30.
3 Meier, *Law and History*, p. 22. Cf. *Vision of Matthew*, p. 30.
4 Meier, *Law and History*, pp. 27-28.

'(*heilsgeschichtliche*) restrictions of Jesus' public ministry' pass away in favor of the universal mission, with its concomitant rescinding of strict fidelity to the Mosaic Law.[1] Meier believes that Matthew conceived of this as a single eschatological event which brought in a new period of 'realized eschatology'. In this new period the expection of the imminent end has receded, and the abiding presence of the exalted Lord is emphasized by the evangelist.[2]

As Matthew's ideological point of view, salvation history helps the evangelist appropriate the world in the narrative of his Gospel because it enables him to include and order the different traditions of hia community according to a 'divine economy'. With the use of salvation history Matthew can include the older Jewish-Christian traditions in his Gospel—even though these are outdated—by fitting them into a salvation historical synthesis. In this manner Meier sees a historicizing tendency operative in Matthew, although he is not as explicit about this point as Strecker and Walker are in their studies.[3] Meier also sees the notion of fulfillment in the concept of salvation history being used by Matthew to express his ethical concerns. Jesus is not only the fulfillment of Jewish Messianic expectations; he is also the eschatological fulfiller of the Law, such that his life and teachings become the basis and norm for the church's morality (cf. 5.17-20; 28.16-20).[4]

Salvation history functions for Matthew's readers, according to Meier's interpretation, as the hermeneutical key which allows them to read the Gospel correctly. This concept reveals to them that the restrictions of Jesus' public ministry have passed away with his death and resurrection, and have been replaced with the universal mission. In this epoch of universal mission, in which the readers find themselves, it is not strict fidelity to the Mosaic law but obedience to Jesus' teaching that is important. Salvation history thus helps the reader understand some of the older Jewish Christian traditions in the Gospel, traditions which highlight the particularism of Jesus'

---

1 *Ibid.*, pp. 30ff.
2 *Ibid.*, pp. 37-40.
3 Cf. *ibid.*, p. 7.
4 *Ibid.*, pp. 87-89, 123ff., 166-69.

mission with its concomitant emphasis on obeying the Law. Placing these traditions in a wider interpretive context, Matthew shows that they belong to a different epoch than the one to which the readers belong. Salvation history also helps the reader understand the importance of obeying Jesus' teaching, because salvation history shows Jesus to be the eschatological fulfillment of God's will to save humanity.

Meier appears to base his scheme of salvation history on two elements in the Matthean narrative. But whereas the textual basis of the one is openly discussed, it appears that the textual basis of the other is simply assumed. The sequential nature of the narrative in general, and the different mission commands in particular (10.5b-6; 15.24; 28.16-20) explicitly account for the notion of 'difference-yet-continuity' in Meier's definition of salvation history. The geographical and ethnic restrictions of Jesus' public ministry that were valid during Jesus' earthly life fall away after his death and resurrection; that is, they were limited to 'one period' of salvation history.[1] Yet the textual foundation in Matthew for the idea of 'schematization', which is so fundamental not only to Meier's, but to any other concept of salvation history, is never openly acknowledged. Perhaps it is the evangelist's use of the Old Testament in his fulfillment quotations (which seems to imply a 'periodizing' of history)[2] which functions as the basis for Meier's assumption that Matthew is concerned with a schematization of history.

4. Summary and Critique

Despite differences of interpretation, the three tripartite salvation history interpretations of Matthew which we have examined are all based upon the temporal experience of reading. This aspect of the reading experience, in which the reader processes information sequentially, is construed by these scholars in terms of a linear concept of time. This results

---

1 Cf. *Vision of Matthew*, pp. 30ff.
2 Cf. Reventlow, *Problems of Old Testament Theology*, p. 75, who points this out with respect to von Rad's *Old Testament Theology*. Through the use of the framework 'promise and fulfillment', von Rad sees a periodizing of history in the theology of the hexateuch itself.

in the use of an idea of 'historicizing' to conceptualize the temporal concerns of the evangelist. The concept of 'historicizing', which is especially prominent in Strecker's and Walker's interpretations, could therefore probably be singled out as the most fundamental characteristic of these tripartite salvation history interpretations.[1] Scholars who have formulated tripartite schemes of salvation history in their interpretation of Matthew have also emphasized the themes of acceptance and rejection in their reading synthesis of the Gospel. It is the teaching of Jesus which is of abiding significance for the evangelist and the readers of his Gospel, and this teaching must be accepted and obeyed. Israel, on the other hand, has rejected Jesus and has thus itself come to be rejected by God.

Wolfgang Iser has observed that 'whenever we analyze a text, we never deal with a text pure and simple, but inevitably apply a frame of reference specifically chosen for our analysis'.[2] The tripartite salvation history interpretations of Matthew which we have examined have all chosen a history of ideas frame of reference as a means of access to the text. Matthew is thus read against the background of the development of doctrine in an effort to ascertain the contributions of the evangelist to emerging Christian theology.[3] In the case of

---

1 Gerd Theissen (*Miracle Stories*, p. 200 n. 6) has pointed out that 'historicizing' is a broad term. He contends that the term always implies an antithesis, and he has identified at least four different shades of meaning in the term as it has been used by New Testament scholars: it can refer (1) to 'a chronological rather than a thematically based composition', (2) to 'a retrospective account rather than immediate kerygmatic appeal', (3) to 'a connected account instead of reports of individual episodes', and (4) to 'an account emphasizing historical fact as opposed to a naive narrative'.

2 Iser, *Act of Reading*, p. 53.

3 Cf. K. Tagawa, 'People and Community in the Gospel of Matthew', *NTS* 16 (1970), p. 152, who has made a similar observation with respect to Strecker's study. Tagawa points out that Strecker's method in analyzing the Gospel is to place 'the evangelist in the development of the history of ideas' while presupposing the main line of this development. He questions, however, whether 'the main concern of the evangelist was to define his own theological concepts on the line of this historical development of theological ideas'. We believe that Tagawa's question should be answered negatively.

Strecker and Walker, Matthew's contribution is seen in terms of the movement away from an originally eschatological kerygma, whereas the emphasis in Meier's study is on Matthew's contribution to the emerging theology of a Gentile community that is moving away from its Jewish roots.

The result of using such a history of ideas frame a reference to read Matthew, however, is that the Gospel is explicated solely in terms of its ideational content as it has been systematically delineated by the interpreter. The organizational strategies of the text are replaced by the personal organization of the interpreter. This produces a text that is purely denotative rather than connotative. In the case of a narrative text like Matthew, such a method results in a greatly impoverished text. As Iser has pointed out, to dispense with the organizational strategies of a narrative text is to produce a text that is 'practically disembodied, being reduced to content at the expense of effect'.[1] In the specific case of Matthew, it would seem that the effect of a text—that is, the way it entangles and involves a reader—is itself an integral part of the Gospel's character as an inclusive story, and it is precisely that dimension which needs to be examined.

The idea of 'historicizing', which figures so prominently in the tripartite salvation history interpretations of Matthew, provides us with a good example of how frame of reference shapes interpretation. With the advent of redaction criticism, it became clear that the evangelists were more than mere compilers of the tradition. A greater appreciation of the literary character of the Gospels was demonstrated, and the evangelists came to be considered as authors and theologians in their own right who creatively shaped their Gospels. Historical concerns were proposed by redaction critics such as Georg Strecker as one possible motive for the compositional plans of the Gospels. He has written that

> whereas form criticism stressed the kerygmatic accentuation of the units of tradition and in some cases the 'sermon' as the basis of the tradition's emergence, redaction critical research seems to imply a tendency to admit that the authors of the Gospels have a historical, not a directly kerygmatic

1 Iser, *Act of Reading*, p. 86.

purpose. This takes up again, although in a greatly modified way that no longer focuses on the authentic life of Jesus, the historically accentuated view of the Gospels held by the liberal life of Jesus research.[1]

What is important to observe for our interests is that within his use of a history of ideas frame of reference to interpret the gospels, Strecker understands the literary activity of Matthew and the narrative character of the Gospel as expressing the ideational concept of a historicizing tendency, rather than seeing it as a vehicle for a kerygmatic appeal. Strecker's interpretation of Matthew assumes that by writing a Gospel in the form of a connected narrative, the evangelist is giving expression to a schematized view of history and thereby contributing to the development of doctrine.

It is not necessary, however, to appeal to this history of ideas frame of reference in order to read Matthew. The appearance of chronology in the Gospels is in part due to the narrative form of composition. The impression of a lapse of time is inevitable when events are narrated sequentially.[2] Although

1 Strecker, 'Concept of History', p. 69. Strecker's use of the term 'historicizing' vacillates between Theissen's two meanings of a 'retrospective account rather than immediate kerygmatic appeal', and 'an account emphasizing historical fact as opposed to a naive narrative'. Cf. Ernst Käsemann, 'Blind Alleys in the "Jesus of History" Controversy', in *New Testament Questions of Today*, transl. W.J. Montague (London: SCM, 1969), p. 49. Speaking of the synoptic evangelists as 'composers of Gospels and not merely the gatherers of certain material which happened to be circulating at the time', Käsemann writes that 'doubtless they are dominated by the interests of kerygma. But they express this in the form of Gospels, which are essentially *not* preaching but reporting.... At the same time they supplement the kerygma with historical touches and employ a historicizing mode of presentation'. The same tension between the two different meanings is thus also present in Käsemann's work.

2 See Theissen, *Miracle Stories*, p. 197, who observes that the narrative form of composition is just one possibility of combining the various synoptic genres. Another possibility would be collections of sayings (e.g. Q or the Gospel of Thomas), which also allow room for some narrative genres. Cf. W. Marxsen, *Introduction to the New Testament*, transl. G. Buswell (Oxford: Blackwell's, 1968), p. 130, who labels this impression that there has been a lapse of time

many students of narrative have identified a connection between narrative and history,[1] it is a misunderstanding, or at the very least an uncritical use of this connection, to postulate salvation history as a heuristic concept to express the ideological point of view of the Gospel. Güttgemanns has argued that one cannot simply correlate 'history' with the moment of 'narration' when other forms are also served by 'narrative'.[2] And as Vorster has pointed out, it is a mistake 'to interpret a narrative in direct relation to the real world, for real world and narrated world need not be one and the same'.[3] The so-called 'historicizing' tendency of the Gospel tradition, identified and postulated as a characteristic of the Gospel genre and figuring prominently in tripartite schemes of salvation history, can be seen as a part of the narrative world of the Gospel created by the evangelist. The different chronological periods which are differentiated in tripartite concepts of salvation history may well evince nothing more than the double temporal perspective characteristic of narratives with an overt intru-

resulting in a retrospective account as 'historicizing'. The sense of temporal distance is in fact simply a part of the narrative world created by the evangelist which arises from his use of the narrative form of composition.

1 See White, 'Value of Narrativity', pp. 5-27 and *Metahistory*, pp. 2ff., for discussions of the way in which modern understandings consider 'historical' representations of 'reality' 'true' only if they possesses the character of narrativity. Cf. James Barr, 'Story and History in Biblical Theology', in *Explorations in Theology* 7 (London: SCM, 1980), pp. 5ff., for a similar discussion of the connection between the categories of 'story' and 'history' in biblical theology. Barr argues that while story and history share many common features, the striking differences between the two mean that the extensive corpus of narrative material in the OT merits the title 'story' rather than 'history'.

2 Güttgemanns, *Candid Questions*, p. 22. Güttgemanns mentions the fairy tale, saga, legend, novella, or myth as other possible forms of narrative. Güttgemanns is criticizing the work of Käsemann who correlates history and narrative when he sees the function of the Gospels as 'recalling the historical Jesus' (cf. Käsemann, 'Blind Alleys', pp. 62-64; *idem,* 'The Beginnings of Christian Theology', in *New Testament Questions*, p. 97).

3 Vorster, 'Kerygma/History', p. 92. Cf. Petersen, *Literary Criticism*, pp. 39ff., for his discussion of the 'referential fallacy'.

sive narrator.[1]

Narratives always establish a sense of the present moment—what Seymour Chatman has labelled the 'narrative NOW'.[2] When the narrator stands outside of the characters and the story as he does in Matthew, however, there are two narrative NOWs present: the narrative NOW of the narrator who is telling the story, and the story NOW when action begins to transpire.[3] These two temporal perspectives are analogous to the time of the church and the time of Jesus in tripartite concepts of salvation history. The third epoch in such schemes, the time of Israel, appears as the background against which the story of Jesus is played.[4]

---

1 The presence of an intrusive narrator seems to be a characteristic of the Gospel genre. The narrators of the other Gospels have been similarly identified. See Culpepper, *Anatomy*, pp. 18ff.; Rhoads and Michie, *Mark as Story*, pp. 35ff.; Hill, 'A Response to Prof. Kingsbury', p. 38.

2 Chatman, *Story and Discourse*, p. 63. Cf. C.P. Casparis, *Tense Without Time: The Present Tense in Narrative* (Swiss Studies in English 84; Bern: Francke, 1975), pp. 9-10, where he redefines the 'historical present' (traditionally defined as a present tense for narrating past action) as simply 'all uses of the Present Tense that are *narrative*'.

3 See Uspensky, *Poetics of Composition*, pp. 67ff. for a discussion of temporal point of view. He also treats the double temporal perspective in which a narrative can be cast.

4 Cf. Kingsbury, *Matthew as Story*, pp. 38ff. He states that what biblical scholars have customarily termed 'the history of salvation' approximates what a literary critic might call 'story-time'; that is, 'the chronological order which all the events cited in a narrative occur' (p. 39). In other words, the story-time of Matthew runs from creation to the consummation, although the greatest interest lies from the time of Abraham to the consummation. We concur with Kingsbury that the story of Matthew is indeed open-ended in the sense that it stretches to the consummation. Yet while this results in the time of the narrator being included with the story-time of the Gospel, Kingsbury's use of this literary category does not adequately distinguish between the different senses of the present moment created by the narrative of the Gospel. It would appear that it is these different senses which interpreters are trying to account for in a scheme of salvation history with separate epochs, and not the general temporal frame in which a story occurs.

The relationship between the narrative mode of discourse and the different periods in tripartite schemes of salvation history can be delineated even more clearly, however. Chatman has pointed out that the English tense system can indicate at least four different temporal periods in a sequence of events. He refers to these narrative periods as 'anterior time', 'past time', 'present time', and 'future time'. He argues that most narratives set their story NOW in the second of these stages, the 'past time', and set the discourse NOW in the third stage, the 'present time'.[1] When we turn to examine Matthew, Chatman's outline of different narrative periods closely corresponds to the different temporal epochs that are delimited in the tripartite salvation history interpretations examined above. The 'time of Israel' corresponds to the earliest 'anterior time'. The 'time of Jesus' corresponds to the story NOW in Matthew, and although it is subsequent to the anterior 'time of Israel', it is still in the past tense in relationship to the time of the author/narrator. The discourse NOW is in the present and corresponds to the 'time of the church'. This 'present' is after Jesus' death but prior to the consummation of history. The latter event corresponds to the final temporal period of the 'future time' in Chatman's scheme.

The different temporal periods which are outlined in tripartite concepts of salvation history are thus part and parcel of the narrative mode of discourse Matthew uses, and so do not necessarily reflect the evangelist's 'theologizing' interest, or his intent to contribute to the development of Christian doctrine. Any temporal distancing of the events of Jesus' life in Matthew is a result of the double temporal perspective in the Gospel, whose narrator tells the story retrospectively. In other words, the so-called 'historicization' of the Gospel traditions ascribed to Matthew in tripartite schemes of salvation history is simply a 'literaturization' which arises from the manner the evangelist chose to tell his story.[2] To propose as Matthew's

---

1 Chatman, *Story and Discourse*, p. 80.
2 This word is borrowed from D.E. Aune, 'The Problem of the Genre of the Gospels: A Critique of C.H. Talbert's *What is a Gospel?*', in *Gospel Perspectives* Vol. II, ed. R.T. France and D. Wenham (Sheffield: JSOT Press, 1981), p. 45. Aune uses it to describe the way

ideological viewpoint an abstract theological concept like salvation history—a concept which developed in the twentieth century in a polemical direction against the proponents of kerygmatic theology who emphasized that salvation is now present in the moment of proclamation[1]—is to obscure the narrative character of the Gospel. Although the idea of 'historicizing' is used in tripartite schemes of salvation history to express the temporal movement of the narrative of Matthew, the sense of this temporal advance or plot is lost as the narrative is reified in a static concept.

Problems other than just the neglect of the narrative character of the Gospel also present themselves. For example, many scholars have questioned the legitimacy of using Conzelmann's Lukan scheme to interpret Matthew.[2] It can

Matthew and Luke augment and alter Mark 'in the direction of an increasing literary sophistication and respectability'. Aune cites the inclusion of genealogies and infancy narratives as an example of such a process, whereas Strecker ('Concept of History', pp. 70ff.) gives these as examples of a 'historicizing' of the tradition. They are in fact part and parcel of the narrative world created by the evangelist.

1 This was primarily directed against Bultmann and his school. Cf. O. Cullmann, *Salvation in History*, transl. S.G. Sowers (London: SCM, 1967), p. 13, who claims in the Foreward of his book that he carried on a 'thorough debate with Rudolf Bultmann and his pupils'.

2 See Frankemölle, *Jahwebund*, pp. 366, 371ff.; Meier, *Law and History*, pp. 26ff.; Tagawa, 'People and Community', p. 152. Even if the Lukan scheme can be transposed onto Matthew, scholars are not unanimous in their agreement about the contours of salvation history in Luke-Acts. See W.C. Robinson Jr, *Der Weg des Herrn* (Hamburg: Evangelischer Verlag, 1964), pp. 30-39, who argues that Luke's story of Jesus has become the story of Jesus' journey to Jerusalem. Robinson (pp. 60ff.) along with numerous other scholars, agues that Luke's scheme of salvation history embraces not three but two epochs which can be characterized by the categories 'promise and fulfillment'. See R.J. Dillon, *From Eye-Witnesses to Ministers of the Word* (AnaBib. 82; Rome: Biblical Institute Press, 1978), pp. 272ff., for a bibliography and discussion of the debate. Frankemölle believes that this corrected conceptualization of Lukan theology calls into question Strecker's and Walker's studies of Matthew which presuppose a linear and chronologically-deter-

also be shown that Strecker's and Walker's so-called historicizing tendency is not carried out consistently throughout the
Gospel. Others have argued that the evangelist 'de-historicizes' the miracles, speeches, and disciples in his Gospel,[1] and
Strecker's and Walker's schemes of salvation history do not
take this phenomenon into consideration. Furthermore, there
are problems with the precise location of the vertical lines of
demarcation between the different epochs on the horizontal
time line. Strecker emphasizes the past reality of Jesus' life
which marks the turning point between the past time of
promise to Israel and the present time of the church. But the
demarcation between Matthew's own time (the 'call of the
Gentiles') and the past of the failed mission to Israel is placed
by Walker at around 70 CE, after the destruction of Jerusalem.
Thus, in Walker's scheme of salvation history, the mission to
the Gentiles does not begin until 70 CE. Matthew 28.18ff. flies
in the face of such a conception, however, for here the mission
to the Gentiles clearly begins with the resurrection.[2]

John Meier has recognized this problem in Walker's tripartite scheme of salvation history, and he tries to solve the
problem by postulating the death and resurrection of Christ as
the vertical line of demarcation between the time of Jesus and
the time of the church. This climax of Jesus' mission serves as
the eschatological '*Wende der Zeit*', the hinge on which
Matthew's scheme of salvation history turns. Meier's strong
emphasis on the death-resurrection of Christ as the eschato-

mined understanding of time (*Jawhebund*, pp. 371ff.). Cf. Kingsbury, *Jesus Christ*, pp. 97ff., who finds in Luke a two-fold division of
salvation history similar to that which he finds in Matthew.

1   Frankemölle, *Jahwebund*, p. 377. See Luz, 'Disciples in Matthew',
pp. 99ff., for a general discussion of the transparency of the disciples
in Matthew, and H.J. Held, 'Matthew as Interpreter of the Miracle
Stories', in *TIM*, esp. pp. 233ff. and 265ff., for the way Matthew
addresses his church through the miracle stories.

2   Frankemölle, *Jahwebund*, pp. 370-71; Meier, *Law and History*, p. 25,
n. 1. Walker recognizes this tension, but merely attributes it to
Matthew's failure to harmonize the material with his redactional
viewpoint. He also admits, however, that 28.18ff. show strong traces
of Matthean redaction (*Heilsgeschichte*, pp. 111-13). The result of
Walker's refusal to treat the problem is that his scheme of salvation
history in Matthew ends in a contradiction.

logical event in Matthew has the effect of superimposing a two-fold division on his tripartite Matthean line of salvation history. This has far-reaching consequences on Meier's scheme, for it implies that Jesus' life up to the death-resurrection belongs to the old age, an age which passes away with the eschatological event and the inauguration of the new 'time of the church'.

Such a conception is foreign to the theological structure of the Gospel. The entire life and teachings of Jesus are viewed by Matthew as the fulfillment of the promises to Israel. This is the purpose of the many fulfillment quotations which are so characteristic of Matthew. Jesus' teachings do not pass away with the turn of the ages at the death-resurrection, but are the very thing the disciples are to teach as they embark on the universal mission (28.20). Meier would assent to these propositions, for he believes that with the abrogation of the Mosaic law at the death-resurrection of Jesus, the old law is replaced by the life and teaching of Jesus which has become the 'norm of morality for Christians'.[1] Yet his view of Matthean salvation history, with its two-fold division superimposed upon a tripartite scheme, results in a scheme where 'the kingdom is realized more fully in history' in each successive period,[2] and such a scheme stands in tension with the affirmation that Jesus' life and teaching is the fulfillment of the Messianic promises and Old Testament law. As Kingsbury has pointed out, Meier's scheme 'places the days of Jesus, the time following Easter, and the consummation, respectively, on a graduated scale whereby each period is regarded as more intensely eschatological than the previous one'.[3] Although there is no doubt that Matthew considers the death-resurrection of Jesus to be the climax of his redemptive mission, Meier's scheme does not do justice to the significance that the evangelist places

---

1 Cf. *Law and History*, pp. 88, 123ff., 166-69.
2 J.P. Meier, 'John the Baptist in Matthew's Gospel', *JBL* 99 (1983), p. 403.
3 Kingsbury, *Structure*, p. 34. Meier openly states this in his essay about John the Baptist when he explains the difficult saying in Mt. 11.11b by writing that 'the time of the Church is distinct from the time of the earthly Jesus and enjoys a heightened eschatological quality over the time of Jesus' ('John the Baptist', p. 404).

on the entire life of Jesus (cf. 1.23).

C. *Two-Fold Schemes of Salvation History in Matthew*

1. *Hubert Frankemölle*

The two recent and most prominent Matthean scholars to postulate a two-fold scheme of salvation history in Matthew, Hubert Frankemölle and Jack D. Kingsbury, both characterize the scheme under the categories of 'promise and fulfillment'.[1] Working independently of one another, the two men reached similar conclusions, Frankemölle publishing his monograph a year before Kingsbury completed his study. Frankemölle, however, shuns the label *'Heilsgeschichte'* for Matthew's theology, preferring instead the designation *'Geschichtstheologie'*.[2] This aversion apparently arises from an association of salvation history with the concept as outlined by Cullmann and Conzelmann. He strongly disagrees with Strecker and Walker, the two Matthean interpreters whose concepts of salvation history are most like Conzelmann's tripartite Lukan scheme. Frankemölle argues that Matthew's intention was not to write a life of Jesus, and he insists that Strecker and Walker distort Matthew's concept of history by claiming this objective for the evangelist.[3] Matthew was not interested in history as 'bruta facta' according to Frankemölle. Rather, his interest was directed to the present situation of his church, as is evident from the way in which the evangelist has 'de-historicized' the narrative material and speeches in his traditions.[4] Matthew operated within the categories of 'prophecy and fulfillment' instead of developing a continuous time line that can be divided into segments. Frankemölle thus contends that what Matthew has composed in reality is a literary and theological document in which the exalted Lord, who is identical with the earthly Jesus, directly addresses the evangelist's community in its own time. Such a

---

1 Cf. Frankemölle, *Jahwebund*, pp. 358, 377; Kingsbury, *Structure*, pp. 31ff.

2 Frankemölle, *Jahwebund*, p. 7, n. 2.

3 *Ibid.*, pp. 372ff.

4 *Ibid.*, pp. 349, 377ff., 388.

document is labelled a 'kerygmatisches Geschichtsbild'.[1]

Frankemölle believes that Matthew's model for his 'kerygmatic portrait of history' is to be found in the history works of the Deuteronomist and the Chronicler. Like his Old Testament forerunners, Matthew theologically reflected on history to show how God has faithfully acted throughout history. This faithfulness or continuity is present throughout the Old Testament and continues in Jesus Christ.[2] Matthew did his 'Bundestheologie', according to Frankemölle, in order to meet a crisis in his community caused by Israel's rejection of its Messiah and the resultant destruction of Jerusalem. Frankemölle conjectures that these events provoked Matthew's community to doubt God's faithfulness and the validity of his promises.[3]

Like Meier, Frankemölle would therefore find a pastoral concern behind Matthew's concept of history: this ideological point of view was developed and used to help the evangelist's community through a transitional crisis. It provided Matthew with a way to solve the problem of a 'geschichtstheologische Spannung' between Old Testament and New Testament or Israel and the Church.[4] In Frankemölle's interpretation, Matthew's 'kerygmatic portrait of history' helps the evangelist appropriate the world in his narrative because it enables Mathew to address the members of his own community through the fictitious past of Jesus' life. Matthew is thus able to project the theological problems of his own time back into the life of Jesus.[5] The emphasis in Frankemölle's exposition of the Gospel is correspondingly on the kerygmatic element. When it comes to the term 'history' in Frankemölle's scheme, the

1 *Ibid.*, p. 398.
2 *Ibid.*, p. 387ff.
3 *Ibid.*
4 *Ibid.*, p. 384.
5 *Ibid.*, pp. 333, 347ff. The following statements are representative of Frankemölle's position: 'Fiktiv spricht Jesus zu seinen Jüngern und zum Volk seiner irdischen Wirksamkeit, faktisch angesprochen aber ist—wie feststeht—die Gemeinde des Matthäus am Ausgang des ersten Jahrhunderts' (p. 342). Matthew makes 'seine Gemeinde fiktiv zu Zuhörern und Mitbeteiligten des irdischen Jesus' (p. 349).

evangelist's concern with the past is simply a literary illusion. The concept which Frankemölle uses to explain the meaning of history in Matthew ultimately dissolves the tension between the two horizons in Matthew's inclusive story—the past of Jesus and the present of Matthew's community—because it essentially ignores the past.

For the readers of Matthew, the evangelist's '*Geschichts-theologie*' de-historicizes both the narrative and the discourses in the Gospel. Readers are thus able to distinguish between the past of Jesus' life that is portrayed in the story and their own situation. If they read the speeches of Jesus correctly with the help of the hermeneutical key of Matthew's kerygmatic portrait of history, they read them all as 'das Testament des Herrn für seine Gemeinde für die Zeit nach seinem Tode'.[1] The readers of the Gospel, as members of Matthew's community, therefore stand as the direct recipients of the speeches, and not Jesus' disciples in some fictitious past of his earthly ministry. Because the speeches function as the last testament of Jesus, the readers are bound to observe and practice what Jesus has taught in them.

If scholars such as Strecker or Walker emphasize those aspects of narrative in Matthew which historicize the Gospel traditions in their formulations of salvation history, Frankemölle emphasizes those elements which he interprets as de-historicizing the tradition. 'Salvation history' in Matthew is thus based on the assimilation between the past and the present. It is interesting to observe that an appeal is made to many of the same elements in the narrative to support the differing interpretations. For example, according to Frankemölle, Matthew's use of the Old Testament fulfillment quotations serves not to historicize the 'Geschichte Jesu', but rather to fill the theological function of showing how the acts of Yahweh in the Old Testament continue in the New Testament.[2] They demonstrate the faithfulness of God. Thus time is not thought of in terms of a linear time-line, but in terms of the theological categories of promise and fulfillment. Moreover, the disciples are not idealized and historicized, but function as types of

---

1 *Ibid.*, pp. 338ff. Cf. pp. 130, 377.
2 *Ibid.*, pp. 358, 387.

2. *The Use of 'Salvation History'* 81

members in the Matthean church, both negative and positive.[1]
The miracles and speeches are also de-historicized and sys-
tematized by Matthew. In the miracles, an emphasis is placed
on the sayings of Jesus. In the speeches, sayings of Jesus are
arranged topically, and they are all to be viewed under the
rubric of Jesus' testament to his church rather than being
seen as addresses to specific situations in Jesus' earthly life.
Frankemölle places great exegetical significance on 26.1-5 in
interpreting the discourses in this manner.[2] Further evidence
of the essentially theologizing structure of the Gospel (as
opposed to a linear-temporal basis) is discovered by Frankemölle in the way Matthew treats the rejection of Israel in
terms of such theological themes such as unfaith, fruit-
bearing, and the faithfulness of God.[3] Finally, Frankemölle
bases his scheme of history-theology on what he sees as parallels between the Old Testament history works of the
Deuteronomist and the Chronicler.[4]

2. *Jack D. Kingsbury*

Kingsbury responds to Frankemölle's study in an excursus in
his book *Matthew: Structure, Christology, Kingdom*. Despite
the parallels between Frankemölle's work and his own,
Kingsbury argues that Frankemölle's outline of Matthew's
'Geschichtstheologie' ultimately fails because he has reduced
the evangelist's 'sense of history to the single point of the present'.[5] To be sure, there is a high degree of assimilation
between the past and the present to be seen in Matthew (in the
transparency of the disciples for example),[6] yet Frankemölle's
collapse of the past into the present in his outline of Matthew's

---

1 *Ibid.*,pp. 150ff., 377.
2 *Ibid.*, pp. 337ff., 351.80.
3 *Ibid.*, p. 357.
4 *Ibid.*, pp. 339ff., 381ff. Some of the parallels cited by Frankemölle
    include 1. a combining of narrative tradition with speech or prayer
    complexes, 2. linguistic parallels in the concluding formula of the
    speeches, 3. a parallel in content with speeches ending in a warning
    of judgment, and 4. a conception of time which is a literary fiction
    aimed at making the past relevant for the present.
5 Kingsbury, *Structure*, p. 39.
6 See Luz, 'Disciples', pp. 98-128.

theology of history fails to do justice to the evangelist's awareness of the passage of time. This is evident in the genealogy
(1.1-17), in the different mission instructions (10.5-6; 28.20),
and in the parables against Israel (21.28–22.14). Despite the
parallels in Matthew between John the Baptist, Jesus and the
disciples, the evangelist also distinguishes between their different ministries—both before and after Easter.[1]

It would appear that Frankemölle developed his outline of
Matthew's theology of history by placing too much emphasis
on the parallels between Matthew and the Deuteronomist and
Chronicler. Some of these parallels cited by Frankemölle
would be applicable, however, to any of the books of the Pentateuch which contain a mixture of narrative and discourse. In
Exodus, for example, narrative is interspersed with legal prescriptions which are binding and which address the needs of
Israel in a period removed from the experiences of Egypt and
the wilderness. Furthermore, Frankemölle's emphasis on the
Old Testament history works does not do justice to the importance which the Gospel of Mark and the prophetic writings
held for the evangelist.[2] Matthew is a 'gospel' and Mark

1 John the Baptist, Jesus and the disciples on a pre-Easter mission all
proclaim the same message, 'the Kingdom of Heaven is at hand'.
Matthew makes a distinction between Jesus' preaching and the
preaching activity of the post-Easter community, however, with the
expression 'the gospel of the Kingdom'. This expression is used in
Matthean summaries of Jesus' ministry (4.23; 9.35), but the evangelist changes it to 'this (*touto*) gospel of the Kingdom' in 24.14 and
26.13 when the expression refers to the proclamation of the post-
Easter church. Contra Kingsbury, *Structure*, p. 130, who has written that 'in Matthew's vocabulary the expression "the Gospel of the
Kingdom" refers without distinction both to the message of the
earthly Jesus and to that of his post-Easter church'. Cf. Kingsbury,
Jesus Christ, p. 63, however, who opines that Matthew used the
expressions 'the Kingdom of heaven is at hand' and 'the gospel of
the Kingdom' 'to divide the "time of Jesus (earthly-exalted)" into the
ministries to Israel of John (3.1-2), of Jesus (4.17), and of the pre-
Easter disciples (10.17) [*sic*] and the minstry to the nations of the
post-Easter disciples, or church (24.14; 26.13)'.
2 G.N. Stanton, 'Matthew as a Creative Interpreter of the Sayings of
Jesus', in *Das Evangelium and die Evangelien*, p. 287, n. 38. See A.
Sand *Das Gesetz und die Propheten: Untersuchungen zur Theologie*

appears to be the evangelist's primary source. The importance of the Old Testament prophetic writings can be seen not only from the frequent citations of them in the fulfillment quotations, but also in the role they play in expressing Matthew's ethical concerns (cf. 9.13 for example). Kingsbury has also rightly questioned whether Matthew was responding to a questioning of God's faithfulness in his community by doing 'Bundestheologie', at least in the sense which Frankemölle intends. He points out, on the contrary, that the 'faithfulness of God and the validity of his promises are exactly what Matthew accounts as certain'.[1] This is plainly evident from the evangelist's use of the fulfillment quotations.

Kingsbury, unlike Frankemölle, uses the term 'salvation history' in his study of Matthew's historical consciousness, although he does not invest the term with the theological qualities presented in Conzelmann's Lukan scheme as Strecker and Walker did. His method for uncovering the Matthean concept of salvation history is a study of time words in the Gospel. He contends that a number of temporal expressions, while vague and indistinct, still contribute chronological or historical movement to the Gospel. Others, however, have an eschatological significance according to Kingsbury, and he argues that the phrase ἐν ταῖς ἡμέραις ἐκείναις in particular is used only eschatologically in the Gospel.[2] Through his investigation of these time words, Kingsbury reaches the conclusion that Matthew considered the entire life of Jesus to have an eschatological significance which extends through to the end of history (cf. 3.1).

Kingsbury therefore postulates that Matthew operated with a two-epoch division of salvation history characterized by the categories of 'promise and fulfillment'. The 'time of Israel' which was preparatory to the coming of the Messiah was the time of the Old Testament and promise. It is followed by the 'time of Jesus' in which 'the time of Israel finds its fulfillment

---

des Evangeliums nach Matthäus (biblische Untersuchungen 11; Regensburg: Pustet, 1974) for a discussion of the importance of the Old Testament prophets in Matthew's theology.

1 Kingsbury, *Structure*, p. 38.
2 *Ibid.*, pp. 27-31.

and which, from the vantage point of Matthew's day, extends from the beginnings of the ministry of John and Jesus (past) through post-Easter times (present) to the coming of the age (future)'.[1] In Kingsbury's scheme Matthew does not have a separate 'time of the church', such as one finds in Conzelmann's outline of Lukan theology. Rather, the alleged time of the church 'is construed as of the nature of a subcategory of the time of Jesus; it is to be subsumed under the 'last days' inaugurated by John and Jesus'.[2] Kingsbury argues that this two-fold scheme is evident in the lack of an ascension narrative in Matthew, as well as in the lack of a theology of the Holy Spirit. Because of the continuing presence of the exalted Lord with his community (28.20), neither is necessary.[3] In contrast to the other conceptualizations of salvation history in Matthew which we have examined, each of which has been temporally delimited by ecclesiological concerns such as the delay of the parousia or the different missions, Kingsbury's outline of salvation history is ultimately determined by the evangelist's christology. According to Kingsbury, it is 'the abiding presence of Jesus with his disciples, both "then" and "now"' which is the constitutive element of salvation history in Matthew.[4]

Salvation history functions as Matthew's ideological point of view in Kingsbury's salvation history interpretation of the Gospel, because it provides the evangelist with a chronological scheme that can delineate the ultimate significance Jesus has for Israel and the Gentiles alike. The chronological dimension of the concept is visible in Kingsbury's study of the different temporal expressions in the Gospel. Unlike Frankemölle's study, Kingsbury's employs salvation history as a heuristic device to help uncover the evangelist's conception of historical passage. It concerns more, however, than the mere highlighting of the temporal element in the Gospel. The concept of salvation history is also used to impose meaning on the passage of time in the Gospel. History is seen to be ordered in a purposeful

1 *Ibid.*, pp. 31-32, 35.
2 *Ibid.*, p. 31.
3 *Ibid.*, p. 32.
4 *Ibid.*, pp. 35-36.

way, it is moving toward a goal. In Kingsbury's scheme this configurational aspect of salvation history is expressed in the two-fold division of history into the epochs of 'Israel/promise' and 'Jesus/fulfillment'. According to Kingsbury, Matthew portrays Jesus as the fulfillment of God's plan and promise of salvation both in his earthly ministry, and in his continued presence with his church in its mission.[1]

For the readers of the Gospel, salvation history reveals the eschatological significance of Jesus' presence both 'then' (earthly) and 'now' (exalted).[2] They should thus realize that the central purpose of the Gospel is not ecclesiological but christological: Matthew seeks to inform his readers of Jesus' relationship to the Father and his mission to save God's people. Such a purpose does not exclude a concern for the church, however, and in Matthew's presentation of the person of Jesus, the readers are also shown what it means to be a disciple. From the perspective of the two-fold scheme of salvation history, the readers of the Gospel can view the disciples as 'representative' Christians.[3]

Kingsbury constructs his scheme of salvation history on a number of different elements in the Gospel's narrative. The wide usage of temporal expressions is construed as reflecting Matthew's interest in the passing of time. The eschatological use of the temporal expression 'in those days' as well as the importance of the theological categories of promise and fulfillment highlight for Kingsbury the eschatological signi-

---

1 Cf. Kingsbury's latest book (*Matthew as Story*, pp. 38ff.), where he uses literary critical categories to correlate story-time and salvation history. According to Kingsbury, Matthew's story-time runs from creation to the consummation of history. Kingsbury's correlation between story-time and the theological concept of salvation history seems to emphasize the temporal dimension of salvation history to the neglect of the configurational dimension which is evident in his earlier work. Kingsbury nonetheless still affirms that salvation history in Matthew shows Jesus as Son of God to be 'of decisive significance' for the salvation of Jew and Gentile (p. 40). Such a claim suggests that if the theological concept of salvation history is to be recast into literary terms, it cannot be simply correlated with the story-time of the narrative.

2 Kingsbury, *Structure*, pp. 36, 161.

3 *Ibid.*, pp. 33ff. Cf. Kingsbury, 'Miracle chapters', p. 572ff.

ficance that Matthew places on the entire life and ministry of Jesus. For Kingsbury the two-fold nature of Matthew's salvation historical scheme is established by these features, viewed both in combination with Matthew's use of post-Easter attributes in his portrayal of Jesus and the earthly disciples, and in the light of the absence of a sharply delimited separate time of the church.

3. *Summary and Critique*

Both Kingsbury and Frankemölle appear to neglect the linear and temporal basis of the reading experience in their salvation historical interpretations of Matthew. Their interest lies in the theology of the evangelist and the result is that their interpretations are based upon the synthesis of certain themes in the narrative. Equal weight seems to be given to every mention of a word, concept, or theme in the Gospel with little consideration of the way elements function in the linear development of the story. This is surprising in some ways. Although Frankemölle emphasizes the literary character of the Gospel and the creativity of the evangelist in addressing his community through the fictitious past of Jesus' life, he is no more sensitive to a literary interpretation of the story than were those who proposed tripartite salvation history interpretations of Matthew. He seems reluctant to highlight the linear-temporal unfolding of the story lest it be understood as a 'historicizing' appeal to the story of Jesus as 'bruta facta'. The alternative for Frankemölle is to see a thorough-going theological structure underlying the Gospel.[1] All the speeches of Jesus, for example, are thus understood under the rubric of Jesus' last testament for his church, even though many have their own functions, understandable within the flow of the story without any appeal to this idea.

Kingsbury, on the other hand, seems to pay more attention to the temporal nature of the narrative with his study of time words in the Gospel. He argues that these show that Matthew was interested in conveying a sense of historical passage in his story. Kingsbury's interest is capable of being misinterpreted, however. For the ultimate purpose behind his study of tempo-

1 Frankemölle, *Jawhebund*, pp. 347-57, 377ff.

ral expressions is to show that the phrase 'in those days' is used eschatologically.[1] Its use in 3.1 is then construed as proving the theological point that Matthew considered the whole of Jesus' life as the eschatological fulfillment of God's purpose.[2] The two-fold nature of the theological concept of salvation history is thus established without any further attention being paid to the way information is temporally and sequentially communicated in the Gospel. In both Frankemölle's and Kingsbury's salvation history interpretations, it is the theological themes of promise and fulfillment which are especially emphasized in the reading synthesis.

It should be pointed out that Kingsbury's and Frankemölle's division of history in Matthew into the two-fold scheme of promise and fulfillment is as much a part of the narrative world created by the evangelist as the historicizing tendency explicated by advocates of a tripartite division of salvation history. Use of the categories of 'promise and fulfillment' also represents a 'periodizing of history', even though Frankemölle criticizes this tendency in tripartite schemes of salvation history in Matthew.[3] The second half of Culpepper's observation, that the 'narrative world of a gospel is not an exact reflection of either the world of Jesus or that of the evangelist', must be stressed in response to these proposals of a two-fold division of salvation history.[4] The so-called 'de-historicizing' of the speeches and miracles identified by Frankemölle simply

1 Cf. Kingsbury, *Structure*, pp. 27-31.
2 Even in Kingsbury's recent literary study of Matthew (*Matthew as Story*, pp. 38ff.), the linearity of narrative communication is ignored, for Kingsbury equates the concept of salvation history with the story time of the Gospel, and this he defines as the whole sweep of world history from creation to the consummation. Such a wide-ranging definition of story time, however, makes it impossible to distinguish between the 'sense of the present' in the story time of Jesus' life and death on the one hand, and the narrative time of the author/narrator telling the story on the other.
3 Cf. Reventlow, *Problems of Old Testament Theology*, p. 75.
4 Culpepper, 'Story and History', p. 472—although Culpepper goes on to state that 'undoubtedly the narrative worlds of the gospels are related in various ways... to both the world of Jesus and the social world of the evangelist'. The narrative world of the Gospels is still, however, primarily a literary creation by the author of a Gospel.

reflects a narrative world in which the sayings of Jesus are emphasized and different characters are given attributes which reflect post-Easter conditions. The narrative world of the Gospel is still a creation of the evangelist and distinct from the world and theological problems of Matthew and his community.

If scholars who use a tripartite scheme of salvation history to interpret Matthew err by making too sharp a distinction between the different temporal perspectives in the narrative, those with a two-fold concept err by blurring the distinction between the 'narrative NOW' and the 'story NOW'.[1] If the notion of 'historicizing' arises from a misunderstanding of the temporal perspective of an intrusive retrospective narrator, the idea of 'de-historicizing' seems to arise from a misunderstanding of the temporal perspective of the implied reader of the narrative. Students of narrative have argued that just as authors have images of themselves inscribed in the text, so readers have literary versions of themselves. The implied reader is thus the recipient of all the rhetorical strategies used by the implied author, and projects the ideal response congruent with the intention of the author as communicated in the text.[2] Since the implied reader/narratee is the correlate to the implied author/narrator, these two textual constructs share the same temporal point of view. In Matthew this perspective is subsequent to the resurrection but prior to the consummation of the ages. In other words, it is identical to the so-called time of the church.[3] Because the implied reader is 'silently' present throughout the narrative, however, Kingsbury and Frankemölle can describe the implied reader's relationship to the world of Matthew's story in terms of 'de-historicizing' or being contained within the 'time of Jesus'. Yet such ways of describing a reading synthesis of Matthew overlook the fact that the temporal point of view—or the 'narrative NOW'—of

1 See our earlier discussion (present chapter) of Chatman, *Story and Discourse*, pp. 63, 79ff. and of the different senses of the present moment which can be established in a narrative text.
2 Cf. Booth, *Rhetoric of Fiction*, pp. 70ff.; Chatman, *Story and Discourse*, pp. 147ff.; Lategan, 'Redescription', pp. 70ff.
3 Cf. Kingsbury, *Matthew as Story*, pp. 36ff.

the implied reader is still distinct from the 'story NOW' of
Jesus' life and ministry, and the two should not be confused. It
therefore may be misleading to speak either of a 'historicizing'
or of a 'de-historicizing' tendency in Matthew. Both characterizations misunderstand the narrative nature of the Gospel.[1]
The aspects of the narrative seized upon in such characterizations are not theologically motivated constructs, but simply
parts of the narrative world of Matthew.

C. *Conclusion*

In the interpretations of Matthew which we have examined,
salvation history has been used as an 'overarching category' of
composition for the Gospel. These scholars have argued that a
concept of salvation history was used by Matthew to hold
together the story and to express his conviction that in Jesus
God was effecting salvation for both Jew and Gentile alike.
When treated as Matthew's ideological point of view, the concept of salvation history explains the way he handled his traditions and composed an 'inclusive' story. For these redaction
critics, the experiences of Matthew's church reflected in the
Gospel, whether seen as the subject of a separate epoch or subsumed in the time of Jesus, can be accounted for by a theological scheme.

It has been clear in studying these formulations of salvation
history that this theological concept is closely tied to the narrative form of the Gospel. Students of narrative have shown
that a narrative is composed of more than a mere chronological succession of events. It must also be configured into some
sort of meaningful, coherent whole.[2] The temporal dimension

---

1 Cf. Luz, *Matthäus*, p. 27, n. 42, who writes that 'Mt. muß also
primär auf der Ebene der Erzählung, nicht auf der Ebene eines theologischen Entwurfs interpretiert werden'. Luz writes his commentary in the traditional style, however, without recourse to the literary critical paradigm and methods which we are using.
2 Ricoeur, 'Narrative Functions', pp. 183ff. Cf. Frank. J. Matera, 'The
Plot of Matthew's Gospel', *CBQ* 49 (1987), p. 235, who also notes the
connection between plot as understood by literary critics and salvation history. He seems to limit the interpreter's concern with salvation history to the passage of time in the Gospels, however, without

of salvation history places the story of Jesus in the wider context of God's dealings with Israel and the church.[1] Some of the schemes examined were in fact based upon the linear unfolding of the narrative. The configurational dimension of salvation history expresses the ultimate significance of Jesus, and is based upon the reading synthesis of certain themes in the Gospel. The themes of promise and fulfillment show Jesus to be the eschatological fulfillment of God's purposes to redeem humanity. Thus the centrality and gravity of the choice faced equally by the characters in the story and by the readers of the Gospel is underlined: one must either accept or reject Jesus and his proclamation of the Kingdom of God.

Notwithstanding this close connection between the narrative form of the Gospel and the concept of salvation history, salvation history seems inadequate as a heuristic paradigm for interpreting the inclusive nature of Matthew, because it paradoxically neglects the narrative character of the Gospel genre. The salvation history interpretations which we have examined have read the Gospel with a history of ideas frame of reference that uses a concept to encapsulate the message of the narrative. The paradox of this approach is that the temporal movement and plot of the Gospel, which are absolutely essential to narrative, are given up and replaced with a static idea. The message or meaning of the Gospel is thus located in something external to the narrative rather than in the narrative's own depiction of characters and events, and the evangelist's rhetoric of entanglement and the reader's participation in reaching the reading synthesis of what the Gospel is 'about' are neglected.

It would appear that the participatory dimension of the reading process is an important, but overlooked, aspect for understanding Matthew as an 'inclusive' story. If the meaning of a narrative is to be found in its plot, that 'on-going interaction of character and circumstance directed toward an end', then this plot should not be considered by itself without also thinking of 'the plot according to whom', for a reader is always involved in construing the possible world which is created by a

also seeing that it is connected to the question of causality.

1 Cf. Kingsbury, *Matthew as Story*, pp. 38ff.

narrative.[1] The specifics of this possible world are not determined solely by textual evidence, but arise from the fusion of horizons between text and reader, as we argued in the introduction. A study using narrative criticism to describe some of the ways in which a reader's experience of the text may be structured by the narrative should therefore help highlight some of the communicative potential in the Gospel, especially given 'the avowed interest of this genre in evoking a response from the reader'.[2] In the case of an inclusive story like Matthew, in which experiences of later readers are in some way considered to be inscribed in the text, it would seem all the more important for interpreters to have some means of describing the ways in which readers come to be included in the narrative, and, for example, how they (or other readers) might recognize their experiences in the story and so involve themselves in interpreting the narrative.

Divergent as the different conceptualizations of salvation history have been, the critics have agreed that in Matthew salvation history emphasizes the ultimate significance of Jesus and his teaching for all humanity. This suggests that it might be the unity of Jesus' life and ministry rather than a theological concept of history which provides the adhesive for the Gospel and gives it its sense of completeness. The message of the gospel is thus to be found within the plot of the narrative rather than in something external to it (such as a concept of history that somehow encloses the story). To argue that the purpose of the Gospel is to put forward the identity of Jesus does not imply that Matthew has written a life of Jesus in the modern biographical sense.[3] Nor does it imply, as Strecker and

---

1 Gary Comstock, 'Truth or Meaning: Ricoeur versus Frei on Biblical Narrative', *JR* 66 (1986), p. 133.

2 Jouette M. Bassler, 'The Parable of the Loaves', *JR* 66 (1986), p. 161. While the fourth Gospel is very explicit in stating this goal (Jn 20.31), it is surely also present in the synoptic Gospels.

3 See Ronald F. Theimann, *Revelation and Theology: The Gospel as Narrated Theology* (Notre Dame, Ind.: Notre Dame University Press, 1985), pp. 112-40, and Kingsbury, *Matthew as Story*, for two recent literary interpretations of Matthew which argue that the purpose of the Gospel is to render an identity description of Jesus through narrative. Cf. also Hans Frei, *The Identity of Jesus Christ:*

Walker state, that Matthew placed Jesus in an unrepeatable holy past.[1] A more balanced approach can be found in Graham Stanton's argument that

> the wholly justifiable insistence that the gospels are not biographies has tended to hide the fact that when they are placed alongside comparable ancient writings, they are seen to tell us a surprisingly large amount about the life and character of Jesus.[2]

In Matthew's life of Jesus the focus is largely on the commands of Jesus, and in this his Gospel is different from Luke-Acts, where the life of Jesus is placed within a larger history of the beginnings of Christianity.[3]

In the following chapters we propose to examine Matthew's inclusive story about Jesus using a literary approach which focuses on the ways a reader appropriates a narrative. We will ask what type of judgments about Jesus might a reader who is included in the story be asked to make by the way Matthew has structured his narrative. In this way the issues of temporal passage and the configurational dimension of narrated events which were raised by the salvation history interpretations of Matthew examined in this chapter, will be examined from the different perspective of their narrative function.

The Hermeneutical Bases of Dogmatic Theology (Philadelphia: Fortress, 1975), who offers a similar narrative interpretation of Mark.

1 See Strecker, *Weg*, pp. 184ff., 194. Walker, *Heilsgeschichte*, pp. 114ff.

2 G.N. Stanton, *Jesus of Nazareth in New Testament Preaching* (SNTS Monograph Series 27; Cambridge: CUP, 1974), p. 136.

3 Cf. Theissen, *Miracle Stories*, p. 223, who opines that Matthew has written a 'didactic gospel life' whereas Luke has written a 'salvation history gospel life'.

Chapter 3

NARRATIVE TEMPORAL ORDERING AND EMPLOTMENT IN MATTHEW'S INCLUSIVE STORY

A. *Introduction*

We argued in the previous chapter that when the theological concept of salvation history has been used to interpret Matthew, it has evinced both a chronological and a configurational dimension that is closely related to the narrative form of the Gospel. The chronological element is expressed in two different senses. On the one hand, the narrative world which is projected by the Gospel has temporal boundaries. That is to say, the story takes place within a certain time-frame. Jack Kingsbury was thus able to argue that the story time—or otherwise put, the history of salvation—in Matthew runs from creation to the consummation, because it is within these temporal limits that Matthew sets his story of Jesus. The chronological dimension is present in another sense, however, since the narrative is made out of events which occur in a temporal sequence. It is this linear unfolding of the story which John Meier, for example, utilized to construct a scheme of salvation history based on the different mission commands in the Gospel. As the story develops, these commands reflect a widening of the scope of the mission.

The configurational dimension of the Gospel's narrative and of the concept of salvation history are visible in the way the narrated events in Matthew are ordered into some kind of meaningful whole. That is to say, literary critics have shown that a narrative is always composed of more than a mere chronological sucession of events. Rather, the narrative world is interpreted and given significance through the rhetorical strategies utilized to plot events so that they tell the story of the

Gospel in a certain way. As readers we must be able to elicit a configuration from the succession, or as Paul Ricoeur has described it, we have to 'understand the successive actions, thoughts and feelings as having a *particular directedness*'.[1] In the salvation history interpretations of Matthew we have examined, the themes of promise/fulfillment and acceptance/rejection have been highlighted in order to give the Gospel its sense of completeness and directedness. In those interpretations based on a two-fold scheme of salvation history, Matthew's Jesus is seen as inaugurating the time of fulfillment to which the Old Testament time of promise pointed. In those interpretations based in a tripartite scheme of salvation history, the theme of rejection is prominent. God's rejection of Israel (which comes about as a result of its rejection of Jesus and the gospel) provides the necessary presupposition for the temporal delimitation between the epoch of Jesus and that of the church in Matthew, the latter epoch containing within itself the concomitant movement of the mission to the Gentiles. The use of these two organizational themes is of course not exclusive to any one type of salvation history interpretation of Matthew, and the configurational dimension of the narrative itself displays temporal features. Information and events are still communicated and read sequentially even when the organizational principle governing the textual order of presentation is something other than a strictly chronological sequencing of events.

One problem which appeared in the salvation history interpretations we examined for the purposes of understanding the inclusive nature of Matthew, was that they were unable to describe the way the experiences of Matthew's church were inscribed in the narrative. Within the history of ideas approach which the salvation history interpretations represented, the readers of the Gospel were not so much included in Matthew's story of Jesus as they were included in a theological construct that was external to the narrative. In this way, the meaning or significance of the Gospel were extracted and isolated from the narrative sequence of the story, rather than being seen as interrelated with the events within the narra-

1 Ricoeur, 'Narrative Time', p. 182.

tive. In the following chapters we propose to explore the inclusive nature of Matthew's Gospel by means of a literary approach sensitive to the way these different aspects of narrative relate and function.

Our analysis of the inclusive nature of Matthew is expedited by the distinction between the chronological and configurational dimensions of narrative, a distinction which has been highlighted by modern literary theorists.[1] Although discussed under a variety of terms, the chronological or episodic dimension is ususally labelled 'story'. This is the 'content' or 'what is told' of a narrative text. The story is composed of a setting, characters, and a chain of events. The means, or 'how', whereby the story is told we will label 'narrative'.[2] This includes not only the order and pattern in which events are presented in the text (which incidentally bears no necessary relationship to the actual or 'objective' order in which the events occurred), but all the other rhetorical techniques utilized to give the story coherence, such as point of view, pacing and closure, to name just a few.[3]

1 The distinction between content and form in narrative has been recognized since Aristotle. The emphasis on recent literary theory on these two aspects of narrative can be traced back to the work of Russian Formalists, however. Cf. Sternberg, *Expositional Modes*, pp. 8-14.

2 We are following the lead of Culpepper in his study of John (*Anatomy*, pp. 53ff.) rather than using the terminology of Chatman who distinguishes between 'narrative' and 'discourse' (*Story and Discourse*, pp. 19ff.). Although such a distinction is more precise, it may lead to confusion because of the connotations of 'discourse' with the five great sections of Jesus' teaching in Matthew. Furthermore, narrative and discourse are often difficult to separate in practice. The term 'narrative' will thus be used in two different ways in our study, at times referring to the text and in other places referring to the 'how'.

3 See Chatman, *Story and discourse*, Gerard Genette, *Narrative Discourse: An Essay in Method*, transl. J.E. Lewin (Oxford: Blackwell, 1980); Petersen, *Literary Criticism*, pp. 35-48; *Rediscovering Paul*, pp. 10-14; Wolterstorff, *Art in Action*, pp. 139-42, for representative discussions of the different strategies and elements which should be discussed in a poetics of narrative. Temporal pacing of narration refers to the amount of time given to telling the story and involves

Although the distinction between the 'what' and 'how' of Matthew's Gospel helps us specify both the sense in which a reader comes to be included in the story and the rhetorical power this has for communicating to readers of the Gospel today, we must remember that the means of telling story also contributes to its 'content'.[1] The narrative of the Gospel is no mere empty structure in which the contents of the story are poured. How a story is told contributes to its meaning and the effect it has on readers. In this chapter we will therefore focus on the way in which the events of the story are plotted in the narrative, and on the temporal boundaries of the narrative world which result from this emplotment. The manner in which the events of the story and experiences of the characters are plotted in the narrative should provide clues to the significance of the plotted story for later readers. In this way we hope to answer provisionally the questions of who is included and how they are included in Matthew's 'inclusive story' of Jesus. In an attempt to fill out our answers, subsequent chapters will focus respectively on the voice within the narrative which tells the story, and on the implied reader (or 'narratee') within the narrative.

B. *Plotted Story and Narrative World*

The two different aspects of a narrative text, story and narrative, present two different levels of information. On the level of the story, characters act, speak, and understand in relation to

such techniques as the use of scenes or summaries (cf. Lanser, *Narrative Act*, pp. 198ff.). Norman R. Petersen, 'When is the End Not the End? Literary Reflections on the ending of Mark's Narrative', *Int* 34 (1980), p. 152, defines closure as 'a sense of literary ending derived from the satisfaction of textually generated expectations'. Cf. also White, 'Value of Narrativity', p. 24; Sternberg, *Expositional Modes*, pp. 70ff.

1 Cf. Lanser, *Narrative Act*, p. 99ff., who wants to overcome the content-form polarity found in many literary theories. She argues that 'aesthetic structures are themselves "content", for they express some organization of the "contents" of social life in such a way as to create a new "content" from the synthesis of social and aesthetic materials'.

one another. On the level of the narrative, however, the narrator gives other information which only the implied reader is allowed to know. The different levels each have their own temporal sequence and are related to one another by the plotting devices used to tell the story.[1] Information and events on the narrative level can be arranged in any order which does not render the narrative nonsensical. Information and events on the story level, however, are by arranged by definition in their 'objective' order of occurrence.

When Matthew is examined, we find a close correlation between the temporal sequence of the story and narrative dimensions of the Gospel narrative. This is true not only of Matthew but of all the Gospels. As ostensibly historical documents, the Gospels each present narratives which are primarily chronological, following the span and contours of Jesus' life.[2] For example, the events which are narrated in Matthew begin with Jesus' birth and end with his death and resurrection. The only major temporal deformation between story and narrative is found in the evangelist's account of John the Baptist's death (14.1ff.). This event occurs much earlier in the story than the events with which it is placed in the narrative.

The relationship between story time and narrative time is, however, more complicated than this simple chronological ordering of the narrative might suggest. Reference is made in Matthew to characters and events both anterior and subsequent to the plotted story of Jesus' life. In this way the narrative text projects a narrative world with temporal boundaries within which Matthew's story of Jesus unfolds. The easiest way to determine the temporal boundaries of Matthew's narrative world is to look for the earliest and latest events referred to in the Gospel. The temporal boundaries which are projected by Matthew, stated in their simplest terms, reach back in the history of Israel to Abraham (1.1-17) on one side, and extend

---

1 Cf. Petersen, *Literary Criticism*, pp. 49ff.; and 'The Reader in the Gospel', *Neotestamentica* 18 (1984), p. 47.
2 See Scholes and Kellogg, *Nature of Narrative*, p. 211, and Sternberg, *Expositional Modes*, pp. 43ff., for discussions of the nature of narrative in historical texts.

into the indefinite future of the coming of the Son of Man (19.28; 24.29ff.; 25.31ff., for example) on the other side. It is within this larger narrative framework that Matthew's story of Jesus' life is told in a specific manner and sequence.

Because this narrative world extends into the indefinite future, it is populated not only by the characters who act in Matthew's story, but also by the narrator/implied author who tells the story and the implied reader to whom it is addressed. By examining the relationships between Matthew's narrative world and his plotted story, we should be able to clarify how later readers (traditionally discussed in terms of Matthean church members) can be included in his story of Jesus. Since our primary interest lies in the question of how a later reader is included in Matthew, we will only briefly note the relationships of the anterior temporal boundaries of the Gospel's narrative world to the plotted story before focusing on the way events and information subsequent to the story are narrated in the Gospel. The categories developed by Gerard Genette in *Narrative Discourse*, a highly acclaimed study of time-relations in narrative, will provide us with a framework to discuss the relationships between Matthew's narrative world and his plotted story.

Since every narrative represents an imaginative world with its own temporal, spatial, and social dimensions within which characters perform certain actions, the reader, as an outsider, must be introduced to what may be a strange and alien world. This is accomplished through 'exposition' whereby the narrator of the story provides the reader with 'the general and specific antecedents indispensable to the understanding of what happens in it'.[1] The genealogy of Jesus (1.1-17) which opens Matthew's Gospel should be considered expositional in this sense, because as Matthew uses it to place his story of Jesus firmly in the history of Israel and thus establish one of

---

1 Sternberg, *Expositional Modes*, p. 1; Chatman, *Story and Discourse*, p. 67. Exposition's primary function is thus explanatory. Cf. Uspensky, *Poetics*, pp. 137-51, for a discussion of how authors 'frame' their narratives with 'beginnings' and 'endings' which facilitate the transition back and forth from the 'real' world to the narrative's represented world.

the temporal coordinates for the narrative world projected by his Gospel.[1] In this way the genealogy lays the basis for the repeated references to the fulfillment of Old Testament prophecy, references which serve as the evangelist's primary literary device for anchoring his story of Jesus to the past history of Israel. With the Old Testament formula quotations Matthew presents Jesus as the fulfillment both of Israel's Messianic hopes, and of God's plans to save his people.

Genette has dubbed allusions in the narrative to past events as 'analepses', and he has defined these as 'any evocation after the fact of an event that took place earlier than the point in the story where we are at any given moment'.[2] The evangelist's use of the formula quotations can be identified more precisely as 'mixed analepses' which are references to events that begin prior to the narrative but which continue into the plotted time of the story.[3] The Old Testament prophecies cited by Matthew were spoken in the history of Israel, but are fulfilled by the events of Jesus' life which Matthew recounts in his Gospel. In this sense, they continue into the time of the story. Sayings such as 5.17ff. (cf. 11.13), which present Jesus as the eschatological fulfiller of the Law, can also be seen as mixed analepses. The Law of course existed prior to Jesus' life, but in Matthew's story it is the life and teaching of Jesus which function as the dynamic expression of God's will.[4]

The effect of these mixed analepses is to link Jesus' life and Matthew's story with Israel and with all the traditions con-

---

1 This literary function of the genealogy has been widely recognized by commentators. Cf. Raymond E. Brown, *The Birth of the Messiah* (London: Geoffrey Chapman, 1977), p. 59, who writes that Matthew uses his genealogy 'to stress Jesus' insertion into a history and a people'.

2 Genette, *Narrative Discourse*, p. 40.

3 *Ibid.*, p. 49.

4 See C.F.D. Moule, 'Fulfillment Words in the New Testament: Use and Abuse', *NTS* 14 (1967-68), p. 316; Robert A. Guelich, *The Sermon on the Mount: A Foundation for Understanding* (Waco, TX: Word, 1982), pp. 142ff., 163ff., for discussions of the disputed question of how Jesus fulfilled the Law. For our purposes in this context, it is sufficient merely to point out that this theme in Matthew helps link Jesus to the prior time of Israel.

cerning the history of God's dealings with this nation. While all the synoptic Gospels place Jesus in the history of God's dealings with Israel, Matthew's use of this type of mixed analepsis particularly highlights Jesus' connection with Israel. The idea of promise and fulfillment which is so characteristic of Matthew can thus be attributed, in part at least, to the way Matthew has temporally plotted the story in his Gospel.[1]

The counterparts of 'analepses' are 'prolepses'. These Genette defines as 'any narrative maneuver that consists of narrating or evoking in advance an event that will take place later'.[2] These anticipations of coming events, like analepses, can be broken down into more precise categories. References to events which will occur within the narrative are called 'internal prolepses'. 'External prolepses' anticipate events which occur entirely after the narrative, and 'mixed prolepses' allude to events which begin within the narrative but continue beyond it.[3] All of these different types of prolepses are used in Matthew and deserve closer scrutiny if we are to explore how Matthew's community is included in the story of his Gospel.[4] We will primarily be concerned with more or less

---

1 The prominence of the theme of fulfillment in Matthean thought was evident in our review of salvation history interpretations of Matthew in the last chapter. Both types of salvation history scheme saw the time of Jesus as the fulfillment of Old Testament Messianic hopes. The literary function and effect of Matthew's Old Testament fulfillment quotations will be discussed in more detail in the next chapter, focussing on their role in the text's overall strategy of creating meaning for the reader.

2 Genette, *Narrative Discourse*, p. 40.

3 *Ibid.*, pp. 68ff.

4 Cf. Luz, *Matthäus*, p. 23, who mentions the presence of 'Signalen' as a characteristic of the evangelist's literary style. According to Luz, these anticipations point out beforehand the meaning ('Sinn') of the whole context and sensitize the reader for later narrative. Luz distinguishes between three distinct types of foreshadowing in Matthew: (1) In the prologue (1.1-4.2) Matthew gives an inventory of the themes of his Gospel, (2) Scenes in the story also anticipate what is to come later and thus have a 'typological' function (2.1-12, for example, anticipates the 'no' of Israel and the positive response of the Gentiles to Jesus and the Gospel), and (3) Sayings of Jesus which are not direct predictions but which have a surplus of mean-

explicit references to specific events, rather than with general allusions which acquire their significance only later after the narrative has been (re)read.[1]

Internal prolepses function in Matthew to advance the plot of the story and to heighten the sense of dramatic intensity. References to and predictions of future events generate expectations in the readers which are later fulfilled in the story. The clearest example of this type of prolepsis or prediction is found in the passion predictions (16.21; 17.22f.; 20.17ff.). The expectations generated by these predictions may be fulfilled almost immediately (as when Jesus came to John for baptism—3.11f), or they may be fulfilled at some point significantly fur-

ing ('Sinnüberschuß') in their immediate context, meaning later disclosed for the believing community by the whole Gospel (3.9; 9.8; and 11.27 for example). While Luz's distinctions are helpful and point out a major plotting device used in the Gospel, the literary categories we will use offer greater precision in identifying the different temporal dimensions operative in Matthew's narrative. See also Moule, 'Fulfillment Words', pp. 293-94, who has distinguished three sets of correlatives in the idea of fulfillment: prediction/verification, beginning/completion, and covenant obligation/consummation. Our category of promise and fulfillment as a plot theme would belong to the first set of correlatives. According to Moule, this set is dominant in Matthew because of his use of the Old Testament formula citations which demonstrate for the evangelist the truthfulness of God in carrying out his predetermined plan (pp. 297ff.). He concedes that the second and third sets of correlatives are also present in the Gospel, although the sense of covenant obligation and consummation is communicated generally through the Gospel rather than in the specific use of fulfillment worlds.

1 Genette, *Narrative Discourse*, p. 75. One of the problems with Luz's categories of 'signals' in Matthew is that he does not distinguish between allusions and explicit references. This is not to deny, however, that both explicit prolepses and suggestive allusions contribute to plot development and to the build up of dramatic intensity in the story. Such a function of suggestive allusions would be heightened in narratives like the Gospels whose story would be well-known through their use in the church. See Ricoeur, 'Narrative Time', p. 179, who has written that 'as soon as a story is well-known ... retelling takes the place of telling. Then following the story is less important than apprehending the well-known end as implied in the beginning and the well-known episodes as leading to the end'.

ther on in the narrative, as is the case with Jesus' scourging, mocking, and crucifixion at the hands of Gentiles (cf. 20.17-19; 27.27ff.).[1] This type of prolepsis will be dealt with in more depth when we look at the way in which Matthew has plotted his story of Jesus.

The other types of prolepses in Matthew are of special interest to our study because they relate the Gospel's story to the time of its readers in Matthew's community. Mixed prolepses, like their counterparts mixed analepses, serve a linking function, anticipating events that begin in the narrative and continue beyond its end. Instead of linking the story of Jesus' life to the prior history of Israel, however, they link Matthew's story with events subsequent to Jesus' death and resurrection. The mixed prolepses in Matthew fall into two categories. First, they are found in sayings of Jesus connected with his actions in carrying out God's plan of redemption. For example, the conditions necessary for Jesus to save the people from their sin (1.21) are fulfilled by the end of the narrative with Jesus' death and resurrection, but the offer of salvation continues in the life and mission of the church. On the basis of Peter's confession, which is plotted in the story, Jesus promises in 16.18ff. to build his church on Peter, but of course the church exists only in the post-resurrection period after the plotted story has ended. Finally, when Jesus calls his first disciples, he promises to make them 'fishers of men' (4.19). Within the story this prediction is presumably fulfilled when the disciples are sent on a mission (10.5-8), but its fulfillment also continues in the post-resurrection mission of the church (28.19-20).

Examples of the second type of mixed prolepsis in Matthew are clustered around the rejection of Jesus by Israel. Thus, in

---

1 Petersen, 'When is the End Not the End', and *Literary Criticism*, pp. 52ff., has also identified this as the major plotting device in Mark. Cf. Paul S. Minear, *Matthew: The Teacher's Gospel* (London: Darton, Longman & Todd, 1984), p. 130, who has written of the passion in Matthew that 'each episode in the dramatic action conveys a prophecy of later episodes'. We will argue that this use of prediction and fulfillment as a plotting device is pervasive throughout the Gospel and not merely limited to the passion account, although admittedly both the frequency and specificity of internal prolepses is greater in the passion accounts than in other parts of the gospel.

27.25 the Jewish people *and their children* accept responsibility for Jesus' death. In a similar vein, the story begun by the leaders of Israel—that Jesus' disciples stole his body from the tomb—continues 'to this day', that is, to the day when the evangelist writes the Gospel (28.11-15). Likewise, the 'field of blood', the field bought by the Jewish leaders with the money Judas received for betraying Jesus, is also still known (27.6-8). Some interpreters would also want to include the prediction of Israel's loss of the Kingdom of God (21.43) among those prolepses which refer to events that are fulfilled within the plotted story of Jesus' life, but which continue beyond the end of the narrative.[1]

The effect of these mixed prolepses, which link the intended readers' experiences with Matthew's story of Jesus, is that the evangelist is also able at least partially to specify the significance of the story for his readers. The mixed prolepses in Matthew reveal that this significance centers around whether the reader will accept or reject Jesus. The negative consequences the resulting both from Israel's rejection of Jesus in the story and from its continued obduracy in the face of the community's proclamation of the Gospel would be evident to the reader. External prolepses in the gospel such as the prediction of the destruction of Jerusalem and the Temple would further support this conclusion by a reader. Conversely, the positive response of acceptance is specified for the reader in terms of observing all that Jesus has taught (28.20). For later readers who find themselves in the time after Matthew's plotted story ends, the essence of their lives as Christians is intimately linked by the evangelist not only with the life and ministry of the earthly Jesus, but also with the lives and witness of his disciples who have heard and passed on Jesus' teaching.[2]

---

1 See. F.W. Burnett, *The Testament of Jesus-Sophia* (Washington, DC: University Press of America, 1981), pp. 111ff., and the literature cited there for arguments that Jesus' departure from the Temple in 24.1 represents the culmination of Jesus' rejection of Israel. According to Burnett, Israel was no longer God's people for Matthew after Jesus left the Temple (p. 164).

2 See Luz, 'Disciples in Matthew', pp. 105-114, for a discussion of the importance for Matthew's concept of discipleship that the disciples

The experiences of Matthew's community may also be reflected in some of the external prolepses. These too fall into two categories in Matthew: 'eschatological' prolepses, which refer to events at the consummation of the ages when the Son of Man comes in glory, and 'historical' prolepses, that refer to events which happen after the evangelist's story of Jesus' life has ended in his death and resurrection, but still within the temporal boundaries of the Gospel's narrative world.[1] Eschatological prolepses are primarily found in the varied images of judgment that are associated with the coming of the Son of Man (8.12; 19.28ff.; 25.31ff. for example). These threats of judgment are used paraenetically by Matthew.[2]

The remaining prolepses found in Matthew are various historical external prolepses. Some of these prolepses do not anticipate specific events so much as they presuppose the general experience of the post-resurrection church. The saying in 12.31 about sinning against the Holy Spirit thus presupposes that the Spirit will be given to the community after the resurrection—even though Matthew himself does not narrate this event as Luke does. In the so-called 'community discourse' of chapter 18, the teaching on discipline in 18.15ff. mentions and presupposes a community with defined boundaries and a shared life. The promise of Jesus' presence in the community in 18.20 also anticipates conditions after the resurrection (cf. 28.20).

Jesus' eschatological discourse in chapters 24 and 25 proves to be a rich source for historical external prolepses, since it looks beyond the plotted story to focus on events which will precede the close of the ages (24.3).[3] Many sayings of these

'hear and understand' Jesus teachings.

1 These categories are drawn from Culpepper (*Anatomy p.* 64). Culpepper notes the difficulty in classifying some prolepses because many of the sayings may be metaphorical and allusive (see pp. 61ff.). It is difficult, for example, to determine whether some of the eschatological predictions should be understood literally or metaphorically.

2 See Bornkamm, 'End Expectation and Church in Matthew', in *TIM*, pp. 15-51, for the classic study of how Mathew uses eschatology in the service of his paraenesis for his community.

3 Cf. Graham Stanton's remark that 'these chapters reflect, perhaps

chapters deal with the mission of the church (24.14; 26.13), and in particular, many deal with the persecution and hardships Christians will face both from Jewish and Gentile sources in the carrying out of their mission (23.34; 24.9; cf. 5.11ff.; 10.17ff.). Besides the hostility from without, the church also faces dissension and problems from within. False prophets (24.11, 24; cf. 7.15ff.) and Messiahs (24.5, 24) will arise, trying to lead the elect astray. Betrayals and divisions between families and other Christians will appear (24.10; cf. 10.21). The destruction of the Temple and of Jerusalem amidst international warfare is predicted, as are famine and earthquakes (24.2, 6ff., 15; cf. 22.7; 23.37ff.).[1] Associated with the destruction of Jerusalem and the Temple will be the flight of many from Judea and widespread tribulation which follows (24.16ff.).

In the midst of the eschatological discourse the narrator intrudes with a comment addressed directly to the readers. They are exhorted to understand the sign of the 'desolating sacrilege' (24.15). This intrusion into Jesus' speech suggests that the events which Jesus is predicting are events about which the reader should have some knowledge; that is to say, they are events which may either be past or present for the implied reader of the Gospel.[2] Matthew not only creates trust in his reliability as a story-teller, but his story gains credibility by showing that he recognizes specific information about past or present events Jesus' predictions in the past. Moreover, the

more clearly than any other part of the Gospel, the setting from which it comes' ('The Gospel of Matthew and Judaism', *BJRL* 66 (1984), p. 281).

1 Although the reference to the destruction of a city in 22.7 appears in a parable, Anthony Thiselton has pointed out that 'it is difficult to see how this sentence could function as a coherent element within the single narrative perspective of the wedding parable . . . .' Rather, the imagery of the 'eschatological kingdom as a festal banquet to which disobedient Israel refused to come triggers a second-level interpretation—the destruction of Jerusalem'—which has been included in the parable's narrative as it is preserved in Matthew ('Reader-Response Hermeneutics', p. 86).

2 Cf. Petersen, 'The Reader in the Gospel', pp. 45ff. for a discussion of what the implied reader already knows, and what new things are learned from a reading of Mark 13.

experiences of later readers (i.e. Matthew's community) also come to be authenticated in a sense, by the story.

External historical prolepses have other literary function besides lending the Gospel credibility. Norman Petersen has argued that 'by rendering the implied reader's present as past, the narrator also relates the problems of that present... to the problems of the past which are recounted in the plotted narration'.[1] A new context for understanding their problems and experiences, the context of the plotted story, is thus provided for the readers. If we are correct in our assumption that some of the external prolepses are reflective of the situation of the readers in Matthew's community, then the hardships and persecution which they are facing are to be recognized as similar to the rejection that Jesus faced in his ministry. In the context of the plotted story, the readers stand in the lineage of God's messengers who have been rejected and persecuted (5.11ff.; 21.31ff.; 23.29ff.). Jesus, however, also stands in this same lineage, and in the story God ultimately vindicates him by the resurrection for his obedience and trust. For the implied readers of the Gospel who are called to accept Jesus and be obedient to his teaching and interpretation of God's will (5.11, 17; 7.21, 24ff.; 12.46ff.; 28.20, for example), this conclusion to the plotted story stands as a word of encouragement (cf. 25.31ff.).

Although our interpretive context is different from that of Matthew and his implied readers—what they know to be past or present, we can only surmise—our experience of the evangelist's mixed and external prolepses evokes certain things which may not be dissimilar to the responses of readers in his community. Included in the references to future events in the prolepses is the prediction that the events which precede the parousia of the Son of Man will occur within the generation of Jesus' disciples (16.28; 24.34). Most scholars place the time of writing for Matthew in the latter part of the first century, sometime between 85-95 CE.[2] If the traditional dating of

---

1 Petersen, 'When is the End not the End', p. 158. Cf. Culpepper, *Anatomy*, p. 68.

2 See W.G. Kümmel, *Introduction to the New Testament*, transl. H.C. Kee (rev. edn; London: SCM, 1975), pp. 119, for a discussion of the

Matthew is accurate, the intended readers of the Gospel are second generation Christians. They would therefore know that this temporal prediction of the parousia had not been fulfilled within Jesus' generation. Matthew accounts for the generation gap and problem of the delay of the parousia in a statement immediately following this prediction in the eschatological discourse (24.36). Here Jesus admits that no one except the Father, not even himself, knows when the day of the parousia will come. His assertion in effect de-temporalizes the eschatological discourse in terms of answering the disciples' question about the parousia and close of the age with temporal language (cf. 24.3 and the use of πότε). This means that although the implied reader may know that many of the external prolepses in Matthew have occurred, they, like readers today, still stand in the midst of an indeterminate time between the end of the plotted story and the parousia of the Son of Man.[1]

The emphasis in the eschatological discourse thus seems to fall on the nature of Christian existence in the indeterminate time preceding the end instead of on the chronology of the end.[2] This is evident from the series of sayings and parables which follows Jesus' statement (24.37-25.46). The two themes which are reiterated throughout the series exhort the disciples to be ready for the parousia and to redeem the time while they wait.[3] Since the prospect of judgment is associated with the

dating of Matthew.

1 Cf. Fred W. Burnett, 'Prolegomenon to Reading Matthew's Eschatological Discourse: Redundancy and the Education of the Reader in Matthew', *Semeia* 31 (1985), pp. 100ff.; and H.J. Bernard Combrink, 'The Structure of Matthew as Narrative', *Tyndale Bulletin* 34 (1983), pp. 89ff.

2 Hans Conzelmann, 'Geschichte und Eschaton nach Mc 13', *ZNW* 50 (1959), pp. 210ff., who has pointed out, with respect to Mk. 13, that unlike other apocalyptic literature the synoptic eschatological discourses do not announce a direct link between contemporary historical events and the arrival of the end.

3 Cf. Terence L. Donaldson, *Jesus on the Mountain: A Study in Matthean Theology* (JSNT Supplement Series 8; Sheffield: JSOT Press, 1985), pp. 165ff., who argues that it is not the imminence but the 'suddenness or unexpectedness' of the end which forms the basis of the exhortations in the eschatological discourse in Matthew.

parousia in Matthew (7.21ff.; 13.36ff., 47ff.; 24.45ff.; 25.31ff.) and since throughout the Gospel the basis of judgment is doing the will of the heavenly Father, the exhortations for watchfulness should be understood in terms of obedience to Jesus' commands. In the context of the plotted story, it is Jesus who correctly interprets and proclaims God's will.

The fact that Matthew uses parables in his account of Jesus' eschatological discourse to encourage watchfulness in the indeterminate time between the end of his plotted story and the parousia contributes to the effect his prolepses have on a reader. It also underlines from a slightly different perspective the similarities between the position of the implied reader of the Gospel and that of other readers vis-a-vis Matthew's 'inclusive story'. Recent studies on parables have emphasized the role an audience plays in contributing to the meaning of a parable. Robert Funk, for example, has written that

> the parable is not closed, so to speak, until the listener is drawn into it as participant. The application is not specified until the hearer, led by the 'logic' of the parable, specifies it for himself.[1]

The reception of the parable, however, is a multi-layered phenomenon. The context within which parables are embedded and the audience to whom they are addressed in the Gospel partially determine their meaning on one hand. The church's tradition in interpreting the parables throughout history as well as the contemporary situation of the reader also contribute to the parables' interpretation on the other. But with the parables in the eschatological discourse which are concerned with life in an indeterminate future, there is a rough

---

See A. Kretzer, *Die Herrschaft der Himmel und die Söhne des Reiches* (SBL 10; Stuttgart: KBW Verlag, 1971), pp. 191ff for a more detailed discussion of the paraenetic purposes of the parables in 24.45–25.46.

1 Robert W. Funk, *Language, Hermeneutic and Word of God* (London: Harper & Row, 1966), p. 133. See Thiselton, 'Reader-Response Hermeneutics', pp. 96-101, and the literature he cites for a general discussion of 'the need for a reader-response approach to the parables'. Thiselton himself, however, does not want to use a reader-response paradigm uncritically without supplementing it with other approaches.

correspondence between the situation of the audience in the Gospel who listen to the parables and that of readers to whom they are directed today. The modern reader or interpretive community, like the disciples to whom the discourse is addressed in the Gospel, does not know when the end will come. This similarity in interpretive context correspondingly means that the interpretation and application of the parables specified in the Gospel may take on more importance in determining modern interpretations of the parables.[1]

Thus, in the context of Matthew's Gospel the parables of the eschatological discourse assert the need for obedience to Jesus' teaching. Like the implied readers of the Gospel, however, every reader of Matthew waits in the indeterminate time between the end of the plotted story and the parousia of the Son of Man with the command to observe all that Jesus taught (cf. 28.20).[2] The specific way in which later readers redeem the time before the parousia by obeying Jesus' commands is determined by their own situations as they read and recontextualize the parables. And yet the indeterminacy of the future which forms the basis of the interpretive context for all readers is the same, so that Matthew's basic interpretation of watchfulness in terms of obedience to Jesus remains valid.

If we return to the question with which we began this chapter, which dealt with the sense in which readers (or Matthean church members, as the question has traditionally been posed) can be said to be included in Matthew's story of Jesus, we note that our survey of time relations in the Gospel has shown that they are included through the use of prolepses. The references to events that will occur beyond the end of the plotted story are found both on the story and narrative levels

---

1 See Thiselton, 'Reader-Response Hermeneutics', pp. 91ff, and his discussion of the work of J. Arthur Baird (*Audience Criticism and the Historical Jesus* (Philadelphia: Westminster, 1969), for the hermeneutical role of the specified audience in the Gospels for interpreting parables.

2 Donaldson (*Jesus on the Mountain*, pp. 166ff.), has pointed out that despite the striking differences in tone and content, both the eschatological discourse and the resurrection appearance in Galilee present 'a view of discipleship centred on the necessity of obedience to the Lord's commands'.

in Matthew, in sayings and actions by Jesus and other characters and in comments by the narrator/implied author. By
these prolepses Matthew projects a narrative world with temporal boundaries which extend into an indefinite future even
though he concludes his plotted story or narrative with Jesus'
death and resurrection. It is within this wider narrative world
that both the narrator who tells the story and the readers to
whom it is addressed are included.

By encoding or inscribing a reader in the narrative,
Matthew is able to specify, in part at least, the significance of
his story for actual readers inasmuch as these readers must
read through the encoded reader if they are themselves to
understand the Gospel. While more work is needed to flesh out
the portrait of the implied reader in Matthew and the way this
construct structures one's reading experience of the Gospel,
we have seen that obedience to Jesus is a major characteristic
demanded of this reader. The importance of accepting Jesus'
teachings will be more evident after we examine the structure
of Matthew's plot.

C. *Emplotment in Matthew*

A discussion of Matthew's plot may seem inappropriate to
some. They might argue that the notion of emplotment is
associated with fiction and with the inventiveness of an
author, whereas the Gospels are historical or history-like documents in which an evangelist recorded 'what happened' in
Jesus' life. It is certainly true that the evangelists were not at
complete liberty to create events or characters as they wrote,
and that the various events which constitute the story of the
Gospels may have been set in the traditions which the evangelists received. It therefore must be acknowledged that the task
of an author of fiction is different from that of the historian or
evangelist. Yet the similarities between their respective tasks
should also not be overlooked.[1] The evangelist had to shape
these events into a coherent story with a discernible beginning,

---

1 See White, 'Value of narrativity', and *Metahistory*, pp. 5-7, for a discussion of the relationships between history as narrative and fictional narrative.

middle and end. This structuring process or element is the plot of a Gospel,[1] and it is the reason why the four Gospels are each distinct even though the evangelists tell essentially the same story. In other words, each evangelist 'emplots' the events which he narrates in order to tell his story in a particular way, to interpret and give the significance of what he tells.[2] According to Seymour Chatman the function of 'plot' is

> to emphasize or de-emphasize certain story-events, to interpret some and to leave others to inference, to show or to tell, to comment or to remain silent, to focus on this or that aspect of an event or character.[3]

A study of the plot of Matthew is thus not only appropriate, given its narrative character, but it is also necessary if we are to form a picture of the implied reader who is 'included' in the Gospel and embodies the response at which the evangelist is aiming. As Norman Petersen has astutely pointed out with respect to Mark, the evangelist creates 'a world of values as well as of events' by his emplotment of the story.[4]

In our survey of time-relations and temporal ordering in Matthew's narrative, two themes which are central to Matthew's plot were uncovered. First, the correlatives promise/fulfillment were used to tie Matthew's story of Jesus to the previous history of Israel and portray Jesus as the fulfillment of Israel's messianic hopes.[5] The theme of promise/

---

1 Abrams, *Glossary of Literary Terms*, p. 137, defines plot in a dramatic or narrative work as 'the structure of its actions, as these are ordered and rendered toward achieving particular emotional and artistic effects'. Cf. Culpepper, *Anatomy*, p. 80, who after surveying recent definitions of 'plot', summarizes its central features as 'the sequence, causality, unity, and affective power of a narrative'.

2 White, *Metahistory*, pp. 6-7, has pointed out that same event 'can serve as a different kind of element of many different historical stories, depending on the role it is assigned in a specific motific characterization of the set to which it belongs'; that is, it may serve as a beginning, transitional, or final element in 3 different stories.

3 Chatman, *Story and Discourse*, p. 43.

4 Petersen, 'Point of View in Mark's Narrative', *Semeia* 12 (1978), p. 108. Cf. Lanser, *Narrative Act*, p. 201, who has written that 'the structuring of "plot" is also a structuring of attitude".

5 Some scholars have even conjectured that events in Jesus' life are

fulfillment also operates within the narrative as a plotting device whereby the story is advanced temporally.[1] Predictions are made which generate expectations and build up dramatic intensity. This plotting device often takes the form of internal prolepses by 'anticipating events which are not clearly defined but gradually come into focus as the narrative proceeds'.[2]

narrated in Matthew simply because they fulfill Old Testament prophecies. See Marxsen, *Introduction*, p. 147, who describes Matthew's procedure in the following way: 'starting from the fragments of tradition before him, he looks for an appropriate passage in the Old Testament which he quotes to make good the claim that the life of Jesus is a fulfillment'. Cf. *Mark the Evangelist: Studies on the Redaction History of the Gospel*, transl. R. Harrisville *et al.*, (Nashville: Abingdon, 1969), p. 97, where Marxsen writes that Matthew uses the Old Testament prophecies in terms of proof, with the result that the focus of the Gospel is on 'the facticity of what happened'. Although Marxsen's insight that the selection of narrated events and plotting of the story is surely correct, we must demur from his claims that the evangelist focuses on the facticity of events. In this respect, Marxsen allow himself to be unduly influenced by the notion that the evangelist 'historicized' the story merely because he presents it as a connected narrative.

1 Theissen, *Miracle Stories*, pp. 198ff. After a study of linking compositions in the synoptic miracle stories, Theissen concludes that time, action and motivation connections are characteristic of Matthew. Nevertheless, the most frequent linking composition is the temporal connection, and the overwhelming majority of these are formed simply with an introductory τότε. Cf. Frankemölle, *Jahwebund*, p. 352, who argues that τότε is often merely the formal designation of a new pericope in Matthew. A.H. McNeile, '*Tote* in St Matthew', *JTS* 12 (1911), pp. 127ff., has pointed out, however, that τότε helps convey the sense that 'the event related is regarded as happening in due sequence to what has gone before'. He argues that Matthew's use of τότε as a connective particle to introduce a subsequent subject or event represents the force of '*waw* consecutive' in Hebrew idiom.

2 Culpepper, *Anatomy*, p. 63. According to Petersen (*Literary Criticism*, pp. 52, 56, 61-63, 78-79), prediction is the major plotting device in Mark. Minear's observation concerning the passion in Matthew, that 'each episode in the dramatic action conveys a prophecy of later episodes' (*Matthew*, p. 130), should not be limited to the passion account. We will argue that the evangelist's use of prediction/fulfillment as a plot device is pervasive throughout the Gospel.

The second theme which is central to Matthew's plot is found in the correlatives acceptance/rejection. J.D. Kingsbury has argued in a recent literary study of Matthew that the element of 'conflict' is central to the plot of the Gospel.[1] According to Kingsbury, the primary conflict is between Jesus and Israel and it is resolved by Jesus' death. A secondary conflict is found between Jesus and his disciples who have difficulty 'thinking the things of God'. Kingsbury correctly observes that this conflict is 'of a fundamentally different order' than the first since the disciples finally 'comprehend that servanthood is the essence of discipleship' (28.16-20).[2] While the importance of conflict to the plot of Matthew cannot be overstated, it appears to be that the correlatives acceptance/rejection give a more precise statement of this plot element than Kingsbury's category of 'conflict'. First, the question of whether to accept or reject Jesus and his proclamation of the Kingdom forms the basis of the literary theme of conflict in the Gospel. The conflict between Jesus and Israel is different from that between Jesus and his disciples because Israel ultimately rejects Jesus, whereas his disciples accept him and observe all that he commanded. Second, the theme of acceptance/rejection is also able to embrace the conflict which Jesus himself faced. In the wilderness and in the Garden of Gethsamene (4.1ff.; 26.36ff.), he too struggled with the temptation of whether or not to obey and accept God's will. The parallel between Jesus and the disciples, an important dimension of Matthew's story, is thus brought into sharper focus by our more specific category of correlatives than by Kingsbury's general statement of plot elements.

In the remainder of the chapter we will offer a reading of Matthew which seeks to follow the flow of the narrative and to focus on the way the plot elements of promise/fulfillment and acceptance/rejection structure the narrative.[3] Since reading is

1 Kingsbury, *Matthew as Story*, pp. 3ff. Richard A. Edwards, *Matthew's Story of Jesus* (Philadelphia: Fortress, 1985) also finds conflict as a dominant theme in his reading of Matthew. Cf. Joseph Tyson, 'Conflict as a Literary Theme in the Gospel of Luke', in *New Synoptic Studies*, pp. 303-27, for a discussion of the theme in Luke.
2 Kingsbury, *Matthew as Story*, pp. 8-9.
3 Moore, 'Stories of Reading', p. 144 would describe my reading as a

a linear and temporal experience in which a reader processes information and constructs a narrative world as the narrative progresses, special attention will be given to the sequence of the plot. This approach is more concerned with the way earlier and later portions of the story are related to one another than it is with imposing a specific outline on the Gospel.[1] The following subdivisions of the narrative are therefore offered not as rigid outline delimitations of the Gospel, but as broad segments within the flow of the narratve, segments which help structure our discussion of Matthew's plot into more easily managed units.[2]

'second story' of reading superimposed upon the first story of Matthew's Gospel.

1 No consensus about the proper outline of Matthew has been reached among scholars. Proposals have centered around repeated formulas in the Gospel with some arguing for an outline modelled on the five discourses, others delineating a tripartite outline, and a third group seeing a chiastic arrangement centered around the parable discourse in chapter 13. See Luz, *Matthäus*, pp. 16-26 who has pointed out the difficulties in specifying a precise outline for the Gospel. He argues instead that the Gospel must be read as a connected narrative which is based on Mark. Cf. Edwards, *Matthew's Story*, pp. 9ff., who also eschews an attempt to impose an outline on the story. Kingsbury (*Matthew as Story*, pp. 38ff.), on the other hand, uses the same tripartite outline in his literary reading of the Gospel which he developed in earlier research (see Kingsbury, *Structure*, pp. 1-25). Bauer, *Structure of Matthew's Gospel*, Combrink, 'Structure of Matthew', pp. 61-90, Matera, 'Plot of Matthew's Gospel', pp. 233-53, provide good discussions of the stucture of Matthew from the perspective of a narrative analysis of the Gospel. Combrink offers a symmetrical outline which is centered around chapter 13 and is based on the alternating sections of narrative and discourse. He connects this symmetrical pattern to a plot outline of the elements: 1) Setting (1.1--4.17), 2) Complication (4.18--25.46), and 3) Resolution (26.1--28.20).

2 We thus recognize that there is an unavoidable subjectivity on the part of the interpreter in deciding what formalized elements of the Gospel should be construed as marking outline divisions. Kingsbury, for example, makes the first division at 4.17 (*Structure*, pp. 7-17), whereas Luz (*Matthäus*, pp. 24ff.) and Edward (*Matthew's Story*, p. 9) make the break at 4.23. In terms of understanding the flow of the narrative, however, it makes no substantial difference which outline division is chosen. Our indifference to a precise out-

1. *Matthew 1.1–4.16*

Literary theorists have shown that authors 'educate' their readers to read their narratives correctly. A model reader is projected or implied by the linguistic code, literary style, and by certain kinds of reading competence which the text presupposes. The text not only presupposes a certain level of competence, however, but it also seeks during the reading process to enhance and 'build up, by merely textual means, such a competence'.[1] The initial information about the attitudes, characters, and narrative world which is projected plays a large part in the process of teaching readers the correct interpretive techniques for reading the text. Because of the 'primacy-recency effect', this information will be retained and will influence interpretations of the subsequent narrative until it is undermined by new information.[2]

The opening chapters of Matthew thus play a critical role in the reader's experience of the Gospel as the evangelist lays the groundwork for what follows. The major characters are introduced, the conflict between Jesus and his opponents is adumbrated, and the plotting devices which are used throughout the narrative are established. We have already seen that the genealogy of Jesus (1.1-17) which opens the book should be considered expositional, since Matthew uses it to place the story of Jesus firmly in the history of Israel. David and Abraham who are mentioned in the superscription of the genealogy (1.1) are pivotal people in Israel's history and Messianic

line of the Gospel does not mean that the Gospel is devoid of structuring elements in the narrative, and our analysis of Matthew's plot will take such elements into consideration.

1 Umberto Eco, *The Role of the Reader: Explorations in the Semiotics of Texts* (London: Indiana University Press, 1979), pp. 7ff.

2 Sternberg, *Expositional Modes*, pp. 93-94, defines the primacy-recency effect as basically 'the proverbial tenacity and enduring influence of first impressions'. He writes concerning a reading experiment that 'due to the successive order of presentation, the first block was read with an open mind, while the interpretation of the second . . . was decisively conditioned and colored by the anterior, homogeneous primacy effect'. See also Perry, 'Literary Dynamics', pp. 47-58. Cf. Minear, *Matthew*, p. 38, who has observed that 'it was the habit of biblical people to find at the outset of a story a kind of preview of all that would follow'.

hopes, and their names also anticipate the basic themes of the first two chapters. The sonship of David and Jesus' work as Messiah of Israel is the focus of the first chapter. As son of Abraham, however, Jesus is also heir to the promise of blessings to the Gentiles. This theme is developed in chapter 2 when the magi come to worship the King of the Jews.[1] The summary to the genealogy (1.17) highlights its structure and contributes to the sense of the providential nature of Jesus' life and ministry, a sense which will be gained throughout the Gospel by Matthew's use of the plotting device of prediction in the Old Testament formula quotations. For Matthew, Jesus' coming as the Messiah is predetermined by God.[2]

The plotted story itself begins in 1.18 with a brief account of the birth and naming of Jesus,[3] and the two major plotting

---

1 Brown, *Birth*, pp. 67ff. These two themes are not limited to the first two chapters, however, but are pervasive throughout the Gospel. Numerous scholars have observed that Matthew shows a heightened interest in both restricting Jesus' mission to Israel while at the same time stressing the universality of the Gospel which offers salvation to the Gentiles. Cf. Marshall D. Johnson, *The Purpose of the Biblical Genealogies* (SNTSMS 8; Cambridge: CUP, 1969), p. 225, who connects the title 'son of Abraham' with 'son of David' and sees both titles elaborating the idea of Davidic Messiahship. Luz, *Matthäus*, p. 93, points out that Jesus is also presented as King of Israel in chapter 2 because he is contrasted with King Herod.

2 See Johnson, *Biblical Genealogies*, p. 208, who argues that this structure of Matthew's genealogy gives his genealogy an 'eschatological—perhaps even apocalyptic—overtone'. Kingsbury, *Jesus Christ*, p. 67, also observes that Matthew alludes to the special activity of God in the coming of Jesus by casting the verb δεννάω in the passive voice (cf. the passive participle in 1.20). Cf. Brown, *Birth*, p. 138, who argues that the idea of 'divine preparation' which dominates the genealogy is underlined by the fact that Jesus is given his name before birth (1.21).

3 See Krister Stendahl, 'Quis et Unde? An Analysis of Matthew 1-2', in *Interpretation of Matthew*, ed. Stanton, pp. 60ff; Adolph Schlatter, *Der Evangelist Matthäus* (6th edn; Stuttgart: Calwer, 1963), p. 25, who observe that Matthew's interest in 1.18ff. appears to be the engrafting of Jesus into the Davidic line, and not the actual birth of Jesus. Cf. Brown, *Birth*, p. 133ff., who expands Stendahl's characterization of the theme of chapter 1 ('*Quis*') with the category of '*Quomodo*' (How). Johnson, *Genealogies*, p. 228, sees a similar

devices used in the Gospel appear immediately in both this
scene and the following infancy stories in chapter 2. In this
opening scene Jospeh is confronted with the choice of either
accepting or rejecting the angel's instructions.[1] He is obedient
to the divine commands first by choosing to marry Mary, and
secondly by naming the child Jesus. In this way Jesus is born
into the Davidic line according to God's plan. Brian Nolan's
observation that 'the keynote of the pericope... is the fulfillment of the will of the Lord in many ways'[2] must be interpreted against the backdrop of Matthew's intertwining of the
correlatives prediction/fulfillment and acceptance/rejection.
The will of God is fulfilled in the predictive sense in that his
predetermined plan is carried out—but it is also fulfilled in the
volitional sense, in that divine instructions are accepted ad
executed by Joseph.

The plot themes of prediction/fulfillment and acceptance/
rejection are closely intertwined in a similar manner in the
infancy stories of chapter 2. The themes of acceptance and
rejection are present as the evangelist contrasts the positive
response and obedience of the magi and Joseph with the rejection of Jesus by Herod.[3] The chapter opens with the magi from

intention for 1.18-25, when he argues that the very *raison d'être* of
the pericope is to answer the question 'how is Jesus the Son of God?'.
1 According to Rudolf Pesch, 'Eine alttestamentliche Ausführungsformel im Matthäusevangelium. Redaktionsgeschichtliche und
exegetische Beobachtungen', *BZ* 10 (1966), pp. 220-45, and 11 (1967),
pp. 79-85, Matthew 1.24-25 represents an obedience formula used in
the Old Testament to express human submission to the will of God
(pp. 229ff.). This tripartite formula is composed of the pattern 1)
reaction to the command, 2) obedience is asserted, and 3) the execution of the command is described. The construction of 1.24ff. closely
parallels the structure of 21.6-7. Cf. Brian M. Nolan, *The Royal Son
of God: The Christology of Matthew 1–2 in the Setting of the Gospel*
(Orbis Biblicus et Orientalis 23; Göttingen: Vandenhoeck &
Ruprecht, 1979), p. 121; Brown, *Birth*, p. 145.
2 Nolan, *Royal Son of God*, p. 130.
3 Cf. Nolan, *Royal Son of God*, p. 132, who has written that 'the magi
scene deftly foreshadows the opposition between faith and worship
and unbelief and persecution that permeates the whole Gospel'.
Brown, *Birth*, p. 183ff., sees in the magi an anticipation of Jesus'
promise to include Gentiles in the Kingdom of Heaven (8.11), and

the East seeking the one born King of the Jews (2.2). This act can be seen as a positive response to a star that they had understood as a sign. Upon reaching Bethlehem their actions continue to be characterized by the positive response of acceptance. First, they worship the child and offer him gifts. Second, in response to a warning in a dream, they do not return to Herod. Since dreams in Matthew 1 and 2 function as a literary convention in which a divine revelation is made through the agency of an angel, the response of the magi can be construed as obedience to God.[1] The obedience of the magi is paralleled by Joseph's obedience throughout the chapter as he accepts the angel's instructions which he receives in his dreams (2.13ff, 19ff.).

The rejection of Jesus by Herod in the chapter stands in sharp contrast to the acceptance and obedience displayed by Joseph and the magi. Whereas the magi came and worshipped Jesus, Herod sought to destroy him. Raymond Brown has conjectured that Matthew chose to place the Old Testament formula quotation in 2.5b-6 in the direct speech of Jesus' Jewish opponents 'to show their obduracy'.[2] If he is correct, the theme of rejection is underlined, and the way in which the correlatives acceptance/rejection control the emplotment of the narrative is plainly visible.[3]

describes the pericope as 'the gospel in miniature'.

1 See Robert Alter, *The Art of Biblical Narrative* (London: George Allen & Unwin, 1981), p. 51, who identifies annunciation as a biblical type-scene with the elements of a fixed convention.

2 Brown, *Birth*, p. 186. If Brown is correct, this formula quotation is also an example of the evangelist's use of irony. Even though the Jewish chief priests and scribes read the Old Testament correctly, they are unable to understand it. This interpetation is strengthened by the parallels between chapter 2 and chapter 26 and 27 where irony is present in the trial and crucifixion of Jesus. People use the correct titles and confessions for Jesus in the passion without realizing it. See Donald Senior, *The Passion of Jesus in the Gospel of Matthew* (Wilmington, Del.: Michael Glazier, 1985), for a good discussion of Matthew's use of irony in his passion account.

3 Cf. Luz, *Matthäus*, p. 122, who sees four 'Auslegungstypen' in 2.1-12: 1) a prelude to the Gospel in which the Gentiles respond and Jerusalem rejects the Messiah of Israel, 2) a christological theme in which men react to Jesus by worshipping as the magi did, 3) a

Throughout the pericopae the one plot theme of accep-
tance/rejection is intimately connected with the other of pre-
diction/fulfillment. Prediction is used both in Old Testament
formula quotations, which show the events of Jesus' infancy to
be the fulfillment of Old Testament prophecy, and in the prediction of events later fulfilled in the narrative. While not
overtly predictive itself, the description of Herod's initial
response to the news of Jesus' birth, 'he was troubled' (2.3), can
be seen retrospectively at the end of the chapter as foreshadowing Herod's violent action towards the male children in
Bethlehem. Herod's slaughter of the children is explicitly predicted, however, in the angel's warning to Joseph (2.13) and
this is fulfilled in 2.16ff.

Herod's rejection functions as part of the plotting device of
prediction/fulfillment in a wider sense as well, because it
proves in retrospect to be representative or anticipatory of the
negative response and rejection of Jesus by the nation of Israel.
It was not only Herod who was troubled by the news of Jesus'
birth, the King of Jews, but 'all of Jerusalem' (2.3). The parallels between Matthew 2 and 26-27 suggest that Jesus' implicit
rejection by Jerusalem in the opening chapters anticipates the
rejection later of the Davidic Messiah and Son of God in the
passion.[1] In chapter 2 Herod sought to kill Jesus, but in chapter
27 Jerusalem succeeds.[2]

paraenetic concern in which the readers identify with the magi and
also worship Jesus, and 4) the idea of God's providential care for his
royal son Jesus. The theme of rejection plays a role in all four of
Luz's categories.

1 Many scholars have observed the parallels between the opening and
closing chapters of the Gospel. For a full discussion of both the linguistic parallels and the analogies of content between chapters 2
and 26-27 see C.H. Lohr, 'Oral Techniques in the Gospel of
Matthew', *CBQ* 23 (1961), pp. 410, 413, 427ff.; Senior, *Passion of
Jesus*, pp. 18-23; Nolan, *Royal Son of God*, pp. 104ff; Brown, *Birth*,
p. 183; Kingsbury, 'Theology of St. Matthew's Gospel', p. 340. Cf. also
Kingsbury, *Matthew as Story*, p. 46 who has written that 'in
Matthew's story, Herod is the precursor of the Jewish leaders, and
his opposition to Jesus foreshadows theirs'.

2 The rejection shown by Herod in the opening chapters of the Gospel
thus contradicts P.L. Shuler's claim (*A Genre for the Gospels. The
Biographical Character of Matthew* (Philadelphia: Fortress, 1982),

The same combination of acceptance/rejection and prediction/fulfillment can be seen in the final narrated incident of the infancy stories. After Herod's death, Joseph again responds positively to the instruction of an angel (2.19ff.). His return from Egypt to Nazareth is interpreted as the fulfillment of another Old Testament prophecy (2.23). In each of the Joseph scenes in the opening chapters, the same form and plotting devices are used by the evangelist.[1] The apearance of an angel in a dream is prefaced with the demonstrative ἰδού (1.20; 2.13, 19), and issues in specific instructions, plus either information (2.20) or predictions (1.20ff. and 2.13ff.). The acceptance of the angel's instructions by Joseph in every instance leads to the fulfillment of Old Testament prophecy.[2] This combination of plot themes in Matthew 1 and 2 proves to be paradigmatic for the reader of the evangelist's manner of emplotment of events throughout the Gospel.

An ellipsis occurs in the narrative following the Old Testament formula quotation in 2.23.[3] The particle δέ in 3.1 is disjunctive and not connective, as the large temporal break in the narrative shows.[4] Nothing more is said about Jesus' infancy or

---

p. 104) that chapters 1-9 in Matthew constitute a 'paradigm of discipleship' because 'there is no direct conflict during this period'. Senior's claim (*Passion of Jesus*, p. 18) that there are 'echoes' of the passion in the birth and infancy chapters appears more accurate.

1 See Hendrikus Boers, 'Language Usage and the Production of Matthew 1.18–2.23', in *Orientation by Disorientation*, pp. 223ff., for a discussion of the formal characteristics of what Boers has labelled 'the cycle of Joseph stories' in Matthew 1 and 2.

2 Cf. E. Schweizer, *Matthäus und seine Kirche* (Stuttgart: KBW Verlag, 1974), p. 19, who argues that the obedience of Joseph which literally fulfills Scripture looks like a description of the later obedience of the disciples (21.6ff.). Combrink, 'Structure of Matthew', p. 77, writes that in Matthew 'Joseph is a prototype of a "follower" of Jesus—obeying exactly what is commanded'. See also Strecker, *Weg*, p. 54; Waetjen, 'Genealogy as the Key to the Gospel According to Matthew', p. 219.

3 According to Chatman, *Stories and Discourse*, p. 70 an 'ellipsis' occurs when the 'discourse halts though time continues in the story'.

4 Contra Kingsbury, *Structure*, p. 13. See Hill, 'Response to Professor Kingsbury's Literary-Critical Probe', p. 43. He considers Mt. 1 and 2

childhood, and the narrative resumes in 3.1 with the appearance of John the Baptist. However, Matthew continues to use the same combination of plotting devices to tell his story. John is introduced by the use of prediction. His appearance is interpreted as the fulfillment of prophecy (3.3). The ministry of the Baptist is then briefly summarized (3.5-6) in a style characteristic of the Gospel as a whole. Throughout the Gospel dialogue is the predominant means of communication, and narration is used sparingly to serve either as a transition between dialogues and discourse material or to summarize briefly the actions of the characters.[1]

The other plot theme of acceptance/rejection is also prominent in Matthew's emplotment of the Baptist's ministry. First, Matthew makes John a preacher of the Kingdom (3.2). His

---

to be 'prologue'; a 'part of the "frame" of the story' (p. 44).

1 See Alter, *Biblical Narrative*, pp. 63-67, where he speaks of the 'biblical commitment to dialogue' in a chapter titled 'Between Narration and Dialogue'. Sternberg, *Expositional Modes*, pp. 14ff, has argued that in every text there are different ratios of represented to representational time. He contends that the time ratio of narrative time span 'generally stands in direct proportion to its contextual relevance' (p. 17). Cf. Lanser, *Narrative Act*, p. 200, who argues that 'whatever is presented through summary tends to remain in the background, while what is scenically represented becomes central'. In narratives like Matthew where summaries are frequently used to condense large time periods and a great breadth of activities (3.5ff.; 4.23ff.; 9.35ff. for example), sections of dialogue and large blocks of discourse material stand out (e.g. the 5 discourses where the represented and the representational time are approximately equal. Such blocks suggest that the evangelist considers Jesus' teaching to be an important element of the Gospel, a fact confirmed by sayings as 7.24ff., 24.35 and 28.20. For this reason, a discussion of the emplotment in the Gospel must also include the teaching material. See Roland M. Frye, 'The Jesus of the Gospels: Approaches Through Narrative Structure', in *From Faith to Faith: Essays in Honor of Donald G. Miller on His Seventieth Birthday*, ed. D.Y. Hadidian (PTMS 31; Pittsburgh: Pickwick, 1979), p. 78, who has written that 'the nature of the gospel narratives is such that we must understand 'event' here as including message and response, for each of the gospel writers is concerned with conveying not only the acts but also the message and meaning of Jesus, and human responses to him'.

message is identical to Jesus' (4.17), and the emphasis is on the imperative of repentance—a message which demands a response from those who hear it.[1] Second, the confrontation between John and the Pharisees and Sadducees is dominated by the theme of rejection. They, along with the chief priests and scribes, become Jesus' main antagonists in the Gospel as the leaders of the Jewish nation. Their appearance immediately elicits a scathing denunciation from John. At this point in the story no reason has been given why they deserve such condemnation. In fact, a reader might assume that their coming for baptism is indicative of acceptance of John's message about the coming Kingdom and the call for repentance. John's denouncement of them in 3.8, however, contains a suggestion about what called forth the condemnation; their actions were incongruous with sincere repentance.[2] John's allusion proves to be accurate later in the story, for Jesus frequently attacks the Jewish leaders for hypocrisy (Mt. 23 for example). Matthew's emplotment of John's encounter with the Jewish leaders also looks back to earlier chapters and draws a contrast between the Jewish leaders, who claim to be sons of Abraham, and Jesus, who has been truly identified as the 'son of Abraham' (1.1).

Matthew's account of the ministry of John the Baptist makes a distinction for the implied reader between the Jewish crowds and their leaders. In contrast to the solidarity between the evil king Herod and all Jerusalem that is found in chapter 2, the crowds respond positively to John's proclamation and come for baptism. The distinction between the crowds and the Jewish leaders remains intact throughout the Gospel until the passion account when the crowds finally join their leaders in

---

1 See J.A. Fitzmyer, *The Gospel According to Luke (I-IX)* (Anchor Bible 28; New York: Doubleday, 1981), p. 184; also Meier, 'John the Baptist', p. 388, who writes that Matthew's concern for 'eschatological morality' is so powerful that 'he co-opts the Baptist as a preacher of Christian repentance'.

2 Cf. Senior, *Passion of Jesus*, p. 24, who writes that the Jewish leaders' 'claim to have "Abraham as our father" is no substitute for integrity'. He argues that 'by stressing an ethical norm for inclusion into the people of God rather than an ethnocentric one, Matthew . . . provided an important opening to the Gentiles.

rejecting Jesus (cf. 27.15ff.).[1] The success which John experiences in his ministry to the crowds anticipates the initial success which Jesus also enjoys (cf. 4.23ff.) and thus contributes to the parallelism between John and Jesus.[2]

The combination of the correlatives prediction/fulfillment and rejection/acceptance to emplot the narrative is continued in a similar manner in the next scene as Jesus comes to John for baptism. Like the preceding pericope, Matthew opens with the plotting device of prediction in 3.11. It takes the form of an internal prolepsis rather than an Old Testament fulfillment quotation, however, as John points to the one coming after him who will baptize with the Holy Spirit and with fire. Jesus immediately comes to be baptized by John with the clear implication that he is the one about whom John talked. John at first resists the request, but finally heeds Jesus' command (3.15b).[3] Instead of using the theme of rejection which is found in the previous scene when the Jewish leaders come to John, Matthew uses the theme of acceptance to plot Jesus' baptism. Jesus' response to John in 3.15a, which for the evangelist provides the answer to the question of how Jesus could submit to John for baptism, highlights the theme of acceptance. In a way similar to the obedience shown by Joseph and the magi in the birth and infancy stories, Jesus' and John's actions in the bap-

---

1 Luz, *Matthäus*, p. 146 argues that it is important for Matthew that the crowds do not simply reject John and Jesus, since the church originates from these people.

2 See Meier, 'John the Baptist', pp. 388 for a thorough discussion of the parallelism-yet-subordination tendency in Matthew's portrayal of John vis-à-vis Jesus. Kingsbury, *Matthew as Story*, p. 55, points out that 'the division in Israel that John occasions foreshadows the division Jesus, too, will at first encounter'.

3 B. Przybylski, 'The Role of Mt. 3.13–4.11 in the Structure and Theology of the Gospel of Matthew', *BThB* 4 (1974), p. 224, has suggested, following the lead of A. Farrer, that Jesus' baptism in Matthew can also be seen as a temptation story, and 'John the Baptist, however innocently, is cast as tempter'. If they are correct, this further supports our claim about the importance of the plotting device of acceptance/rejection in Matthew's telling of the story. Jesus is offered the alternatives of accepting or rejecting God's will in the decision as to whether or not to be baptized.

tism are done in obedience to the will of God.[1] The saying of
3.17, which follows Jesus' baptism and voices divine approval
of him, accomplishes two purposes from a literary perspective.
First, it looks back to earlier Old Testament quotations (1.23
and 2.15) and explicitly reaffirms Jesus' true identity. Secondly, it serves to confirm and commend the positive response
of accepting the will of God.[2]

The scheme of acceptance/rejection is also used to plot the
account of Jesus' temptation which follows the baptism. The
evangelist summarizes forty days and nights of fasting in a
single verse (4.2) before recounting the temptations in a manner which emphasizes the dialogue between Jesus and his
tempter. A number of scholars have shown that the story
should be seen against the background of Israel's experiences

1 A literary study of the way in which Matthew plots his narrative
   thus supports the view that Jesus' fulfillment of all righteousness
   should be interpreted in an exemplary or ethical sense rather than
   in a *heilsgeschichtlich* sense. Contra, Meier, *Law and History*, p.
   79; Barth, *TIM*, pp. 139ff. Cf. Strecker, *Weg*, p. 180; E. Schweizer,
   Matthäus und seine Gemeinde, p. 19; Kingsbury, 'Theology of St.
   Matthew', p. 346; *idem, Matthew as Story*, p. 49, who all interpret
   Jesus' baptism in an exemplary sense.
2 Contra Edwards, *Matthew's Story*, p. 17, who sees the statement in
   3.17 as expressing God's pleasure 'on who Jesus is, rather than on
   what he has done or said'. While God's statement affirms Jesus'
   identity, Edwards' interpretation downplays the importance of
   Jesus' obedience to God's will in Matthew's portrayal of Jesus. J.D.
   Kingsbury ('The Figure of Jesus in Matthew's Story: A Literary-
   Critical Probe', *JSNT* 21 [1984], pp. 10ff., *idem Matthew as Story*,
   pp. 50ff.) also emphasizes the former narrative function of the divine
   voice when he argues that God's baptismal announcement makes
   God's point of view of Jesus as Son of God normative for the Gospel.
   Our analysis of the plotting device of acceptance/rejection suggests
   that the later narrative function is equally important. See Hill,
   'Response', pp. 41-43, for a critique of Kingsbury's position. Hill
   argues that Isa. 42.1 is as important as Ps. 2.7 in the divine voice,
   and that Kingsbury neglects the Servant-of-the-Lord aspect of Jesus'
   sonship in Matthew. An important emphasis in the Servant
   imagery is that it stresses Jesus' humble obedience to God, which is
   further evidence to corroborate the importance of the plotting device
   of acceptance/rejection. Cf. Hill, 'Son and Servant: An Essay on
   Matthean Christology', *JSNT* 6 (1980), pp. 2-16.

in the wilderness. The conjunction of the Son statements with
the quotations from Deuteronomy suggest that the temptation
is centered around 'an attempt to induce Jesus to be unfaithful
to a pattern of Sonship conceived in terms of the relationship
between ideal Israel and the divine Father'.[1] In contrast to
Israel the first Son, however, Jesus withstands the temptations
and accepts the way of humble obedience to God (cf. 4.4).[2]

Although the plotting device of prediction/fulfillment is not
explicitly used in the temptation account, the temptations
foreshadow future events narrated in the Gospel.[3] They play
an important part in preparing for the passion for example.
Jesus rejects Satan's final advance with the phrase Ὕπαγε
Σατανᾶ (4.10) which is echoed after Peter attempts to deflect
Jesus from the path of suffering at Caesarea Philippi (16.23).
Jesus is also later tempted to prove that he is 'the Son of God'
by coming down from the cross and avoiding suffering and

---

1 Donaldson, *Jesus on the Mountain*, p. 92. Cf. B. Gerhardsson, *The Testing of God's Son (Mt 4.1-11): An Analysis of an Early Christian Midrash*, transl. J. Toy (Lund: Gleerup, 1966), pp. 43ff., 51; Kingsbury, *Matthew as Story*, pp. 52ff.; G.H.P. Thompson, 'Called—Proved—Obedient: A Study in the Baptism and Temptation Narratives of Matthew and Luke', *JTS* 11 (1960), pp. 6ff.

2 Cf. Donaldson, *Jesus on the Mountain*, p. 99, who comments that by Matthew's extension of the quotation of Deut. 8.3 in 4.4 (cf. Lk. 4.4), Jesus' reply is changed 'from a negative statement that food is not of ultimate significance for the Son of God to the positive one that humble obedience to the word of God is'. Donaldson uses the concept of salvation history, however, to interpret Matthew's view of Jesus' sonship as corporate which 'incorporates a recapitulation of the Israel wilderness ideal' (pp. 92, 95, 104). We would argue that appeal to such a theological system is not necessary. Rather, Matthew's presentation of Jesus' temptation can be seen in terms of the way he has plotted the story using the alternatives of acceptance or rejection.

3 See Luz, *Matthäus*, p. 164, for a listing of the points of contact between the temptation account and later texts. Cf. Przybylski, 'Role of Mt. 3.13–4.11', pp. 224ff., who argues that the individual temptations foreshadow specific incidents in the story: the first temptation foreshadows the two feeding narratives, the second temptation and baptism foreshadow the Transfiguration, and the third temptation foreshadows the conclusion (28.16ff.).

death (27.40).[1] The links between the baptism/temptation stories and later incidents in the Gospel underline the importance
of these early stories in establishing the nature of Jesus' sonship and ministry: he is the Son of God who is fully obedient to
God's will, and by the use of the plotting device of accep-
tance/rejection Matthew shows that in his obedience Jesus is
exemplary for discipleship.[2]

After the temptation, news about John's arrest (4.13)—
which presumably came about while Jesus was in the wilderness—prompts Jesus to move from Nazareth to Capernaum
and actively begin his ministry. The theme of prediction and
fulfillment governs the narrative as Matthew utilizes an Old
Testament formula quotation (4.14ff.) to interpret the move as
the fulfillment of prophecy. The account of Jesus' movement
in 4.12ff. with its concomitant formula quotation is linked with
earlier descriptions of his travel. In 2.23, which also contains
an Old Testament formula quotation, Matthew narrates
Jesus' move to Nazareth. In both places the use of a formula
quotation gives the impression that Jesus' travels are 'divinely
ordained'.[3] This impression contributes to the evangelist's use
of the acceptance/rejection plotting device; Jesus, or Joseph in
2.23, could have chosen to reject the divine plan thus thwart-
ing the fulfillment of Old Testament prophecy and God's purposes.

Mt. 4.17 marks the beginning of Jesus' active public ministry. Before we examine the way Matthew emplots Jesus'

1 Donald Senior, 'The Death of Jesus and the Resurrection of the Holy
  Ones (Mt. 27.51-53)', *CBQ* 38 (1976), p. 323, has written that 'the
  prime issue of the death scene has become a challenge to Jesus'
  Sonship. While the mockers question Jesus' identity as Son—or
  perhaps more accurately, the quality of his sonship—Jesus himself
  is portrayed as the obedient Son who prays in the face of death and
  who dies with an attitude of reverent obedience'. Donaldson (*Jesus
  on the Mountain*, pp. 99ff.) also sees the Matthean temptation foreshadowing both Jesus' suffering and vindication as Son of God.
2 Cf. Schweizer, *Matthäus und seine Gemeinde*, p. 19; Kingsbury,
  'Theology of St. Matthew', p. 345ff.; *idem, Jesus Christ*, pp. 69-70,
  73ff. Luz, *Matthäus*, p. 162, stresses, however, that the paraenetic
  meaning of the temptation account is only indirectly manifested in
  Matthew.
3 Kingsbury, *Structure*, p. 16.

public ministry, let us summarize what the opening chapters of the Gospel have revealed to the implied reader. First, Matthew presents the protagonist of his story, Jesus.[1] He is the Messiah-King of Israel from the lineage of Abraham and David. The meaning of these titles will become evident for the implied reader in the rest of the narrative as Jesus' actions cohere with the names given him.[2] Preeminently, however, Jesus is portrayed as the Son of God. The genealogy shows how God has guided Israel's history until it reaches its culmination in Jesus, and God's providential care continues even after Jesus' birth. The origin of Jesus can be traced back to God (1.16, 18, 20) and he is presented to the reader as 'God with us' (1.23).[3] The filial relationship between Jesus and God is subse-

1 See Perry, 'Literary Dynamics', p. 53, who observes that the first character introduced will be regarded 'as the protagonist for as long as it has not been displaced by another character'. Contra Edwards, *Matthew's Story*, p. 15, who argues that the 'primary purpose' of 1.17–2.23 'was to verify the reliability of the narrator who reports to the reader that these events are in full accord with God's intentions'. While the opening chapters of the Gospel accomplish this effect, particularly by the liberal use of Old Testament fulfillment quotation, Edwards certainly overstates his case and overlooks the role the chapters play in introducing to the reader the characters and conflict in the story. Cf. Edgar Krentz, 'The Extent of Matthew's Prologue: Toward the Structure of the Fist Gospel', *JBL* 83 (1964), p. 410, who recognizes this literary function of Matthew's opening chapters. These constitute 'Matthew's preliminary statement of the significance of Jesus. It is the Matthean "preunderstanding" of Jesus necessary for the reader properly to evaluate Jesus' words and actions in his ministry, death, and resurrection'.

2 Cf. Frei, *Identity of Jesus Christ*, p. 96. Combrink, 'Structure of Matthew', p. 77, points out that the titles given to Jesus imply the giving of a commission which is fleshed out in 1.18-25. Cf. Robert Tannehill, 'The Gospel of Mark as Narrative Christology', *Semeia* 16 (1978), pp. 57-95. Tannehill argues that since Mark has little description of the inner state of a character, a study of character can only be apprehended through a study of the Gospel's plot. In particular, he bases his study of Mark's christology on a narrative analysis of the commissions which Jesus accepts and fulfills in the unfolding story.

3 See Burnett, 'Prolegomenon', pp. 95ff., who argues that the description of Jesus as 'God with us' becomes 'paradigmatic for all later

quently reaffirmed in 2.15 and 3.16-17. Second, while the nature of Jesus' sonship remains to be fleshed out in the course of the narrative, Matthew indicates in the opening chapters that obedience to God's will is central to Jesus' sonship (3.15; 4.1-11).[1] Third, the implied reader is informed of Jesus' role in the story: he has come to 'save his people from their sins' (1.21), and his proclamation of the Kingdom issues in a call to radical obedience (4.18ff.). Finally, the opening chapters adumbrate the different responses Jesus will evoke: the worship of the magi and acceptance by the crowds of John the Baptist are contrasted with the obduracy and rejection of Herod and the Jewish leaders. Because of this rejection from the Jewish leaders, the implied reader is confronted with the question of how Jesus will accomplish his saving task when the people are prepared to reject him. The stage is thus set for Matthew's story of Jesus' ministry.

2. *Matthew 4.17–11.1*

J.D. Kingsbury has argued that the formula 'from that time Jesus began', a distinctive Matthean formula, is used by the evangelist in 4.17 and 16.21 to demarcate the three broadest divisions of the whole Gospel: 1.1–4.16 is about the person of Jesus Messiah, 4.17–16.20 is about the proclamation of Jesus Messiah, and 16.21–28.20 is about the suffering, death, and rejection of Jesus Messiah.[2] There is little doubt that the formula marks important transition points in Jesus' life; in the first instance Jesus actively and openly pursues his public ministry, and in the second case Jesus begins specifically to teach his disciples in private about his coming suffering and death in Jerusalem. Kingsbury probably overstates his case,

scenes involving Jesus'. Cf. Kingsbury (*Matthew as Story*, pp. 41-55; 'Figure of Jesus', pp. 7-11), who also stresses the function of the opening chapters of Matthew in presenting Jesus to the reader as Son of God.

1 Luz, *Matthäus*, pp. 156, 162, 167.
2 *Structure*, pp. 7-25. Cf. Kingsbury, *Matthew as Story*, pp. 38-42. See also Bauer, *Structure of Matthew's Gospel*, pp. 73-108, who agrees with Kingsbury's tripartite division of Matthew. Bauer was one of Kingsbury's students. Cf. the full discussion by F. Neirynck, 'ΑΠΟ ΤΟΤΕ ΗΡΞΑΤΟ and the Structure of Matthew', *ETL* 64 (1988), 21-59.

however, in making this formula mark the major divisions in a topical outline of the Gospel.[1] A break or ellipsis already occurs between 2.23 and 3.1, and the phrase in 4.17 is just one of many stereotyped Matthean formulas used which could also be construed as formal outline markers (4.23ff. and 9.35, or 5.17 and 10.34 correspond to each other, for example).[2] Kingsbury's division at 16.21 also breaks the clearly delineated scene of Peter's confession at Caesarea Philippi (16.13ff.), and leads Kingsbury to interpret Peter's confession from a too favorable perspective.[3] Furthermore, 4.17 and 16.21 appear in contexts that are introduced by an aorist circumstantial participle (4.12; 16.13) in which the temporal idea dominates, so that the formula 'from that time Jesus began...' looks with equal emphasis back to the incidents referred to by these participles, and forward to future events.[4] Thus, it was *when* Jesus heard about the arrest of John the Baptist that he began his active public ministry. This event signals a new use of the plotting device of rejection by the evangelist. The rejection of John the Baptist, manifested in his arrest, leads to the beginning of Jesus' ministry.[5]

1 Cf. Robert H. Gundry, *Matthew: A Commentary on His Literary and Theological Art* (Grand Rapids: Eerdmans, 1982), p. 10, who comments that the formula in 4.17 and 16.21 seems 'to mark turning points in Jesus' life, not in Matthew's gospel'. Gundry concludes that Matthew is 'structurally mixed' (p. 11).
2 See Luz, *Matthäus* pp. 18ff., 24ff., and 85, for a critique of the use of 4.17 as an outline marker. While we are following Kingsbury in considering 1.1–4.16 as a large narrative unit, it must be stressed again that we are not interested in rigidly defending any one outline. Luz's outline of the Gospel is based in part in Matthew's use of Markan material, whereas Kingsbury's delimitations are based on considerations which are internal to Matthew's text.
3 See Kingsbury, 'Jesus in Matthew's Story', p. 14. Cf. also Hill, 'Response', p. 45.
4 Cf. Frankemölle, *Jahwebund*, p. 344. Contra Kingsbury, *Structure*, p. 8.
5 Cf. Senior and Stuhlmueller, *Biblical Foundations*, pp. 243, who see the rejection of Jesus on different levels in the Gospel become part of a pattern of sacred history: 'In each instance the act of rejection becomes a paradoxical impulse to a new life-giving stage in God's plan of history' (p. 244). Edwards, *Matthew's Story*, p. 18, writes that

The content of Jesus' proclamation (4.17) is identical to John's (3.2), and in a similar manner it confronts those who hear it with the same challenge of whether to accept or reject it.[1] One of the first activities that Matthew therefore narrates is Jesus' calling of some disciples (4.18ff.). Just as the evangelist uses exposition and the illustrative scene in chapters 1 and 2 at the beginning of the Gospel to introduce who Jesus is to his readers, so illustrative scenes and exposition are used to give the reader a brief overview of Jesus' ministry at the beginning of that ministry.[2] The calling of two sets of brothers is plainly illustrative, since it recounts incidents that are typical of Jesus' ministry; the calling of people to leave home, family and possessions to follow him (cf. 8.21; 9.9; 10.35ff.; 19.27). The theme of response is utilized again by the Matthew as the brothers accept Jesus' call. In this way their actions prove exemplary for later Christians.

Matthew continues to illustrate what is typical of Jesus' ministry with a summary in 4.23-25. The acts of ministry and response to them are not concrete and specific, but are presented as habitual and recurrent in a manner which is in no way dynamic or developmental. The geographical setting is deconcretized and is narrated merely to show the breadth of

---

John's arrest is 'a signal for a beginning, not a retreat'.

1 Cf. Luz, *Matthäus* p. 176, who writes: 'Wo das Evangelium Jesu vom Himmelreich verkündet wird (4,17), werden Menschen in radikalen Gehorsam gerufen'.

2 See Sternberg, *Expositional Modes*, pp. 24, 29, for a discussion of the narrative features of illustrative scenes and exposition. He defines illustrative scenes as scenes in which the quantitative time-ratio approximates that of the first scenic occasion, but which narrate incidents that are "deconcretized, habitual or illustrative' in nature. The incidents are 'in no way dynamic or developmental in terms of the action'. Cf. Ernst Lohmeyer, *Das Evangelium Matthäus*, ed. Werner Schmauch (2nd edn; Göttingen: Vandenhoeck & Ruprecht, 1958), p. 65, who observes that Matthew has removed all historical detail from his opening account of Jesus' proclamation (4.17); no mention is made of the place of proclamation or its addressees. This has the effect of generalizing the proclamation by placing it in the 'Sphäre eschatologischer Gültigkeit, die den Glauben der Gemeinde umfaßt'.

Jesus' ministry.[1] Jesus' initial success is not only reminiscent of John the Baptist's success, the description in the summary anticipates a future summary of Jesus' ministry (9.35) and thus helps structure the narrative.

After briefly giving this overview of Jesus' ministry, the evangelist provides the reader with detailed examples and commentary of the summary in chapters 5-9. The Sermon on the Mount first illustrates Jesus' teaching and preaching ministry. An extended discourse such as the Sermon is obviously plotted and arranged differently from narrative, in part at least because of the difference in the nature of the material. Nonetheless, the themes of acceptance and rejection are still prominent both in individual sayings and in the discourse as a whole. The entire discourse is concluded and summed up by the parable of the wise and the foolish men, a parable which exhorts the listeners to hear and practice the words of Jesus (7.24ff.). As Hans-Dieter Betz has observed, the relatively frequent occurrence of the term 'doing' suggests that 'the "doing" must be the goal of the Sermon on the Mount itself'.[2] The other plotting device of prediction-fulfillment is, however, not neglected in the Sermon. The Sermon in Matthew should not be seen merely as a collection of teaching but also as 'part of an event of eschatological fulfillment'.[3] In the structure of

---

1 Theissen (*Miracles*, p. 205) describes summaries as a typifying device which 'takes individual motifs from a few stories and makes them a constant feature of the whole story described in the framework form'. See Kingsbury, *Matthew*, pp. 20ff., who sees 4.23ff. as a part of one of the set of summary passages which 'alert the reader to direction of the plot of the gospel story'. Mt. 4.23ff.; 9.35; and 11.1 describe Jesus as the Messiah to the people of Israel in word and deed, but they reject Jesus (chapters 11-12). The second set of summaries is made up of the passion predictions (16.21; 17.22ff.; 20.17ff.), which set the tone for the final part of the Gospel. Cf. Kingsbury, *Jesus Christ*, p. 75.

2 H.D. Betz, 'The Sermon on the Mount: Its Literary Genre and Function', *JR* 59 (1979), p. 289.

3 Donaldson, *Jesus on the Mountain*, pp. 114ff. He points to the connection between the Sermon and 4.23ff., which is an actualization of the Old Testament formula quotation in 4.14ff. Cf. 11.2-6 where it is also clear that Matthew considers teaching to be an important element of Jesus' Messianic vocation. See Guelich, *Sermon on the*

the entire Gospel, the mountain of the Sermon where Jesus teaches also points ahead to the mountain of commissioning where Jesus 'commands his disciples to propagate his teaching'.[1]

There is, however, a noticeable absence of temporal references in the Sermon, which could be plotted on a time line. Many of the sayings utter a sort of timeless truth which are relevant in any time period (5.3-10; 6.19ff.; 7.1 for example). Other sayings include an eschatological element—such as those which warn about Gehenna (5.29f.) or the final judgment (7.22). Sayings such as these would be meaningful in any period that is prior to the eschaton, since the prediction is always in the future. Even those sayings which are temporally and culturally limited by the imagery used can be classified as examples of what Robert Tannehill has labelled the 'focal instance'. This form of saying uses imagery that is specific and extreme in order to point beyond the literal sense of the commands to the many situations in which the hearer encounters others: 'it is not "just that" which is commanded but "even that"'.[2] The effect of this lack of specific temporal reference in many of the sayings is that the meaningfulness and relevance of the discourse is not limited to the original listeners of Jesus but can be more easily and directly extended to later generations of readers.[3] This is an important effect for an evangelist

---

Mount, pp. 25ff., 163ff. for a discussion of the role of the Sermon in Matthew's christological portrait of Jesus. Guelich argues that Matthew has a 'fulfillment christology' to which the Sermon contributes by presenting Jesus as the Messiah who fulfills the Old Testament promise for the coming age of salvation, the one who brings about God's sovereign rule by his ministry.

1 Donaldson, *Jesus on the Mountain*, pp. 120ff.

2 See Tannehill, *The Sword of his Mouth*, p. 72.

3 See Perry V. Kea, 'The Sermon on the Mount: Ethics and Eschatological Time', *SBL 1986 Seminar Papers*, ed. K.H. Richards (Atlanta: Scholars, 1986), pp. 96-97, who argues that the Sermon on the Mount belongs in the 'middle-time', whether this be understood in terms of the plotted story of Jesus' life in the Gospel narrative, or in terms of the situation of the implied reader between resurrection and parousia. Cf. Betz, 'Sermon on the Mount', pp. 296ff., where he argues that the literary genre of the Sermon on the Mount is that of an epitome. Although Betz's theory has not won wide acceptance,

who wants to emphasize the teaching of Jesus.

Following the completion of the discourse with his stereo-typical concluding formula (7.28), Matthew narrates a second element in Jesus' ministry in more depth—his healing.[1] In chapters 8-9 Matthew recounts a series of miracles which highlight the alternative responses of acceptance and rejection to Jesus' ministry. The positive response of acceptance is present in the stories, sometimes being explicitly mentioned as faith (8.10; 9.2, 22, 27), and at other times remaining implicit (8.2; cf. 8.25ff.) as people with a need come to Jesus for help. The negative response of rejection is juxtaposed with this positive response, however. Israel is compared unfavorably with the faith Jesus found in a Gentile (8.10), and he predicts Israel's rejection in the Kingdom of Heaven (8.11ff.) even though specific incidents of unbelief and rejection have not yet been narrated and the response of the crowds in general has been positive (4.24ff.; 8.1; 9.8, 33). The Jewish leaders respond negatively to Jesus' healings with accusations of blasphemy (9.3) and of acting in collusion with the prince of demons (9.34). Rejection is not limited, however, to Israel alone. It is also expressed by Gentiles when the Gadarenes ask Jesus to leave their region (8.34). In this pericope the element of faith has been replaced 'by an implicit element of cost: the loss of the

---

most scholars would agree with him that the Sermon 'is not "law" to be obeyed but theology to be intellectually appropriated and internalized, in order then to be creatively developed and implemented in concrete situations of life'.

1 Numerous commentators have drawn attention to the way in which Matthew juxtaposes the ministries of teaching and healing in the initial stages of his account of Jesus' ministry. Eduard Schweizer, *The Good News According to Matthew*, transl. D. Green (London: SPCK, 1976), p. 233, is representative when he writes that in chapters 5–9 Matthew is presenting Jesus as 'Messiah in word and deed'. This effect is achieved in part by Matthew's use of the summary passages in 4.23ff. and 9.35 to enclose these chapters. Cf. J.D. Kingsbury, 'Observations on the "Miracle Chapters" of Matthew 8–9', *CBQ* 40 (1978), p. 567, who writes that in chapters 8–9 Matthew expands both the breadth of Jesus' healing ministry (4.24) and the picture of Jesus being followed by great crowds from all Israel and Decapolis (4.25).

pigs is more important than the healing of the two men'.[1]

Chapters 8-9 also contain other events besides miracles (8.18-22; 9.9-17), and the narration of these incidents, which are related to Jesus' teaching, reveals how the themes of acceptance and rejection control the plotting of events in the two chapters.[2] In the first pericope of teaching material, Jesus is approached by two men wishing to follow him (8.18ff.). When challenged with the cost that following Jesus entails, however, the would-be disciples apparently reject the call. Their response contrasts sharply with the response of both the two sets of brothers (4.18ff.) and with that of Matthew the tax collector (9.9), all of whom obediently left family and livelihood to follow Jesus.[3] The second section of teaching material begins with the calling of Matthew and the controversy with the Pharisees over Jesus' table fellowship with sinners (9.9-12). The contrast between the negative response of the Pharisees who were self-sufficient and the positive response of those in need is underlined in the following teaching about fasting (9.13-17). Fasting is not as important as commitment to the

1 J.P. Louw, 'The Structure of Mt. 8.1–9.35', *Neotestamentica* 11 (1977), p. 95.
2 Cf. Kingsbury, 'Miracle Chapters', p. 563, and C. Burger, 'Jesu Taten nach Matthäus 8 und 9', *ZTK* 70 (1973), pp. 284ff., who deal with the divergent material by a thematic organization in the two chapters: (1) Christology (8.1-17), (2) discipleship (8.18-34), (3) questions pertaining to the separation of Jesus and his followers (9.1-17), and (4) faith (9.18-34). Certain features of the narrative do not fit smoothly into their thematic outline, however (faith is also a prominent element in 8.5-12, for example). Held, *TIM*, pp. 169ff., also divides the chapters into 3 thematic groups. The formal outline of Louw, 'Mt. 8.1–9.35', p. 91 is therefore to be preferred. He divides the chapters into 3 groups of 3 miracles (8.1-17; 8.23–9.8; 9.18-34) which are separated by two teaching stories (8.18-22; 9.9-17), although the final group (9.18-34) probably has 4 rather than 3 miracles. See Davies, *Setting*, p. 87.
3 See J.D. Kingsbury, 'On Following Jesus: the "Eager" Scribe and the "Reluctant" Disciple (Matthew 8.18-22)', *NTS* (1988), pp. 45-59. According to Kingsbury this pericope underlines 'two cardinal tenets of discipleship: one cannot summon oneself to the life of discipleship . . . ; still once entered, this life brooks no divided loyalties'.

bridegroom (Jesus).[1]

These pericopae in the midst of the miracle stories reveal that the miracles should be read in the context of Jesus' teaching about the cost and commitment of discipleship. This reading of the miracle stories is further underlined by the commonly observed phenomenon that Matthew has enhanced the element of direct speech in his telling of the stories to the point where the focus of the story appears to be the dialogue.[2] This formal trait of the Matthean miracle stories means that 'emphasis is placed on personal encounter'[3] between Jesus and others, and in this encounter the characters in the story are confronted with the choice of accepting or rejecting Jesus. The alternatives of acceptance or rejection which are plotted in the miracle stories challenge the readers of the stories as well.[4]

The correlatives of promise/fulfillment are also operative in Matthew's emplotment of Jesus' healing ministry to Israel. Another formula quotation is used in 8.17 to show how Jesus' healing fulfills Old Testament prophecy. One external prolepsis takes the form of an eschatological prediction in 8.11ff. which looks forward to the inclusion of the Gentiles and exclusion of Israel in the Kingdom. This anticipates the future acceptance of the Gospel by Gentiles and the rejection of it by Israel. The question addressed to Jesus by the Gadarene demoniacs (8.29) contributes to the plot's development by raising the question as to what is meant by 'the time' when Jesus will torment the demons. It appears to look forward to the crucifixion and resurrection, and introduces a new ele-

---

1 Louw, 'Mt. 8.1–9.35', p. 96.
2 See Held, *TIM*, pp. 233ff., 242ff.
3 Kingsbury, 'Miracle Chapters', p. 570.
4 Cf. *ibid.*, pp. 572ff., where Kingsbury writes that the miracle stories function as 'paraenetic paradigms' for Matthew and his church: 'Paradigmatically, these chapters set forth for the members of Matthew's Church the cost and commitment of discipleship and the ways in which they are distinct from contemporary Israel... Paraenetically, they invite these Christians, as persons of faith, to approach the exalted Son of God, under whose lordship and in whose presence they live, and to offer to him their petitions for help in sure knowledge that he desires to hear them and will exploy his divine power to aid them in time of trial and need'.

ment of suspense into the story.[1]

A summary identical to the summary which opened Matthew's account of Jesus' ministry (4.23) closes the section in 9.35. The summary not only looks back to form an inclusio around Jesus' teaching and healing ministry, but it also serves as a transition for the discourse that follows. The disciples share in Jesus' ministry by being sent to the cities and villages to preach and heal (10.1, 7, 11). At the completion of the discourse Jesus resumes his own preaching tour of the cities (11.1).[2] An internal prolepsis is used in the transition between the sections as Jesus' sending of the disciples on a mission (10.1) appears to answer the prayer Jesus commands his disciples to pray (9.38). As with Jesus' ministry, Matthew uses summary to provide an overview of the activities of the disciples' mission (10.1). A hint about the rejection Jesus is to face is found in Matthew's simple identification of Judas Iscariot as 'the one who betrayed him' in the listing of the twelve 'apostles' (10.2ff.).

The discourse itself begins at 10.5 with Jesus' instructions for the mission. At its end, Matthew will use his concluding formula for the second time in the Gospel (11.1). Although the instructions in 10.5-15 allow for the possibility of both a positive or negative response to the mission, the juxtaposition of the following predictions of persecution (10.16-23) highlights the negative response of rejection.[3] Neither the prediction of

1 Cf. Hill, *Matthew*, p. 168, who writes that 'Jesus' action with these demoniacs is an anticipation of the overthrow of Satanic forces'. Hill also conjectures that this incident 'may be intended to anticipate the rejection of the Church in certain Gentile areas' (p. 169), although interpreting the prediction in this way as an external prolepsis would be dependent on the situation of the actual readers of the Gospel and the information which they bring to the reading experience.

2 Cf. Scheweizer, *Matthew*, p. 233, who sees the inclusio formed by 4.23 and 9.35. Schuyler Brown, 'The Mission to Israel in Matthew's Central Section (Mt. 9.35–11.1), *ZNW* 69 (1978), p. 77, interprets 9.35 and 11.1 as forming the inclusio around the mission discourse.

3 Cf. Hare, *Jewish Persecution*, p. 98, who has observed that a large proportion of material in chapter 10 is concerned 'with the non-acceptance of the gospel and the hostility with which the missionaries are treated'. Cf. A.D. Jacobsen, 'The Literary Unity of Q', *JBL*

persecution nor the prediction of the coming of the Son of Man are actually fulfilled within the temporal boundaries of the narrative.[1] In fact, Matthew does not give an account of the disciples' mission. The predictions of persecution and rejection, however, cohere with the rejection which Jesus faces in the story.[2] This principle of solidarity between Jesus and his disciples is emphasized by the logion in 10.24ff. which appears to provide the organizing principle for the variegated material in the discourse.[3] The mission of the disciples is to parallel Jesus' mission, and their fate will also be the same as Jesus' fate. As 10.40ff. makes clear, the mission of the disciples is to be 'mysteriously interlocked' with Jesus' mission so that people's reactions to the disciples—'in accepting or refusing, in faith or disbelief'—are people's reactions to Jesus and to the Father.[4]

No report of the disciples' mission is given, and the discourse is simply concluded with Matthew's stereotypical formula and the resumption of Jesus' ministry (11.1). In this section of

101 (1982), p. 379, and *idem*, 'The Literary Unity of Q. Lk. 10.2-16 and Parallels as a Test Case', in *Logia*, ed. J. Delobel (Leuven: University Press, 1982), p. 423, who argues that in Q the note of rejection is so strong in the mission discourse that the mission is more of an errand of judgment than a mission. The same might be said for Matthew, and it is interesting to note that some scholars have suggested that the Deuteronomistic and Wisdom traditions have influenced Matthew in a way similar to the manner in which Jaocobsen believes that they shaped Q.

1 Contra L. Sabourin, 'The Coming of the Son of Man (Mt 10.23b)', *BThB* 7 (1977), pp. 9ff., who connects 10.23b with such texts as 16.27ff. and 13.14 in order to argue that Jesus first comes as Son of Man at his resurrection.

2 Kingsbury, *Matthew*, p. 50, notes that the negative results of the disciples' mission sketched in the discourse adumbrate the rejection Jesus experiences by all segments of Israel in chapters 11-12. This is another example of the way in which the evangelist combines his two major plotting devices. Cf. Kingsbury, *Matthew as Story*, p. 73.

3 See J. Radermakers, *Au fil de l'évangile selon Saint Matthieu* (Heverlee-Louvain: Institut d'Études Théologiques, 1972), pp. 135-38; and Brown, 'Mission to Israel', p. 77.

4 W. Trilling, *The Gospel According to St. Matthew* (NT for Spiritual Reading 1; London: Sheed & Ward, 1969), p. 196. Cf. Burnett, *Testament of Jesus-Sophia*, p. 398, who argues that the disciples' rejection is a direct result of their proclamation of Jesus' message'.

the narrative Matthew has demonstrated Jesus' authority in his ministry of preaching, teaching, and healing to Israel. While Jesus' encounters with the Jewish leaders give hints of the rejection to come, the overall tone of his ministry is one of acceptance in this section. The section concludes with the disciples being commissioned for a similar ministry to Israel that is portrayed as an extension of Jesus' ministry. The rejection which is predicted of their ministry, however, foreshadows the rejection Jesus will face as the story continues.

3. *Matthew 11.2–16.20*

The next narrated incident looks back past the sending of the disciples on a mission to the previous accounts of Jesus' ministry.[1] John the Baptist questions if Jesus is the Messiah because his ministry of mercy and healing did not fit John's prediction (cf. 3.11).[2] Jesus' answer recounts the miracles just narrated and functions as part of the plotting device of prediction/fulfillment by showing that Jesus' ministry fulfills Messianic hopes (11.4ff.). More explicit use of the theme of promise/fulfillment is utilized later in the chapter with a formula quotation. Jesus affirms that John is the forerunner of the Messiah—which the narrator has already told the implied reader (3.3)—by citing the Malachi prophecy (11.10). For Matthew, John is a part of the fulfillment which he himself had predicted.[3]

If the emphasis in Matthew's use of the plot themes of acceptance/rejection when narrating Jesus' healing ministry in chapters 8 and 9 was on acceptance, the tone changes in chapter 11. Rejection becomes the primary response, and this negative reaction is not limited to the Jewish leaders.[4] Refer-

---

1 It is this structural connection between 11.2ff. and chapters 5-9 which has led Schulyer Brown to label 9.35–11.1 'the central section', and to treat it as an insertion in the main flow of the story. See 'Mission to Israel', pp. 77ff. Cf. also Luz, *Matthäus*, pp. 19, 25, who sees all of chapter 11 serving a transitional function in the structure of the Gospel.

2 Meier, 'John the Baptist', pp. 392ff.

3 *Ibid.*, p. 394.

4 Cf. B.C. Lategan, 'Structural Interrelations in Matthew 11-12', *Neotestamentica* 11 (1977), p. 128, who believes that Matthew is con-

ence is made in 11.16 and 11.20 to Jesus' earlier ministry, but
the response is now portrayed negatively as rejection. The
cities where Jesus performed his miracles are upbraided for
their lack of repentance (11.20ff.) even though Matthew had
not narrated such a systematic lack of response.[1] The generation of Jesus' contemporaries is mentioned five times in chapters 11-12, and each time the reference is pejorative, pointing
to the people's rejection of Jesus (11.16; 12.39, 41, 42, 45). The
intensity of opposition to Jesus increases in chapter 12 as the
evangelist focuses on the rejection of the Jewish leaders in a
series of controversy stories.[2] The Pharisees question Jesus
about his disciples breaking Sabbath laws (12.1ff.) and about
his own healing on the Sabbath (12.9ff.). The report that the
Pharisees went out to plot how to destroy Jesus after he healed
on the Sabbath is the first explicit mention in the narrative of
Jesus' manner of death (12.14). The healing of the demoniac
in 12.22ff. looks back to earlier incidents in the narrative, and
by repetition emphasizes the persistent opposition of the Jewish leaders. Their accusation against him that he was acting in
consort with Beelzebul, the prince of demons (12.22ff.), combines the terminology of 9.34 and 10.25. Jesus' words of condemnation which follow are reminiscent both of John's condemnation against them in 3.7ff. and of Jesus' own warnings

structed on an antithetical basis. In chapters 11-12, the antithesis 'is
centered around the attitude towards Jesus with the dual possibility
of acceptance or rejection'. We have argued that this antithesis is
not limited just to these chapters, however, but that it is one of the
fundamental plotting devices by which the evangelist tells his story.

1 J.D. Kingsbury (*The Parables of Jesus in Matthew 13* [London:
SPCK, 1969], p. 15) conjectures that Jesus' woes against the cities
reflect an unsuccessful mission in the region of Galilee by
Matthew's church. Although the open-ended nature of the mission
discourse in chapter 10 supports this thesis, it is a secondary reference at best and would be dependent upon information which readers from Matthew's church bring to the Gospel. On the level of the
narrative, the woes are uttered as a result of the lack of response to
the ministries of Jesus and John the Baptist.

2 Cf. Schweizer, *Matthäus und seine Gemeinde*, p. 26, who sees the
characteristic viewpoint of 12.1–16.12 summed up in the division
(caused by Jesus' miracles) between the rejection of the Pharisees
and the faith of the disciples and Gentiles.

against false prophets in 7.15-20. The effect of this repetition is that the implied reader sees Jesus' repudiation of the Jewish leaders as being justified after the second incident. Their opposition and rejection has persisted, and has perhaps even grown (cf. 12.14).[1]

The theme of rejection is also developed in these chapters by reverse example when it is contrasted with the opposite response of acceptance in the pericopae which close chapters 11 and 12.[2] These two pericopae are connected by the concept of the 'family of God' and the theme of acceptance and commitment to Jesus. In 11.25ff. it is the relationship between Jesus and the Father which is emphasized, whereas in 12.46ff. it is the relationship between Jesus and those that are his disciples. In contrast to the rejection Jesus has faced from his contemporaries, Jesus offers an invitation to accept his yoke, which is the yoke of discipleship.[3] Those who accept his invitation do the will of the Father (12.46ff.), and it is these who

---

1 See Janice Capel Anderson, 'Double and Triple Stories, The Implied Reader, and Redundancy in Matthew', *Semeia* 31 (1985), pp. 74ff., for a discussion of the rhetorical effects of anticipation, retrospection, and repetition with variation in Matthew. Cf. W.R.G. Loader, 'Son of David, Blindness, Possession, and Duality in Matthew', *CBQ* 44 (1982), pp. 577, 585, who argues that Matthew uses 'Son of David' in the two healings of the demoniacs (9.27ff.; 12.22ff.), and elsewhere in the Gospel, to emphasize Israel's unbelief. The rejection of the Jewish leaders is contrasted with those who are healed and respond to Jesus as Son of David, which is the appropriate response of Israel to its Messiah.

2 See Senior, *Passion of Jesus*, pp. 36ff., who point out that 'one of the functions of the opponents is to portray, in negative terms, the meaning of authentic discipleship'. Opponents also alert the implied reader to the cost of discipleship, as the parallels between Jesus and the disciples make plain.

3 See G.N. Stanton, 'Salvation Proclaimed: Matthew 11.28-30', *ExT* 94 (1982), pp. 6-7, who argues against interpreting the logion against a Wisdom background. It is not Jesus as Sophia who issues the invitation, but Jesus as the humble Servant of God. Stanton further argues that the invitation is issued to the disciples, who are the 'weary and heavy laden', because of the costly nature of discipleship. The disciples, as a character group in the plotted story, are absent from the scene, however, and we will argue in chapter 5 that the invitation is directed to the implied reader.

constitute the real family of God.[1]

The correlatives prediction/fulfillment are also present in these chapters depicting Jesus in conflict with different segments of Israel. In the midst of all this rejection, Matthew uses one of his formula quotations to show how Jesus is the fulfillment of Old Testament prophecy (12.15ff.). The citation from Isaiah correlates with the description of Jesus as the Son who is gentle and humble-hearted (11.29), and reinforces information given in earlier chapters: that God chose Jesus, gave him his Spirit at baptism, and is well pleased with him. By using an Old Testament prophecy which promises hope and salvation to the Gentiles, the rejection of Israel is underlined. It also functions as a prolepsis that anticipates the future acceptance of the Gospel by Gentiles. Another internal prolepsis is found in the Jonah logion (12.40) which looks ahead to Jesus' death and resurrection.

The theme of rejection is continued in the third of the so-called five discourses in Matthew, the parable discourse of chapter 13. The plotting device of acceptance/rejection actually divides the discourse in half and places it in its context in the Gospel. Jesus teaches the crowds in 13.1-33 and they do not understand the parables. The disciples are taught privately in 13.36-52, however, and they understand (13.51). An Old Testament formula quotation is used by the evangelist to help divide the discourse in half and show that Jesus' teaching in parables fulfills prophecy (13.35). Jesus himself cites a prophecy from Isaiah to explain the lack of positive response and understanding by the Jewish nation (13.14ff.). It is thus possible to see the first half of the discourse as Matthew's apology for the rejection and lack of understanding displayed by Israel. The crowds are contrasted with the disciples and their positive response of understanding which has as its object the doing of God's will (13.23; 52).[2] The contrast is also evident at

---

1 Cf. Lategan, 'Matthew 11-12', pp. 120-21.

2 See Kingsbury, *Matthew 13*, pp. 13, 16, 130ff. Kingsbury argues that Jesus' turning from the crowds to the disciples in the middle of chapter 13 marks an important structural turning point in the entire Gospel. Jesus focuses his teaching on the disciples throughout the rest of the Gospel as a result of Israel's rejection of him. Cf. J.C. Fenton, 'Inclusion and Chiasmus in Matthew', in *Studia*

the end of chapter 13 when the understanding of the disciples at the completion of the discourse is juxtaposed with the rejection of Jesus by his own home town. The people there can know him only as the son of a carpenter (13.54ff.).

In chapter 14 the only major temporal deformation in the ordering of events in the Gospel occurs. Herod mistakenly identifies Jesus as the resurrected John the Baptist (14.1ff.), and Matthew pauses in his story to recount the Baptist's death. This story provides another instructive example of the way Matthew has combined his two plot themes. The rejection of John not only foreshadows Jesus' own fate,[1] but Herod's mistaken assumption of John's resurrection correctly anticipates Jesus' resurrection. The news of John's death is used by the evangelist to provide the impetus for Jesus to withdraw to a lonely place (14.13) even though this news is temporally misplaced in the story. In this lonely place Jesus has more success in his ministry when he heals the sick and feeds the five thousand (14.14ff.). In a second scene about Jesus stilling a storm (14.22ff.), the theme of acceptance appears to be used ambiguously. The disciples are full of fear and Peter is reproached for his doubt and little faith. The plot has developed, however, for unlike the first incident (8.27), the miracle ends this time with a correct confession instead of a question (14.33). The disciples have progressed in their understanding of Jesus' identity.[2]

Although the response of the crowds to Jesus' ministry is mixed at this point in the story, sometimes being positive especially with respect to the healing ministry, but other times negative, reflecting rejection and a lack of understanding, the response of the Jewish leaders is uniform—they are opposed to

---

Evangelica I, ed. K. Aland and F.L. Cross (Berlin: Akademie-Verlag, 1959), p. 79; Lohr, 'Oral Techniques', pp. 427ff. Those two also see the discourse in chapter 13 having a pivotal function in the structure of the Gospel.

1 Cf. Meier, 'John the Baptist', pp. 399ff., who argues that this is another example of the way Matthew parallels Jesus and John the Baptist. They are both rejected by Israel and martyred as end-time prophets.

2 Cf. Anderson, 'Double and Triple Stories', pp. 73ff.

Jesus.[1] In 15.1ff. Matthew narrates the dispute over purity laws between Jesus and the scribes and the Pharisees. In the middle of the controversy Jesus cites another prophecy from Isaiah to show how the rejection fulfills the Old Testament. Their rejection is contrasted with the disciples' acceptance in spite of the fact that the disciples' understanding is flawed: only after Jesus' explanation do they fully understand (15.15ff.; 16.12; 17.13).[2]

The Jewish leaders' rejection of Jesus is also contrasted with the faith of the Canaanite woman (15.21ff.), whose faith is exemplary because it comes from one with marginal status.[3] The repetition of a second feeding miracle (15.32ff.) reinforces the wavering nature of the disciples' faith and understanding.

1 Cf. Joseph A. Comber, 'The Verb *Therapeuo* in Matthew's Gospel', *JBL*, 97 (1978), p. 433, who has observed that Matthew continues to narrate examples of Jesus' healing after 11.1 when his ministry of teaching and preaching to Israel stopped because of its rejection. Matthew is thereby able to distinguish between the crowds, who respond positively to Jesus' healings, and the Jewish leaders, who consistently reject Jesus. Even this kind of positive response is not adequate for the evangelist, however, as is made clear both in the passion story when the Jewish crowds ultimately reject Jesus (27.15-25), and in logia which stress the cost of following Jesus (cf. 8.19ff.; 10.34ff.; 16.21ff.). See Kingsbury, 'Verb *Akolouthein*', pp. 57-62, who argues that the elements of personal commitment and cost must be present for ἀκολουθέω to be interpreted metaphorically and not literally in Matthew.

2 See Luz, 'Disciples', pp. 102ff. Luz shows that the theme of understanding is a crucial concept in the Matthean portrayal of the disciples. If the disciples themselves did not understand Jesus' teachings, they would be unable to fulfill the commission to teach others to observe all that Jesus taught (28.20).

3 Anderson ('Double and Triple Stories', pp. 78ff) and Donaldson (*Jesus on the Mountain*, pp. 132ff.) see in this pericope an anticipation of, and justification for, the extension of the mission to the nations at the conclusion of the Gospel. Cf. Loader, 'Son of David', p. 578, who writes that Matthew has turned this incident into 'a symbolic narrative which highlights the faith of a Gentile woman, who recognizes the Son of David, Israel's Messiah, and thus foreshadows the faith of Gentiles to come.... A daughter of the Gentiles is set free from demon-possession in contrast to Israel's continuing bondage'.

Not only does their faith pale in comparison with the faith of the Gentile woman, but they seem not to have learned anything from the preceding feeding miracle and intervening events. The motif of bread seems to tie the incidents together, and the pattern repeats itself in the first half of chapter 16, where one finds rejection by the Pharisees and Sadducees followed by partial understanding on the part of the disciples. The incident in which the Pharisees and Sadducees ask for a sign is a repetition of an earlier scene (cf. 16.1-4 and 12.8-42), although this time the request is specifically identified as an attempt to 'tempt' Jesus. The effect of this repetition is that the implied reader 'sees the Jewish leaders becoming more perverse in the course of the narrative'.[1] Jesus' answer to the Jewish leaders criticizes them for being unable to discern the 'signs of the times'.[2] The sign of Jonah is mentioned again (16.4), but no interpretation is given because it is not necessary. The implied reader already knows what it means from the previous episode (12.40) and the Jewish leaders will not understand it. Matthew juxtaposes this incident with Jesus' warning to the disciples about the 'leaven of the Pharisees and Sadducees', in which the disciples finally obtain understanding (16.12), and this highlights the fact that understanding is an important element in Matthew's use of the themes of acceptance and rejection. This section of narrative closes with an act of understanding when Peter correctly confesses who Jesus is at Caesarea Philippi (16.13ff.). Even this understanding is defective, however, as subsequent events show.

In summary, Matthew has narrated in more detail the response to Jesus' ministry in this section of the narrative. For Israel, the response has primarily been negative with the Jewish leaders leading the opposition. Their rejection of Jesus has become more persistent and resolute as the narrative progresses. In the face of such rejection, Jesus turns to the disciples and privately directs more attention to them (13.36ff.).

---

1 Anderson, 'Double and Triple Stories', p. 80.
2 Cf. Hill, *Matthew*, p. 257, who interprets this pericope to mean that the Jewish leaders were unable to understand that the person and activity of Jesus in their midst 'signify that these days are decisive for repentance and judgment'.

Despite the progress made in the disciples' understanding of Jesus' identity, their faith and understanding is still wavering. The positive response to Jesus by some of society's marginal characters in this section of the narrative thus serves as a foil for revealing both the perversity of the Jewish leaders and the dullness of the disciples.

4. *Matthew 16.21–20.34*

The disciples are the primary recipients of Jesus' teaching in the next section of the Gospel, and much of this teaching deals either with Jesus' mission of suffering as he talks openly about the passion or with matters that concern the church. In the second half of chapter 16 the evangelist uses the plotting device of prediction to project incidents beyond the temporal boundaries of the plotted story. The predictions about the coming of the Son of Man (16.28ff.) occur outside the plotted story, and the founding of the church (16.18) begins in the narrative but continues outside it.[1] Only Jesus' passion prediction is fulfilled within the temporal boundaries of the story by Jesus' crucifixion and resurrection (16.21). These predictions are closely connected with the themes of rejection and acceptance. Peter's confession is approved by Jesus (16.17), but the following rebuke reveals that Peter has not fully understood (16.22ff.). Jesus chooses to accept the path of obedient suffering which began with the temptations in the wilderness (cf. 4.10 and 16.23).[2] The logia in 16.24ff. challenge the disciples to accept Jesus' fate as their own, although the saying about taking up the cross (16.24) only makes sense at this point in the plotted story because Jesus has not explicitly mentioned the manner of his death (cf. 10.38) prior to this. Peter's difficulty in accepting the way of suffering Jesus has chosen

1 Cf. Kingsbury, *Jesus Christ*, p. 87, and J. Grassi, 'The Last Testament-Succession Literary Background of Matthew 9.35–11.1 and its Significance', *BThB* 7 (1977), p. 175, who see Matthew's portrayal of the earthly Jesus founding the church as reflecting his concern to assert the continuity between Jesus and his church's doctrine and praxis.
2 Cf. Hill, *Matthew*, p. 264, who writes that 'the words of Peter are a return of the temptation to other ways of fulfilling the messianic role than by sacrifice and obedience'.

typifies the conflict with his disciples that Jesus will face throughout the rest of the Gospel as he seeks to instruct them to accept his evaluative point of view concerning servanthood.

Immediately after Jesus' first passion prediction, the evangelist narrates Jesus' transfiguration, in which a divine voice expresses approval of him (17.5). The link between this event and the baptism are widely recognized,[1] and the heavenly voice functions in a similar way to confirm Jesus' obedience. In 3.17 Jesus' obedience to God's will is confirmed in a general way as he acts 'to fulfill all righteousness' (3.15). In 17.5, however, Jesus' obedience is given more specific content when it is confirmed as a way of suffering and death (16.21).[2] The command to the disciples to listen to Jesus emphasizes the importance of Jesus' teaching (cf. 28.16ff.) and highlights the exemplary character which Jesus' acceptance of God's will has for the disciples. A subtle type of prolepsis is used in 17.9 since the saying presupposes that the Son of Man will be raised from the dead. The interchange with the disciples also has a retrospective glance back to John the Baptist when Jesus identifies him as Elijah (17.10ff.) and predicts that the Son of Man will suffer the same rejection John suffered.

The response of rejection continues to govern the rest of the incidents plotted before the next great teaching discourse. An epileptic boy is healed in 17.14ff., but instead of being plotted according to the theme of acceptance as so many of the healing stories are, the incident provokes an exasperated remark from Jesus about his unresponsive contemporaries (17.17). Matthew's interest in the incident is obvious when he uses the

1 See Przybylski, 'Mt, 3.13–4.11', pp. 227ff., and Donaldson, *Jesus on the Mountain*, p. 152, for a discussion of the way Matthew has assimilated the two sayings to one another.

2 Donaldson, *Jesus on the Mountain*, pp. 151ff., stresses that it is Matthew's 'Son-of-God' christology which links together the baptism, the temptation, Peter's confession, and the transfiguration in the Gospel. Although Donaldson is correct on this point, it must be stressed that Matthew defines Jesus' sonship in terms of his obedient suffering according to the will of God. The plotting device of acceptance/rejection plays an important role in this definition as Jesus is tempted throughout the Gospel to deviate from this path (4.1ff.; 16.21ff.; 26.36ff.; 27.40, 43).

event as an occasion for Jesus to teach about faith to the disciples rather than concluding the scene with a reference to the faith of the father or the cured boy.[1] A second passion prediction follows, underlining the approaching dangers and challenges which will test the faith of the disciples (17.22ff.).

The fourth of the great discourses appears in chapter 18 and forms the center of this narrative section. The reference to the church (18.17) implies a situation outside of the temporal boundaries of the plotted story. The correlatives acceptance/rejection are used differently in this discourse, becoming applied to the relationships among members of the community, rather than to people's response to Jesus and the proclamation about the Kingdom of Heaven. Jesus uses the example of a child to teach that greatness in the Kingdom is defined by childlike humility (18.1-4), and this general norm is applied to specific situations which may arise in the church: 'the evil of scandal (vv. 5-9), the care of a sheep going astray (vv. 10-14) and the reconciliation of a brother who has sinned (vv. 15-20)'.[2] The discourse closes with a parable which stresses that the community must live on the basis of God's grace (18.21ff.). There is the warning that if disciples do not accept and forgive one another as they have been forgiven by God, then God will take back his forgiveness and reject them (cf. 6.14ff.). The themes of acceptance and rejection are thus operative throughout the discourse as the disciples are exhorted not to cause offense to their fellow Christians. It is this use of the acceptance/rejection theme that connects the discourse with the controversy about paying the temple tax (17.24f.). Christians are to avoid being a stumbling block to those outside the community as well as those within the church.[3]

The Matthean concluding formula closes the discourse in 19.1, and the evangelist uses a summary to recount more healing successes (19.2). This success is immediately followed

1 Cf. Schweizer, *Matthew*, p. 352.
2 W.G. Thompson, *Matthew's Advice to a Divided Community. Mt. 17,22–18,35* (AnaBib 44; Rome: Biblical Institute Press, 1970), p. 247.
3 Cf. *ibid.*, pp. 50ff., and Schweizer, *Matthew*, pp. 357ff., for discussions of how 17.24ff. functions as an introduction to the following discourse. Despite the Christians' freedom, they should continue to pay the tax to avoid offending the Jews.

by controversy with the Pharisees about divorce. Matthew
continues to contrast the completely negative response of the
Jewish leaders with the mixed response of the crowds. The
trusting acceptance of children is held up as an example for
the disciples (19.13ff.) as it was earlier in the community discourse (18.1ff.), and this trust is contrasted with the self-
reliance of the rich young man (19.16f.). Jesus does not criti-
cize the young man's obedience to the law, but charges that
the extra needs by the man to obtain perfection is full obedience and commitment to Jesus. The man's rejection of the call
to discipleship is also contrasted with the disciples who have
accepted the poverty arising from their commitment to Jesus
(19.27).

The final passion prediction is found in 20.17ff., and an
increasing specificity is observable in each succeeding prediction. The role of understanding in Matthew's use of the plotting device of acceptance/rejection can be seen in the disciples'
continued inability to comprehend fully the nature of Jesus'
ministry and mission, despite the teaching and predictions.
This inability is obvious from the misunderstanding about
positions in the Kingdom which follows the final passion prediction (20.20ff.). A prolepsis concerning the fate of James and
John is utilized, although their martyrdom is not fulfilled
within the temporal limits of the plotted story.

The section of narrative closes with a second episode of Jesus
healing two blind men (cf. 9.27-31). The major differences
between this event and the earlier scene involve the response
of the healed men and of the crowd. The differences are
related to the episodes' context in the narrative and reflect the
development of the Gospel's plot. In the first episode the blind
men exhibit faith, but fail in their obedience to Jesus (9.31),
whereas in the second healing the blind men 'follow' Jesus
(20.34) once healed. Whether or not this 'following' should be
understood as expressive of discipleship has been debated
among commentators, but at the very least, the second group
is portrayed more favorably than the first group who dis-
obeyed. In the development of the plot which has seen opposition increasing among the people of Israel, the positive
response of the blind men is contrasted with the 'blindness'

Jesus faces in the Jewish leaders.[1] The crowd's rebuke of the blind men in the second episode (20.34) should be seen in light of the movement towards Jesus' death, when the crowds will join with their leaders in rejecting Jesus. Their initial attraction to Jesus is giving way to a more ambiguous response.

5. *Matthew 21.1–25.46*

The next section of the narrative recounts Jesus' ministry in Jerusalem, and the theme of rejection dominates the emplotment of events. The section opens with Jesus' entry into Jerusalem, and Matthew's plotting of the event underlines the humility of Jesus who is willing to accept God's way of suffering and service (20.28). Matthew has abbreviated the Septuagintal citation of Zech. 9.9 which attends Jesus' triumphal entry into the city (21.5). This abbreviation has the effect of emphasizing the paradox of Jesus the humble king.[2] While the crowds acknowledge Jesus as 'Son of David' (which is a correct title for Jesus: cf. 1.1.), its use nonetheless appears ironic, for they have unwittingly spoken the truth (21.11).[3] The evangelist's intertwining of the two plotting devices is clearly evident in this scene. Jesus tells the disciples precisely what to do (21.2ff.) and his instructions are obeyed. Their actions contribute to the fulfillment of an Old Testament prophecy as Matthew uses one of his formula quotations (21.4ff.).

Jesus' first act in Jerusalem is the cleansing of the Temple,

---

1 See Kingsbury, 'Verb *Akolouthein*', pp. 57ff., and Anderson, 'Double and Triple Stories', pp. 77, 86, for discussions of how 'following' should be read in this pericope. Anderson points out that part of the difference in interpretation depends upon whether discipleship is 'defined as becoming a member of the character group, "the disciples", or as the response of faith' (p. 86, n. 7).

2 Barth, *TIM*, p. 130; Hill, *Matthew*, p. 291; Schweizer, *Matthew*, p. 405.

3 Kingsbury, *Matthew as Story*, p. 81. Contra Edwards, *Matthew's Story*, p. 73, who argues that Matthew's emplotment of Jesus' entry creates 'a positive image of the acclamation of the crowd'. See Kingsbury, *Structure*, pp. 99ff., who argues that Matthew uses the title Son of David to stress Jesus' ministry to Israel as the royal Messiah. This Davidic Messiah is not a political or military figure in the Gospel, however, but a humble king who is primarily engaged in a healing ministry.

an act which challenges the authority of the Jewish leaders (21.12ff.). This event sets the tone for the remainder of Jesus' stay in Jerusalem, for he continues to act and teach in the Temple prior to the delivery of his eschatological discourse, provoking opposition from the Jewish leaders as he does so. Matthew uses the same nexus of motifs in the cleansing of the Temple to show the rejection of Jesus by the Jewish leaders: Jesus heals the sick and is acclaimed 'Son of David' by children (i.e. characters on the margin of society) which provokes indignation and rejection from the chief priests and scribes. The irony of the scene should be apparent for the implied reader, who knows the true identity of Jesus: 'the Jewish leaders have heard the children hail Jesus as the Son of David but cannot perceive the truth of their words'.[1] The subsequent controversy story looks back at the fate of John and shows that the Jewish leaders' rejection of Jesus parallels their rejection of John (21.23ff.).

In response to such rejection, Jesus tells a series of parables reflecting the history of the rejection of the Jewish leaders both inside and outside of the temporal boundaries of the plotted story.[2] In each parable Israel has failed to respond properly to the rule of God: they do not act (21.28ff.), they do not bear fruit (21.33ff.), and they do not accept the invitation to the wedding feast (22.1ff.). The first parable looks at their rejection of John and his message. The second parable points to the rejection and killing of Jesus, the Son of God, by the Jewish leaders. An

---

1 Kingsbury, *Matthew as Story*, p. 83. See Senior, *Passion of Jesus* for a thorough discussion of irony in Matthew, particularly in the passion account where the evangelist's use of irony is more frequent.

2 See Schweizer, *Matthäus und seine Gemeinde*, pp. 116-125, and *idem, Matthew*, pp. 401-403, who has identified in these parables, and in chapters 21–25 in general, a pattern in which Israel and its leaders are put on trial for their rejection of Jesus and his envoys. The patterns consists of a twice repeated trial schema involving a verdict, a sentence, the execution of that sentence, and a warning for the Matthean community. Cf. David Garland, *The Intention of Matthew 23* (Leiden: Brill, 1979), pp. 30ff. N.A. Dahl, 'The Passion Narrative in Matthew', in *Matthew*, ed. Stanton, p. 50, believes that the parables in 21.28–22.14 and the discourse in ch. 23 play an important part in assigning guilt to the Jews for Jesus' death.

Old Testament quotation is cited to support the Messianic meaning of the parable (21.42), and the parable closes with a prediction of Israel's loss of the Kingdom (21.43).[1] Although the fulfillments of these predictions have not yet occurred in the narrative, they would have been patently obvious to later readers of the Gospel. The evangelist himself reveals within the temporal boundaries of the plotted story that the Jewish leaders realized Jesus was talking about them (21.45), and the implied reader has already been told that the leaders are actively planning to destroy Jesus. The fact that the Jewish leaders 'understood' the parable highlights the perversity and tenacity of their rejection of Jesus. The parable in 22.1-14 forms a climax to the series as a thinly disguised allegory of the destruction of Jerusalem. In this parable two sets of servants are sent who represent respectively Old Testament and New Testament prophets. The focus is on the second set, however, and the destruction of Jerusalem is Israel's temporal punishment for their rejection of Jesus' disciples.[2] While this

1 See Stanton, 'Matthew and Judaism', pp. 269-70, for a novel interpretation of the parable. Because of 21.43, he believes that the 'stone' in 21.42 is a reference to Matthew's own community rather than Jesus. His arguments, however, are not convincing. First, his interpretation goes against the primary thrust of the parable where the son who is rejected and killed is almost certainly an allegorical reference to Jesus. Second, the narrative conclusion of the parable in 21.45—where the Pharisees understand that the parable is 'about them' (περὶ αὐτῶν)—does not preclude interpreting the parable christologically. They are rejected in favor of the ἔθνος which produces fruit not because they have rejected this ἔθνος, but because they have rejected Jesus. The idea of bearing fruit is a prominent Matthean theme, and he connects it with obedience to God's will (cf. 3.8, 10; 7.16ff.; 12.33). Matthew's use of the plotting device of acceptance/rejection which we have delineated supports this interpretation. Finally, the emphasis in the following parable on the rejection of the church's missionaries does not necessarily support Stanton's interpretation. It can be seen as part of the progression of Israel's rejection of God's envoys—John the Baptist, Jesus, and now the church's disciples (cf. 23.34f.). Cf. Trilling, *Wahre Israel*, p. 65, who writes that with verse 43 Matthew has inserted an interpretation which repeats verse 41 'ohne Bild'. According to Trilling, the purpose of this addition is to emphasize Israel's guilt.
2 See Hare, *Theme of Jewish Persecution*, pp. 121ff.; Stanton,

destruction is not fulfilled within the temporal limits of the plotted story, post 70 CE readers would easily have recognized the allusion.

The themes of acceptance and rejection appear to be operative on another level in the parable trilogy, however, for the evangelist's paraenetic interests for his community become visible in the addition of 22.11-14 to the last parable. There are now two acts of judgment; one on the invited guests who refuse the invitation (22.7), and one on a person who has accepted the invitation but who fails to fulfill the requirements of proper dress (22.13). This second judgment suggests that some members of Matthew's community, members who appear to have accepted the gospel of the Kingdom, will be rejected in the final judgment if they do not continue to be obedient to God. Israel thus provides Matthew with a concrete example and illustration of the fate of those who will not hear and understand the word of the Kingdom (13.19). Members of the Matthean church must also act, bear fruit, and accept the invitation of the Kingdom if they are to escape Israel's fate.[1] The links with chapter 13 reveal what it means for 'a nation producing fruits' of the Kingdom (i.e. the church) to be 'given' the Kingdom (21.43). They will hear and understand the word of the Kingdom (13.11ff., 19, 23).[2]

The theme of rejection continues to be used as the plotting device as the evangelist narrates a series of controversy stories. The circle of Jewish leaders who debate with Jesus grows ever wider, and the series of debates is only concluded when

---

'Matthew and Judaism', pp. 269-70 and van Tilborg, *Jewish Leaders*, pp. 48ff., for arguments that the two sets of servants in the parable represent two different groups of messengers.

1 See Kretzer, *Die Herrschaft*, pp. 150ff. Kretzer summarizes the paraenesis in the trilogy with the formula 'Verweigern der Tat (21.28-32) führt zur Fruchtlosigkeit (21.33-44) und schließlich zum Gericht'. Kretzer is correct in seeing the trilogy building to a climax in 22.1-14, although it should be noted that the element of judgment is present in each of the parables. Cf. Schweizer, *Matthew*, p. 422, who also notes the paraenetic function of vv. 11-14 and so warns against interpreting the parable solely as a description of Israel's apostasy and resulting judgment.

2 *Ibid.*, p. 166.

Jesus confounds his opponents with a question (22.46). Jesus' silencing of the Jewish leaders stands in sharp contrast to the way he was able to answer all their questions. Unable to best Jesus in a debate, his opponents withdraw and Jesus launches a scathing attack against the Jewish leaders in chapter 23. The theme of rejection is obviously dominant in this speech of woes against the scribes and Pharisees. The woes close with a retrospective glance at the way the ancestors of the Jewish leaders also rejected the Old Testament prophets (23.29ff.) and with a prediction of the rejection Jesus' messengers will face (23.34).[1] The latter prediction is not fulfilled within the temporal boundaries of the plotted story but the two temporal references highlight the pattern of rejection which has characterized the course of Israel's history. The prediction of the forsakenness of the house of Israel (23.38) is fulfilled for Matthew when Jesus departs from the Temple (24.1).[2]

After Jesus leaves the Temple, he delivers his eschatological discourse to the disciples privately in chapters 24-25, the last of the great discourses in Matthew.[3] The way in which the discourse predicts events which will occur beyond the temporal boundaries of the plotted story has already been examined. The correlatives of acceptance/rejection are utilized both in

1 Matthew's use of the present tense ἀποστέλλω in 23.34 makes it clear that Christian disciples are the ones who will be persecuted. See Garland, *Matthew 23*, pp. 173ff.; Kingsbury, *Matthew*, pp. 76, 79.
2 See Burnett, *Testament of Jesus-Sophia*, pp. 130ff., 164ff., and Garland, *Matthew 23*, pp. 26ff., 200ff., who argue that for Matthew, Jesus' departure from the Temple represents Israel's loss of the presence of Jesus' and hence the presence of God (cf. 1.23; 18.20; 28.20); since Matthew has appended Jesus' withdrawal from the Temple directly to the woes and lament over Jerusalem (cf. Mk. 12.41ff. and Lk. 21.1ff., where the story of the 'Widow's Mite' comes immediately after the Jerusalem logion).
3 Kingsbury, *Matthew as Story*, p. 84, points out that just as there was an expansion of Jesus' ministry at the beginning of the Gospel from the disciples (4.18ff.), to the crowds (4.23ff.), and to the Jewish leaders (9.2ff.), so there is a corresponding narrowing as the Gospel comes to its climax. Jesus first withdraws from involvement with the Jewish leaders (22.46) when he addresses the crowds and disciples together (23.1) before the disciples alone receive Jesus' final discourse.

projecting a future of tribulation and rejection for the church as well as in the paraenesis for the disciples to stand firm in the face of persecution and to continue to accept Jesus by the doing of the heavenly Father's will.

6. *Matthew 26.1–28.20*

The discourse of chapters 24 and 25 is closed with the final concluding formula (26.1), and Matthew makes it plain by deviating from the other formulas which have closed Jesus' teaching that Jesus' teaching ministry is completed: all that remains is his obedient death. The final section of the Gospel is introduced with a prediction of the imminent passion and crucifixion during the Passover feast (26.2) which gives the implied reader the impression that Jesus is in full control of his destiny. Prediction is used to plot events in the passion narrative, although in contrast to the preceding discourse, the overwhelming majority of the predictions are fulfilled within the temporal limits of the plotted story by the events of the passion.[1] Rejection is the predominant theme in the narrative as Jesus comes into conflict both with the people of Israel, who completely reject Jesus at the urging of their leaders, and with his disciples, who cannot accept Jesus' path of suffering, and who fail to remain faithful to Jesus during the passion and crucifixion.

The theme of rejection is encountered immediately as Matthew reports the Jewish leaders planning a way to kill Jesus (26.3ff.). This theme reappears in the disciples' failure to understand the true nature of Jesus' ministry in the next narrated incident, Jesus' anointing at Bethany (26.6ff.). In this passage, the uncomprehending dullness of the disciples is contrasted with the loving act of service performed by the woman. The incident points ahead to the passion regardless of whether the anointing is understood as a messianic anointment before Jesus' sufferings, or as a burial anointment to prepare for Jesus' death. Likewise, the prediction about the future preaching of the gospel in all the world (26.13) points to the scope of the church's mission, although this mission occurs outside of the boundaries of the plotted story. The theme of

1 Cf. Minear, *Teacher's Gospel*, p. 130.

rejection continues in 26.14ff. as Matthew narrates Judas' collaboration with the Jewish leaders in planning Jesus' arrest. If events in narrative are 'correlative and entailing'— not only in a linear, but also in a causative way, as traditional literary theorists have argued[1]—then the placement of Judas' cooperation with Jesus' opponents at this point may imply that his actions could have been motivated by the misunderstanding of Jesus' mission that has been characteristic of the disciples throughout the Gospel. Donald Senior has pointed out the irony in the activity of Judas and the Jewish opponents, who share the same goal as Jesus: 'the deliverance of the Son of God into the hands of sinful people'.[2]

Matthew continues to show Jesus in full control of his destiny by using the correlatives promise/fulfillment to emplot the last supper. The preparation for the passover meal is plotted with the device of prediction as Jesus' instructions are immediately fulfilled by the disciples (26.17ff.). At this meal Jesus predicts which disciple will reject and betray him although this information is not new to the implied reader (10.4; 26.14ff.). The intertwining of prediction and rejection continues as Jesus predicts Peter's denial and the flight of the disciples (26.30ff.). In the scene at Gethsemane Matthew focuses on the repeated prayer of Jesus, and the evangelist uses the acceptance/rejection theme in a manner which has been utilized earlier in the Gospel. This too is a test in which Jesus is confronted with the possibility of accepting or rejecting the fate of suffering and crucifixion which lies ahead. In contrast to the failure and misunderstanding of the disciples,[3] and in a

---

1 See Chatman, *Story and Discourse*, p. 45.

2 Senior, *Passion of Jesus*, p. 57. Καιρός is the root of the word which is used in 26.16 (ἐυκαιρία). Jesus uses καιρός in 26.18, and throughout the Gospel the word has been used with an eschatological connotation (cf. 8.29; 13.30). Cf. Combrink, 'Structure of Matthew', pp. 84ff., who speaks of the 'dramatic irony of Jesus' own commission with the plan of his opponents'.

3 Senior (*ibid.*, p. 78) points out that Jesus' command to 'watch' (26.38) recalls Jesus' instructions in the final discourse (24.42; 25.13). Not only does this connection reflect Matthew's conviction that Jesus' death and resurrection are of eschatological significance, but it also underscores the failure of the disciples. The hour has come and the

decision consistent with his earlier decisions, Jesus accepts God's will (26.40). He embraces the cross in obedience to God.[1]

The last half of chapter 26 narrates incidents that fulfill earlier predictions: Jesus is betrayed by Judas, forsaken by the disciples, denied by Peter, arrested, tried and condemned by the Jewish leaders. The theme of fulfillment is also present in its wider use which sees the fulfillment of Old Testament prophecies in Jesus' life and ministry. For the first and only time in the Gospel, the formula used by the narrator in the Old Testament fulfillment quotations is expressed in the words and point of view of Jesus himself (26.54, 56).[2] Judas repents of his deed in 27.3ff., but his subsequent suicide fulfills not only Jesus' earlier prediction in the story (26.24) but also leads to the fulfillment of an Old Testament prophecy which the evangelist plots with one of his formula quotations (27.9ff.).

The theme of rejection colors the narrative in all these events as Matthew stresses the perversity of the opposition by the Jewish leaders. They seek 'false testimony' at the trial so they can condemn Jesus to death (26.59ff.) and they are unsympathetic towards Judas when he repents of his betrayal of Jesus. They take the money which was paid Judas to buy a field (27.6ff.), but 'their concern with legality is mocked by their admission that the money is tainted by the blood of betrayal'.[3] Finally, the Jewish leaders urge the people to ask Pilate to crucify Jesus (27.20ff.). The evangelist no longer presents the crowds in an ambiguous light, some of the time

---

disciples were not prepared. Cf. Edwards, *Matthew's Story*, p. 87.

1 See Kingsbury, 'Theology of St. Matthew', p. 355, and *idem*, *Jesus Christ*, p. 84, who argues that Jesus' experience at Gethsamane is a test.

2 Jesus' statement in 5.17 uses the active rather than the passive form of πληρόω. The concept of point of view on the 'phraseological plane' is developed by Uspensky (*Poetics of Composition*, pp. 15ff.). By this term Uspensky means the 'strictly lingustic means of expressing a point of view'. Cf. Senior, *Passion of Jesus*, p. 89, who draws attention to Matthew's use of ὅλος in 26.56: 'Because the passion of Jesus was the final expression of Jesus' mission of salvation the evangelist presents it as the ultimate fulfillment of the Scripture of the prophets'.

3 Senior, *Passion of Jesus*, p. 106.

accepting Jesus and other times rejecting him. The rejection is now complete as the crowds accept responsibility for Jesus' death (27.25). The question of whether to release Jesus or Barabbas represents the culmination of Matthew's use of the correlatives acceptance/rejection to plot his Gospel. As Donald Senior has pointed out, throughout the Gospel

> those confronted by Jesus and his message must ultimately choose either to accept or reject him... Now those many choices to reject Jesus would be forged into a final 'no'.[1]

Jesus continues to act with absolute integrity and consistency during the passion, in contrast to the other major characters in the drama. Jesus' fearless confession before the Sanhedrin stands in obvious contrast to Peter's denial (26.59ff.). Unlike Peter (26.72) and Caiaphas (26.63), Jesus refuses to swear an oath (cf. 5.33ff.; 23.16ff.). He voluntarily accepts his humility and suffering as he is tormented and mocked by the Roman soldiers. Even at the moment of crucifixion Jesus is tested, when the Jewish leaders and crowds mock Jesus, challenging him to prove his sonship by saving himself (27.41-43).[2] Jesus, however, obediently fulfills the will of God as he has throughout his ministry, and dies in an act of obedience, yielding up his spirit to God (27.50). The fact that Jesus dies outside of Jerusalem in Matthew 'seems to capture that abject rejection' which Jesus faced throughout his ministry and which is used to emplot the story of the Gospel.[3] The rejection and opposition of the Jewish leaders, however, continues to manifest itself even after Jesus' death. Not only do they post guards by Jesus' tomb to prevent the disciples from stealing

1 *Ibid.*, p. 113. He argues that the incident with Pilate's wife (27.19) also emphasizes the element of choice, since dreams function in Matthew as a literary convention for the mediation of a divine message.
2 See Barth, *TIM*, pp. 143ff., for a discussion of the way Matthew presents the passion as an act of obedience to God. Cf. Birger Gerhardson, 'Gottes Sohn als Diener Gottes', *ST* 27 (1973), pp. 96-103; Senior, *Passion of Jesus*, pp. 132ff.; Donaldson, *Jesus on the Mountain*, p. 99; Kingsbury, *Jesus Christ*, p. 84 (cf. *idem*, *Matthew as Story*, p. 89) who all argue that the crucifixion in Matthew is a test.
3 Senior, *Passion of Jesus*, p. 124.

Jesus' body (27.62ff.), but they also spread this rumor after his resurrection (28.11ff.).

In the midst of all this rejection in Matthew's account of Jesus' passion, individuals who do not reject Jesus stand out: the Roman centurion confesses Jesus as Son of God (27.54), women who watch the crucifixion are named (27.55), and Joseph of Arimathea provides Jesus with a tomb (27.57ff.). The acceptance which is exceptional in the account of the passion and crucifixion, however, becomes the major plotting device in the resurrection stories in chapter 28. The women accept the task given to them to report to the disciples what they have seen (28.7ff.), and the disciples go to Galilee as Jesus directed them (28.16). The Gospel closes with the disciples being given the commission to make disciples by teaching people to observe (i.e. accept) all that Jesus has commanded. Jesus' trust in and obedience to God has been vindicated by the resurrection. His resurrection fulfills earlier predictions in the story, and the Gospel closes with an open-ended promise/prediction of the resurrected Jesus' presence with the disciples. Both this promise and the assertion of Israel's continued rejection (see 'to this day', 28.15) have the effect of extending the temporal boundaries of the narrative into the time of the implied reader. The implied reader is thus challenged with the disciples to obey all that Jesus commanded.[1]

D. *Conclusion*

If Matthew is an inclusive story about Jesus' life and ministry,

1 Janice Capel Anderson, 'Point of View in Matthew: Evidence', paper read at AAR-SBL Meeting in San Francisco, December 1981, pp. 16-17, has written: 'The Great Commission places all four (Jesus, disciples, narrator, and implied reader) temporally in the same position: the period of mission following the resurrection and prior to the close of the age.... If one may be permitted an historical inference, the actual author wanted the actual readers or hearers to carry over the ideological viewpoint adopted in assuming the role of the reader or hearer in the text into real life and obey the final commission'. Quoted from Combrink, 'Structure of Matthew', pp. 89-90. See chapter 5 for our discussion of the strategies utilized by Matthew to involve a reader in the text.

then who is included in it, and how are they included? By prolepses or predictions of events which lay beyond the end of the
temporal boundaries of the narrative, Matthew projects a
narrative world within which Matthew's plotted story occurs.
These are found on both the story level in predictions by Jesus
and on the narrative level in comments by the implied
author/narrator. Because the implied readers find themselves
in a world that shares the same temporal boundaries as the
narrative world of the Gospel (i.e. the time prior to the coming
of the Son of Man), they can be said to be included in the narrative.

The open-ended nature of the temporal boundaries of the
narrative world is not sufficient in itself, however, to specify
the identity of the implied reader who is included in the story.
Matthew is further able to specify the characteristics of the
implied reader through the way in which the story is emplotted. Internal prolepses were used to advance the story temporally, but the correlatives acceptance/rejection provides the
dominant plot device or theme. Matthew opens his Gospel by
introducing his protagonist Jesus, the Son of God, whose mission is to save his people from their sins. His coming provokes a
crisis as characters in the story are confronted with the choice
of accepting or rejecting him and his proclamation of the
Kingdom of God. Acceptance or obedience to Jesus' teaching is
the proper response according to the evangelist, and the
implied reader is challenged to respond correspondingly in the
open-ended conclusion to the Gospel.

The themes that are used to emplot the story in Matthew
can be studied from the perspective of both the author and the
reader. As C.H. Holman has pointed out, plot 'is the chief principle for selection and arrangement' for the author, whereas
for the reader 'it is something perceived as structure and
unity'.[1] When considered as plotting mechanisms used by the
author to tell his story, the correlatives promise/fulfillment are
thus used to create expections which may be fulfilled later.
With the correlatives acceptance/rejection, events are plotted

---

1 C.H. Holman, *A Handbook to Literature: Based on the Original by
William Flint Thrall and Addison Hibbard*, (3rd edn; Indianapolis:
Odyssey, 1972), p. 397, from Combrink, 'Structure of Matthew', p. 74.

so that characters are confronted with the option of accepting or rejecting Jesus. When considered from the perspective of the reader, the plot themes help explicate how readers create meaning in the text. The correlatives promise/fulfillment describe the temporal or successive reading activities. Expectations and hypotheses are formed by the reader which are either fulfilled or disappointed later in the story. The correlatives acceptance/rejection describe the way the reader must make judgments as he or she reads and decides afresh whether or not to accept the claims of Jesus and his teaching. In the following chapters we will examine the plot themes in a more differentiated manner, treating them from the perspectives of the implied author/narrator and implied reader in an effort to understand both the poetic and pragmatic dimensions of Matthew's inclusive story.

Chapter 4

IMPLIED AUTHOR, NARRATOR AND POINT OF VIEW IN MATTHEW'S INCLUSIVE STORY

A. *Introduction*

Narrative art by definition presupposes a story-teller, a story, and an audience.[1] In the previous chapter we focused on the middle component in this triad of narrative elements by sketching the narrative world projected by Matthew and by tracing the emplotment of Matthew's inclusive story. In the next two chapters the roles of the participants in the communicative transaction, the story-teller and the audience, will be highlighted. A study of the story-teller is germane to our discussion of Matthew's inclusive story because of his ability to shape the role of any reader who might be 'included' in the story.

The readers of narrative text start off as outsiders to the narrative world in which the story unfolds, and they must not only be introduced to it but they must also be guided through the narrative. This task is accomplished by the story-teller who is able to use a wide range of rhetorical techniques and strategies to cajole, impress, persuade, assure—in short, to communicate with—the reader. By means of these strategies, the story is told in a particular way and the story-teller indicates how he or she sees the significance of the story. Perhaps one of the most important means of shaping the audience's response to the story is point of view, because it involves the perspectives by which the narrative is both presented and experienced.[2] In the previous chapter we argued that

1 Scholes and Kellogg, *Nature of Narrative*, p. 240.
2 Recent literary theorists have pointed out that, in some formalist-structuralist approaches to point of view, the designation point of

Matthew's inclusive story is emplotted according to a point of view in which acceptance and obedience are portrayed as the proper response to Jesus and his teaching. In this chapter the craft and role of the Matthean story-teller in communicating this point of view will be examined.

Before we begin, some clarification in terminology is needed. The story-teller and audience who are essential to narrative art are multi-faceted concepts or characters. There are actual flesh-and-blood authors and readers who as extratextual persons compose and read the narrative. There are also, however, intratextual parties to the communication who are encoded or implied in the literary text. These authors and readers are said to be 'encoded' because they are 'linguistically present in the text in the form of first and second person pronouns or their equivalents in the subjects and predicates of verbs'.[1] They may be explicitly mentioned, as happens in Luke-Acts when the implied reader or narratee is encoded through both the pronoun 'you' and the proper name 'Theophilus', and when the implied author or narrator is encoded through the first person personal pronouns 'I' and 'we' (Lk. 1.1-4; Acts 1.1; and the 'we' passages in Acts; cf. Jn 20.31; 21.25). Alternatively,

view is limited solely to the narrative voice which speaks in the story. This practice, however, isolates the text from its dynamic relationship between author and reader and neglects those aspects of point of view which cannot be quantified. It also overlooks the fact that authorial presence and perspective is always encoded into the text since it is the author who ultimately creates and establishes all the narrative strategies used to communicate. According to Lanser (*Narrative Act*, p. 13), point of view is 'essentially a *relationship* rather than a concrete entity'. We will be following Lanser's typology in using point of view in this broader sense which encompasses all the narrative strategies used to structure 'the relationships of speaker to verbal act, the audience, and the propositional material' in a narrative (Lanser, *Narrative Act*, p. 79). By using point of view in a more inclusive sense, we will be able to understand more precisely how Matthew's inclusive story functions. For example, a narrator who explains and persuades is quite different from one who judges and warns, even though they can be described in the same formalist categories, Cf. also Wolterstoff, *Art in Action*, pp. 136ff.; Walhout, 'Texts and Actions', pp. 63ff.

1 Petersen, 'Reader in the Gospel', p. 39.

implied author and reader may be the implicit interlocutors behind third person narration and the person to whom it speaks, as is found in the other Synoptic Gospels Matthew and Mark.

These intratextual communicants are further differentiated by literary theorists. The voice which tells the story is the narrator. This rhetorical device may be dramatized as a character in the story or it may be left undramatized. The narrator is to be distinguished from a third party in the narrative act, the implied author. Wayne Booth, who coined the term, defines the implied author as 'an ideal, literary, created version of the real man; he is the sum of his own choices'.[1] Such authors are 'implied' in the sense that they must be reconstructed or inferred from the text by the reader through the intricate network of literary devices and strategies in the narrative text.[2] Unlike narrators, implied authors have no voice of their own and so cannot communicate directly to the reader. Rather, the implied author stands as the literary impression or 'principle' who creates not only the narrator, but everything else in the narrative and thus 'establishes the norms of the narrative'.[3] It is important to distinguish between the implied author and the narrator because the

1 Booth, *Rhetoric of Fiction*, pp. 74-75. Cf. Lategan, 'Reception, Rediscription, Reality', p. 70, who describes the implied author as 'a textguided image of the author'.

2 The implied author is thus not as completely an inhabitant of the text as Janice Capel Anderson implies ('Matthew: Gender and Reading', *Semeia* 28 (1983), p. 8, n. 19) when she contrasts him with the implied reader. According to Anderson, the implied author is entirely within the text, whereas the implied reader is 'both textual structure and structured act'. This formulation overlooks, however, the role of the reader in constructing an image of the implied author in the reading process. Lategan more correctly formulates the relationship between the two: 'Author and reader stand in a chiastic relationship to one another: the implied reader is a construct of the real author, and the implied author is a construct of the real reader. The first is necessary to prepare the expected response to the text, the latter is a textguided image in order to get a grip on this intended response' ('Reception, Redescription, Reality', p. 73).

3 Chatman, *Story and Discourse*, p. 149.

narrator may prove to be limited or untrustworthy as a guide
to the story. A narrator is 'unreliable' when he or she is at odds
with the values and norms of the implied author which
inform and support the narrative.[1]

While it has become commonplace in literary theory to distinguish between the author and narrator—the narrator
(who tells) is a creation of the author (who wrote)[2]—the distinction should not be absolutized. The distance between
author, implied author and narrator can be expressed along a
spectrum of possibilities ranging from equivalence to separation. Moreover, certain types of narrators are more easily
associated with the extratextual authorial voice than others. A
public, undramatized, reliable, and omniscient narrator for
example is the type of narrator who 'most closely approximates the implied author'.[3] This phenomenon has led one literary critic to postulate the following general rule:

> In the absence of direct markings which separate the public
> narrator from the extrafictional voice, so long as it is possible
> to give meaning to the text with the equation author = narra-
> tor, readers will conventionally make this equation.[4]

---

1 The term 'unreliable narrator' is another coinage of Wayne Booth's.
  See *Rhetoric*, pp. 158-59; Chatman, *Story and Discourse*, pp. 148ff.,
  233-37.
2 Monroe Beardsley (*Aesthetics* [New York, 1958], p. 147) argues that
  'the speaker of a literary work cannot be identified with the author'.
  From Chatman, *Story and Discourse*, pp. 147-48. Cf. Wayne Booth,
  'Distance and Point of View: An Essay in Classification', *Essays in
  Criticism* 11 (1961), p. 65, who writes that 'one of the most frequent
  reading faults comes from a naive identification of such narrators
  (omniscient narrators) with the authors who create them. But in
  fact there is always a distinction... '; also cf. Sternberg, *Expositional Modes*, p. 256.
3 *Ibid.*
4 Lanser, *Narrative Act*, p. 151. Lanser qualifies this potential identity
  by defining the term 'author' as a 'textually encoded, historically
  authoritative voice kin to but not identical with the biographical person who wrote the text' (p. 152). In other words, her author is little
  different from our implied author. The equivalence of author and
  narrator thus functions on 'the levels of imagination, ideology, and
  even narrative style' rather than on 'the level of referentiality' (p.
  153).

The characteristics of the other party in the communicative transaction, the audience, will be examined in detail in the next chapter. It is sufficient to note here that for every author-figure or narrator present or implied in the text, there is a corresponding reader or narratee. The presence of these intra-textual interlocutors in the narrative effectively renders any communication between a flesh-and-blood author and audience indirect: such communication is mediated through the interplay between the encoded voice(s) and listener(s). The importance of these intratextual communicants is that they 'to some degree create the competence of all actual readers to decode the significance of the text'.[1] That is to say, readers must read 'through' the experiences of the implied reader if they are themselves to appropriate, understand, and be influenced by the narrative. For this reason, it is important for us to be sensitive to the interaction between encoded story-teller and audience in Matthew. In this chapter we will focus particularly on how the implied author/narrator creates, shapes, and controls an encoded reader as the story of Jesus unfolds in the Gospel.

We will begin by identifying and labelling the narrator in Matthew since his presence is plainly visible as the voice in the Gospel which narrates the story. The ways in which he communicates his point of view in the narrative, thus influencing and controlling the reader, will then be examined in more detail. While the characteristics of the Matthean narrator have yet to be delineated, we will discover that he is the type of narrator who is virtually identical with the implied author. The lack of distance between the two means that both narrator and implied author espouse the same system of values in Matthew. The traditional terminology 'Matthew' or 'the evangelist' will therefore be used to refer to the narrator even though we recognize the distinction on the theoretical level between 'narrator', 'author' and 'implied author'.[2]

---

1 Petersen, 'Reader in the Gospel', p. 40. Cf. Lanser, *Narrative Act*, pp. 116ff.
2 See Anderson, 'Gender and Reading', pp. 7, 22-23; Kingsbury, *Matthew as Story*, pp. 30ff.; *idem*, 'Jesus in Matthew's Story', pp. 4ff., all of whom also point out that the narrator functions as the

B. *The Matthean Narrator and Aspects of Point of View*

The Matthean narrator shares many characteristics with the narrators of the other Gospels, and these similarities lead one to speculate whether a specific kind of narrator might be typical of the Gospel genre.[1] It is immediately apparent that the narrator—or story-teller—in Matthew is undramatized. He is not a character in the story, and he speaks in the third-person as one outside the action.[2] He is intrusive in the sense that the reader is aware of his presence addressing an audience which exists outside the story world of the Gospel.[3] The narrator can thus be characterized as a 'public narrator', and one of his functions is to define the story world in which he is creator and authority.[4] He is autonomous and feels free to interrupt

reliable voice of the implied author in Matthew.

1 See Culpepper, *Anatomy*, pp. 20ff., and Petersen, 'Point of View', pp. 97ff., for detailed discussions of the narrators in John and Mark respectively. Cf. also Rhoads and Michie, *Mark as Story*, pp. 35ff., and Hill, 'A Response to Prof. Kingsbury', p. 38, who also identify the narrators of the Gospels as overt and intrusive. See Kingsbury, *Matthew as Story*, pp. 30-36 for a discussion of the implied author and narrator in Matthew. The most useful categories for defining narrators are spelled out in the work of Booth, 'Distance and Point of View', Uspensky, *Poetics of Composition*, and Lanser, *Narrative Act*.

2 Matthew's account of Jesus' baptism provides a good example of third person narration: 'Then Jesus came from Galilee to the Jordan to John, to be baptized by him. John would have prevented him ... ' (3.13-14). The Matthean narrator tells his story as an observer.

3 The most obvious places in the Gospel where the implied author/ narrator addresses an audience outside the story world are 1) in the aside in the eschatological discourse, 'Let the reader understand' (24.15), 2) the temporal references 'to this day' in 27.8 and 28.15, and 3) in the OT fulfillment quotations. Matthew's use of these and other narrative techniques will be discussed in more depth later in the chapter.

4 Lanser, *Narrative Act*, pp. 138ff., distinguishes between public and private narrators. The difference is that the former sort is capable of addressing a reader-construct who represents the public, whereas the latter can only address another person in the fictional world. According to Lanser, 'public narrative acts are closest to authorial speech acts' (p. 140). The role of the public narrator in creating the

the flow of the narrative—commenting on characters, evaluating their actions, and interpreting the significance of events as he tells the story.[1] Wayne Booth has argued that the typology of person is the 'most overworked distinction' used to classify narrators.[2] Yet the choice of third-person narration in the Gospel genre has an important effect in the experience of reading the narrative. The third person narrator is perceived as an observer which 'produces the illusion of pure reference'—an important effect for a narrative which is ostensibly historical.[3]

The illusion of pure reference in the narration of the story is heightened by other characteristics of the narrator in the Gospel. The Matthean narrator displays what has been commonly called an omniscient point of view. M.H. Abrams defines this label as the assumption

> that the narrator knows everything that needs to be known about the agents and events; that he is free to move as he will in time and place, and to shift from character to character, reporting (or concealing) what he chooses of their speech and actions; and also that he has 'privileged' access to a character's thoughts and feelings and motives, as well as to his overt speech and actions.[4]

Abrams' definition refers to several different aspects of point of view which correspond to the different planes of point of view identified by Boris Uspensky in his study: the ideological (evaluative norms), the phraseological (speech patterns), the spatial (location of narrator), the temporal (time of narrator),

---

story world of Matthew is visible in the genealogy (1.1-17) where the reader is introduced to the antecedents of the story.

1 Abrams, *Glossary of Literary Terms*, p. 143. The Old Testament fulfillment quotations are a prominent example of the Matthean narrator's habit of interrupting the flow of the narrative to interpret the story for the implied reader.

2 Booth, 'Distance and Point of View', p. 64, and *idem*, *Rhetoric of fiction*, p. 150. Cf. his qualification of this statement, however, in the afterward to the second edition of *Rhetoric of Fiction*, p. 412.

3 Kermode, *The Genesis of Secrecy*, p. 117. The full quotation reads 'the advantage of third-person narration is that it is the mode which best produces the illusion of pure reference'.

4 Abrams, *Glossary*, p. 143.

and the psychological (internal and external views of characters).[1] While the most important privilege offered by omniscience is no doubt the ability to obtain an inside view of a
character—the omniscient narrator can tell a reader what
'no one in so-called real life could possibly know'[2]—this
knowledge also has temporal and spatial dimensions. A
discussion of omniscience should thus not be limited to the
psychological level. Uspensky's categories will therefore be
utilized to explicate the characteristics and point of view of the
Matthean narrator.

1. *The Phraseological Plane*
The phraseological plane, as 'the strictly linguistic means of
expressing a point of view',[3] perhaps stands as the most obvious dimension of point of view in terms of the surface level of
the narrative, for it allows a reader to distinguish the various
voices of characters and narrator within the text. For example, we have identified the Matthean narrator as an undramatized, third person, public narrator on the basis of his
speech and diction as he narrates his story of Jesus. The
phraseological aspect of point of view is not purely a grammatical issue, however, for the speech patterns and diction
used impinge upon other dimensions of point of view and a
reader's experience of the narrative. For example, the Old
Testament fulfillment quotations in Matthew are all spoken
by the narrator, and the authoritative nature of the Old Testament conveys a sense of authority and reliability to the narrator's speech acts.[4] The choice of pronouns in the phrase

---

1 Uspensky, *Poetics*, Cf. Lanser, *Narrative Act*, pp. 184-222.
2 Booth, *Rhetoric of Fiction*, pp. 3, 160.
3 Uspensky, *Poetics*, p. 15. Cf. Lanser, *Narrative Act*, p. 185, who
  writes that 'the choice of phraseological stance delimits the spatial-
  temporal, psychological, and ideological possibilities the text may
  generate ... '.
4 See Kingsbury, *Matthew as Story*, pp. 33ff., and *idem*, 'Jesus in
  Matthew's Story, pp. 6ff., who emphasizes the role of the OT in
  establishing the credentials of the Matthean narrator for the
  reader. Cf. Lars Hartman, 'Scriptural Exegesis in the Gospel of St.
  Matthew and the Problem of Communication', in *Matthieu*, ed.
  Didier, p. 134, who lists as one possible reason an author will quote

'their synogogue(s)' (4.23; 9.35; 12.9; 13.54; cf. 10.17 and 23.34
['your'], where the expression is placed on Jesus' lips) likewise
reflects a particular perspective on the part of the narrator
vis-à-vis this Jewish institution, and this has led to much
speculation among modern Matthean scholars as to the relationship between Matthew's church and Judaism.[1]

The implied author/narrator's influence on the phraseological plane is also operative in the other narrative voices.
Although characters in the story may speak directly, their
speech is ultimately the creation of authorial actions. Their
speech may be expressed in either direct or indirect discourse.
Jesus' first passion prediction (16.21) is indirectly reported by
the narrator in his own voice, for example, but the next two
predictions are recorded in Jesus' direct speech (17.22ff.;
20.18ff.). The narrator is involved even when direct discourse
is used because he is responsible for translating the spoken into
the written word.[2] The different ways of introducing speech,
the descriptors utilized and the punctuation chosen all
influence the implied reader's perception and experience of
direct discourse. In Matthew the narrator's use of a concluding formula to end large sections of Jesus' teaching (7.28; 11.1;
13.53; 19.1; 26.1) has thus led commentators to perceive five
large discourses in Matthew, even though there are other
narrative sections with extensive teaching material.[3] More-

from another, 'He wants to reinforce his opinion with the authority
of somebody else'. This effect would be intensified if the authority is
considered to be none other than the Word of God itself (cf. Mt. 1.22;
2.15; 15.4; 22.31). Matthew's use of the OT fulfillment quotations will
be discussed more fully later in the chapter.

1 See Graham Stanton, 'The Origin and Purpose of Matthew's
Gospel: Matthean Scholarship from 1945 to 1980', in *Aufstieg und
Niedergang der römischen Welt*, II, 25, 3 ed. H. Temparini and W.
Haase (Berlin: Walter de Gruyter, 1985), pp. 1910-1921, for a discussion of this Matthean phrase and of the different interpretations of
the relationship between Matthew and Judaism.
2 Cf. Lanser, *Narrative Act*, pp. 190ff.
3 B.W. Bacon (*Studies in Matthew* [London: Constable, 1930], pp. 29,
40ff., 81ff.; numerous other commentators follow him) thus argues
that Matthew's Gospel contains five books which are analogous to
the Pentateuch. The large amount of teaching material in Matthew
outside these discourses have led others to propose the existence of

over, Matthew's use of the historic present λέγει to introduce
many of Jesus' sayings plays an important role in the narrative strategies of his inclusive story, as we will see later.
Because of the pervasive effect which codes on the phraseological plane have in structuring and communicating point of
view in narrative, it will be well to examine further not only
the characteristic patterns and vocabulary of the Matthean
narrator's own speech, but also the interplay between the narrator and characters on the phraseological plane, as we explicate other dimensions of point of view in Matthew.

2. *The Spatio-Temporal Plane*

Like the phraseological plane, the spatial and temporal planes
of point of view also function primarily as a means of
structuring and communicating the psychological and
ideological dimensions of point of view in a narrative.[1]
Uspensky defines these planes as 'the verbally-established
spatial and temporal relations of the describing subject (the
author) to the described event'.[2] In Matthew the narrator
appears to hover spatially and temporally above all the scenes,
able to see the overall picture as well as to enter into individual
episodes as a kind of unseen observer. He is never spatially
confined to individual scenes or characters. He is
simultaneously present at Jesus' trial before the chief priests
and council (26.57) and at Peter's denial in the courtyard of
the high priest (26.69). In short, the narrator is omnipresent:
that is, he has the 'capacity to report from vantage-points not
accessible to characters, or to jump from one to another, or to
be in two places at once'.[3]

Despite the capacity to be omnipresent, the spatial relation
of the narrator to his story is closely aligned with Jesus. The
narrator follows Jesus in much the same way as a movie

six (adding ch. 23; Walker, *Heilsgeschichte*, p. 146, n. 112) or even
seven discourses (adding chapter 23 and 11; H.B. Green, 'The Structure of St. Matthew's Gospel', in *Studia Evangelica IV* (Texte und
Untersuchungen zur Geschichte der altchristlichen Literatur 102;
Berlin: 1968), p. 48) in the Gospel.

1 Lanser, *Narrative Act*, pp. 184ff.
2 Uspensky, *Poetics*, p. 57.
3 Chatman, *Story and Discourse*, p. 103.

camera, so that between Jesus' baptism and crucifixion, the times when the narrator does not accompany Jesus are exceptional.[1] Kingsbury has correctly pointed out that even prior to Jesus' baptism and subsequent to his death, Matthew follows minor characters primarily 'in the interest of conveying information to the reader about Jesus'.[2] The narrator's spatial stance towards Jesus during his story of Jesus' ministry (3.13-27.56; 28.9-10, 16-20) is what Uspensky has labelled 'suprapersonal' because it follows Jesus but also encompasses a view of him. In other words, the narrator 'accompanies the character but does not become embodied in him', so that 'he can portray the particular character; he could not do so if they shared one perceptual system'.[3] An almost complete alignment between the narrator and Jesus on the spatial dimension of point of view thus results from the narrator following Jesus. This alignment plays an important role in the rhetoric of Matthew's inclusive story, for it provides a way of focalizing on Jesus without giving up the authority or privileges associated with a third person, omniscient, public narrator.[4]

The temporal dimension of point of view encompasses two aspects of the narrator's relation to the story world: the temporal distance between the encoded moment of telling and the narrated events, and the pace of narration.[5] The temporal distance between the Matthean narrator and Jesus shows the same two-fold relationship as we found on the spatial plane of point of view. On the one hand, the narrator's temporal point of view is not limited to the temporal perspective of any single character. He is able to know both the past and the future in a way not open to characters in the narrative. He shares the

---

1 Matthew's accounts of the death of John the Baptist (14.3-12) and Peter's denial (26.58, 69-75) are the sole exceptions.

2 Kingsbury, *Matthew as Story*, p. 34.

3 Uspensky, *Poetics*, p. 58.

4 Literary critics have used the concept of a 'focalizer' or 'focalization' to refer to a 'point of view character' who provides a 'medium' through whom the narrator may record the events which are narrated. See Lanser, *Narrative Act*, pp. 141-42, 212-14, for a more detailed discussion of the types of focalization in narrative.

5 Lanser, *Narrative Act*, p. 198.

author's temporal viewpoint which means that 'he knows how the story will end'.[1] The narrator is thus able to identify Judas Iscariot as the apostle 'who betrayed him' (10.2) and so anticipate Jesus' death well in advance of its place in the plot of the story.[2] From this point of view, which is external to the ongoing narration, the narrator retrospectively tells his story of Jesus' life and casts events in past time.[3] The narrator is able to cite Old Testament prophecies to show how the events of Jesus' life fulfilled Jewish Messianic hopes, or to report Jesus' predictions of his passion, death, and resurrection in summary fashion (16.21). Since the Matthean narrator overtly stands outside of the story, a double sense of the present moment—what Seymour Chatman has labelled the 'narrative NOW'—is established in the Gospel.[4] There is the narrative NOW of the narrator who retrospectively tells the story, but there is also a story NOW when action begins to transpire.

Although most of the story takes place in the past of the narrator and implied reader, the narrative NOW and the story NOW seem to coincide at certain points. The temporal position of the narrator, and thus correspondingly that of the implied reader, becomes synchronized with that of Jesus when the narrator uses the historic present, records extended speeches of Jesus, or introduces direct discourse with the

1 Uspensky, *Poetics*, pp. 66ff.
2 See Edwards, *Matthew's Story*, pp. 33-34; Daniel Patte, *The Gospel According to Matthew: A Structural Commentary on Matthew's Faith* (Philadelphia: Fortress, 1987), p. 143. Although Jesus has faced opposition from the Jewish leaders in the infancy stories (ch. 2) and in the miracle stories of chapters 8-9, the Pharisees' antagonism and harmful intentions towards Jesus are not mentioned in a definite statement until 12.14. Jesus' own passion predictions do not begin in the story until 16.21.
3 Mt. 2.1 is an example of the way the narrator looks back on the life of Jesus and recounts events in past time: 'Now after Jesus had been born in Bethlehem of Judea in the days of Herod the King, behold, wise men from the East came to Jerusalem...'. See Kingsbury, *Matthew as Story*, p. 34.
4 Chatman, *Story and Discourse*, p. 63. Uspensky, *Poetics*, pp. 67ff., also discusses the double temporal perspective in which a narrative can be cast. Cf. C.P. Casparis, *Tense Without Time*, pp. 9-10.

present participle of λέγω.[1] The historic present functions in narrative to take the implied reader directly into the action of the story. The effect of this device is to eliminate the distance between narrator and the story's characters so that the implied reader occupies the same position as the characters, and experiences the action as they experience it.[2] One of the striking features in Matthew's use of the historic present is the predominance of its use in conjuction with locutionary verbs. Moreover, most of its occurrences are connected to Jesus' speech. Of the narrator's 80 uses of the historic present, λέγει is used 46 times (with Jesus as the subject 43 times), λέγουσιν 14 times (13 times when the subjects are speaking to Jesus), and φησίν once.[3] The upshot of Matthew's use of the historic present in conjunction with Jesus' speech is that the focus is placed on his words, and the implied reader is addressed by them together with characters in the story.[4]

1 See Anderson, *Gender and Reading*', pp. 24ff., Kingsbury, *Matthew as Story*, pp. 34ff., Combrink, 'Structure of Matthew', pp. 88ff., for discussions of the pragmatic or rhetorical effect of temporally aligning the narrator and Jesus.

2 See Uspensky, *Poetics*, p. 71, A.A. Mendilow, *Time and the Novel* (New York: Humanities Press, 1965), p. 98, and F. Blass, A Debrunner, and R. Funk, *A Greek Grammar of the New Testament and Other Early Christian Literature* (Chicago: University of Chicago Press, 1961), p. 321, for discussions of the function of the historic present.

3 These statistics are taken from Anderson, 'Gender and Rhetoric', p. 24, n. 58. She has revised the list of Matthew's historic presents compiled by J.C. Hawkins, *Horae Synopticae* (Oxford: Clarendon, 1899), pp. 118ff. Cf. also Wolfgang Schenk, 'Das Präsens Historicum als makrosyntaktisches Gliederungssignal in Matthäusevangelium', *NTS* 22 (1976), pp. 464-75, who bases his study on Hawkins' figures. The Matthean tendency to use the historic present in conjunction with Jesus' speech is highlighted by the fact that 11 of the 20 historic presents taken over from Mark are λέγει.

4 Cf. Schenk, 'Präsens Historicum', pp. 468, 73ff., who concludes that Matthew's use of the historic present has both a formal and material function. Formally historic presents mark the high point of a pericope, and materially they point to the christological promise of Christ's presence with the church. Schenk writes that the historic present 'ist die besondere matthäische Gestalt der Anwesenheit der christologischen Gegenwartsverheißung in den einzelnen

This temporal alignment of Jesus and narrator is evident in other rhetorical devices present in the Gospel. A.A. Mendilow has argued that discourse in narrative produces 'the illusion of immediacy and presentness in the reader'.[1] Jesus' teaching is arranged into five great discourses by the narrator in Matthew, and the length of these uninterrupted discourses enhances this effect. The narrator's use of the present participle λέγων to introduce both these extended discourses (5.2; 10.5; 13.3; 23.1-2) and shorter sections of dialogue (for example 1.20; 8.2; 9.30; 22.42) further contributes to the temporal synchronization of narrator, implied reader and Jesus. As Janice Anderson points out:

> The action denoted by the present participle, speech, occurs at the same time as the action denoted by the main verb. Thus the main verb freezes the moment of action and the participle indicates what was said at that moment as if it were being spoken in the present.[2]

The effect of the temporal alignment of narrator and Jesus in Matthew is that Jesus' teachings are addressed to the implied reader as well as to the designated audience in the Gospel. In this way this narrative strategy makes a significant contribution to one's experience of Matthew as an 'inclusive' story, because Jesus' teachings become the 'medium' for the implied author's ideological point of view.[3] The temporal position of the Matthean narrator and the implied reader is both posterior to the story which is narrated and yet contemporaneous in the recounting of Jesus' teaching, thus giving the impression of an 'inclusive' story.

The other aspect of point of view on the temporal plane, the pacing of narrative, also supports our conclusions about the importance of Jesus' teaching in the rhetoric of Matthew's inclusive story. Temporal pacing of narration determines whether happenings become presented in the narrative as summary or scene. Literary theorists have shown that what

Perikopen, deren Höhepunkt sie markieren' (p. 474).

1 Mendilow, *Time and the Novel*, p. 112.

2 Anderson, *Gender and Reading*, p. 25.

3 *Ibid.* Anderson writes: 'Through the medium of Jesus the implied author presents his or her ideology in the moment of reading'.

is presented as summary tends to remain in the background while what is scenically represented becomes foregrounded. Temporal pacing in narrative can thus serve as an indicator of what the narrator/implied author considers to be important.[1] A reader only needs to note the extensive discourses of Jesus' teaching in Matthew—in which the reading time closely approximates the duration of the act of speaking in the story—or to recognize the narrator's tendency to highlight dialogue in the miracle stories,[2] to appreciate the way the evangelist has foregrounded the sayings of Jesus in his Gospel.

3. *The Psychological Plane*

The relation of the narrator to the story on the psychological plane is an extremely complex aspect of point of view. As Susan Lanser points out, this aspect encompasses the broad question of 'the narrator's distance or affinity to each character and event (indeed, perhaps to almost everything) represented in the text'.[3] A crucial issue in this respect, although certainly not the only factor in determining point of view on the psychological plane, is whether or not a narrator can provide an inside view of characters.[4] In Matthew, the narrator is able to penetrate the consciousness of characters and tell what no external observer could possibly know. He can describe the thoughts, emotions, and motives of characters. Thus, Joseph is described as a just man, and the reader is given insight into the working of Joseph's mind as he ponders whether or not to divorce Mary (1.17). The narrator knows that Jesus often acted out of compassion or pity (9.36; 14.14; 20.34) and that Pilate knew the envy of the chief priests and elders and their motivation for Jesus' arrest (27.18).

The narrator in the Gospel, however, does not provide just an internal point of view of the characters on the

---

1 See Lanser, *Narrative Act*, pp. 200ff.
2 Cf. Held, *TIM*, pp. 233ff.
3 Lanser, *Narrative Act*, p. 202.
4 See Uspensky, *Poetics*, p. 83. Kingsbury, *Matthew as Story*, p. 35, and Culpepper, *Anatomy*, pp. 21ff., unduly restrict their discussion of the Gospel narrator's psychological point of view to questions of access to characters' consciousness.

psychological level. The Matthean narrator is an example of a narrator who can simultaneously assume both internal and external points of view.[1] He tells what characters think and feel but he does it as a third-person observer. This dual position of the narrator is most obvious in places where the narrator is able to describe the content of private conversations (8.3; 16.7) or people's mental and emotional condition when they are completely alone, such as Jesus' feelings of sorrow and trouble in the Garden of Gethsemane (26.38).

The implied reader's detachment from or involvement with the persons and events in the story world is also determined by the quantity and quality of information shared by the narrator. 'Subjective' information which reveals a character as perceiver (temperament, personality, beliefs, etc.) creates greater affinity than 'objective' information which merely conveys a description of the person.[2] By these criteria we are again able to see how the Gospel focuses on Jesus. Quantitatively, the narrator provides more information about Jesus than any other character or character group in the Gospel, as our investigation of the spatial and temporal dimensions of point of view has revealed. Qualitatively, the narrator portrays Jesus as a conscious human subject; he has compassion on people (9.36; 14.14; 20.34), can be troubled (26.38), and is aware of private conversations, thoughts, and motives of characters (9.3, 21; 12.15; 16.7-8; 22.18; 26.10) to cite a few examples.

The questions of psychological affinity between narrator and character and the narrator's ability to shape the implied reader's attitude cannot be answered on formal grounds alone, however, as if the story were told in a context devoid of values. Psychological affinity is ultimately dependent upon the narrator's judgment of any character.[3] No narrator/implied

---

1 Uspensky, *Poetics*, pp. 95ff. See Petersen, 'Point of View', p. 116, who describes the Markan narrator in similar terms as one who is 'in one and the same scene both external and internal to his actors; he is both objective and subjective . . .'.

2 Lanser, *Narrative Act*, pp. 205ff.

3 Lanser (*ibid.*, pp. 214-15) summarizes this fact in the following way: 'In the end, psychological affinity between any two textual figures (characters and narrator, narrator and narratee, character and narratee) is to a considerable extent a function of the relationship

author is absolutely impartial or objective in the telling of a story, but will draw the implied reader's interest, sympathy, and affection toward certain characters, claims, and interpretations, and away from others.[1] One of the reasons a narrator/implied author provides an inside view of characters is to shape the implied reader's response and attitude to them. In Matthew the implied reader is never led to disapprove of Jesus, while other characters are viewed with both approval and disapproval. The narrator's approval of Jesus is expressed in a number of ways. Jesus is identified as 'God with us' early in the narrative (1.23), and through the Old Testament fulfillment quotations he is portrayed as the fulfillment of God's redemptive purposes. By his actions and teaching Jesus also fulfills and expounds God's will in the unfolding story (cf. 3.15; 4.1-11; 5.17ff.; 26.39, 42). God himself voices approval of Jesus at the baptism and transfiguration of Jesus (3.17; 17.5).[2] Finally, those who oppose Jesus are pictured in a negative manner. The Jewish leaders, for example, are described as acting without integrity. They seek 'false' testimony against Jesus (26.59), act out of 'envy' (27.18), and lie about the events of the resurrection (28.11-15).

The question of the narrator's approval or disapproval of events and characters in the story brings us to the ideological plane of point of view. According to Uspensky, this is not only the most basic of the different levels of point of view, but also the most complex and difficult to retrieve. This level raises the problem of how the narrator/implied author 'evaluates and perceives ideologically' (i.e. conceptually) the world which the

between the persona (including the persona's behavior) and the norms of a given culture, individual, or group'. If the Matthean narrator had been sympathetic to the ideological point of view of the Jewish leaders for example, their rejection of Jesus would not have been judged so harshly in the Gospel. It is possible to conceive of the events in Matthew being narrated in such a manner that the actions of the Jewish leaders in crucifying Jesus would be presented as a justified and proper response to the claims of Jesus' ministry.

1 Booth, *Rhetoric of Fiction*, pp. 78ff.
2 See Kingsbury, 'Jesus in Matthew's Story', pp. 5ff., for a discussion of the rhetorical importance of this direct discourse by God.

narrative describes.[1] R. Alan Culpepper considers the reliability of the narrator to be an essential aspect of the ideological point of view in John.[2] The characteristic of reliability, however, tells us nothing about the evaluative norms of a work themselves. Rather, it merely describes the relationship between a narrator and those norms. Wayne Booth, who coined the term 'reliable narrator', defines such a narrator as one 'who speaks for or acts in accordance with the norms of the work (which is to say the implied author's norms)'.[3] The Matthean narrator is a reliable proponent of the evaluative norms of the Gospel. Such reliability results from the close alignment, almost identification, between implied author and narrator in Matthew. The narrator in effect serves as the voice of the implied author.

An 'honest and honorable relationship between narrator and reader' is also established because the narrator shares unreservedly with the reader the privilege of his omniscience.[4] From the beginning of the Gospel the reader is told who Jesus is and the significance of his life and mission (1.18ff.).[5] This open communication continues throughout the

---

1 Uspensky, *Poetics of Composition*, p. 8. Cf. Lanser, *Narrative Act*, pp. 215-22.

2 Culpepper, *Anatomy*, pp. 32ff.

3 Booth, *Rhetoric of Fiction*, p. 158. Biblical scholars who have used literary criticism are quick to point out that reliability as a literary category is completely separate from questions about the historical accuracy of the narrative or the truth of the ideological point of view. As Culpepper, *Anatomy*, p. 32 has stated, '"Reliability" is a matter of literary analysis, historical accuracy is the territory of the historian, and "truth" is a matter for believers and theologians'. Cf. Petersen, 'Point of View', pp. 113ff.

4 Sternberg, *Expositional Modes*, p. 270.

5 Menakhem Perry, 'Literary Dynamics', p. 53, has argued that at the beginning of a text there are no expectations of the reader other than cultural ones. Sternberg, *Expositional Modes*, p. 94 discusses this phenomenon under the rubric of the 'primacy-recency' effect. He writes: 'Due to the successive order of presentation, the first block (of information) was read with an open mind, while the interpretation of the second ... was decisively conditioned and colored by the anterior, homogeneous primacy effect'. This means that that information at the beginning of Matthew has a formative influence

Gospel as the implied reader receives information (the Old Testament fulfillment quotations for example) and becomes privy to scenes with Jesus which characters in the story would not have known (4.1-11 for example). The implied reader thus has an overwhelming advantage over other characters in the story, and never faces the problem of misunderstanding who Jesus is in the same sense that they do. The reliability of the narrator as someone who can be trusted to guide the implied reader to the meaning of Jesus' life and death is further enhanced by his ability to explain the meaning of words such as Jesus' name (1.23), Golgotha (27.33), or Jesus' Aramaic cry from the cross (27.46). While the Matthean narrator's reliability does not therefore tell us anything about the content of the narrative's ideological point of view, it does mean that the narrator's own speech will help us explicate the system of values which is operative in the Gospel.

C. *Commentary and Ideological Point of View*

Direct commentary is one of the most visible ways a narra-tor/implied author's ideological point of view can be expressed since it is in direct commentary that the narrator explicitly addresses the implied reader. Literary theorists have argued that commentary is a 'function of the social role of literature' by the way it 'contextualizes' a narrative text.[1] When a narrative or some element in it is somehow 'strange' because it does not conform to known or agreed societal codes and norms, commentary can be used by an author either to reduce or to reinforce the 'significance of the strangeness' by supplying the reader with information which places either the narrative or the nonconforming element in its proper context.[2]

on how the rest of the Gospel is read.—for example, cf. 1.23ff., where the reader is told that Jesus' name means 'God with us', and that he has come to save his people. See Burnett, 'Prolegomenon', pp. 95ff.

1 Ross Chambers, 'Commentary in Literary Texts', *Critical Inquiry* 5 (1978), pp. 327-28.

2 *Ibid*. Chambers distinguishes between 'meaning' which can be understood 'as the object of semantic analysis' and 'meaningfulness' which is 'the meaning *bestowed on* a set of rela-

The presence of commentary thus presupposes the existence of an agreed system of general cultural codes or values held by people outside the text. Such an agreed system may cohere with the value system of the text, in which case commentary seeks to reinforce and confirm codes and values already shared, or it may conflict with it, in which case the commentary seeks to bring about an agreement by moulding the beliefs and values of the readers.[1] In either case, commentary provides an interpreter with important clues about how the implied authors/narrators conceptually view the world, because it enables one to see directly what system of values and cultural norms they espouse.

Seymour Chatman has identified three different kinds of explicit commentary used in literary texts: interpretation, judgment, and generalization.[2] All three types of commentary are present in Matthew. 'Interpretation' can be seen as the broadest category, and in some ways it encompasses all three types. If 'interpretation' is conceived of as explanation then 'judgment' would categorize explanations that are moral evaluations, and 'generalization' would denote an explanation that compares the narrative or elements in it with the real world. More specifically, however, Chatman reserves the category of 'interpretation' for commentary which 'is the open explanation of the gist, relevance, or significance of a story element'.[3] In Matthew interpretation can be seen in the translation or explanation of the meaning of such words as Jesus' name (1.23), Golgotha (27.33), or Jesus' Aramaic cry from the cross (27.46). This type of commentary has the effect of both creating and bridging a gap between the implied reader and narrative, because it assumes that the implied

tionships by an act of interpretation'. Commentary is used by an author when it is felt necessary to make 'meaningful' what is not 'naturally so'. Cf. Chatman, *Story and Discourse*, p. 245.
1 Chambers, 'Commentary', p. 328. Cf. Booth, *Rhetoric of Fiction*, p. 177, who emphasizes the way commentary is used to shape the moral norms of the narrative, and Chatman, *Stories and Discourse*, p. 149, who believes that the norms are not necessarily moral but can be general cultural codes.
2 Chatman, *Story and Discourse*, p. 228.
3 *Ibid.*

reader is not competent in the cultural and linguistic codes used. It also heightens the reader's dependence on the narrator as one who can bridge the gap between narrative and reader.[1] Direct addresses to the implied reader to pay attention to specific warnings and signs—as in the eschatological discourse (24.15)—can also be categorized as interpretation.[2] The category of 'judgment' contains commentary which 'expresses moral or value opinions'.[3] Examples of judgment in Matthew are to be found in the evaluation that Joseph was a just man (1.19), that Jesus taught with authority (7.29), or that the Jewish leaders acted out of envy when they arrested Jesus and turned him over to Pilate (27.18). The final category of 'generalization' involves commentary which 'makes reference outward from the fictional to the real world, either to 'universal truths' or to actual historical facts'.[4] This category of commentary is primarily represented in Matthew by the Old Testament formula quotations. Since we are trying to ascertain the ideological point of view which governs the Matthean narrative, we will concentrate on the latter two types of commentary, because they are most transparent to the values and norms used to guide and order the narrative.

1. *Judgment Commentary*

Judgment-type commentary may perhaps be most directly pertinent for our concerns, since it is explanation that is made on the basis of moral evaluation. At times this commentary is supplied as a description of characters' attitudes or feelings which could have been deduced on the basis of their actions. Herod's rage because the wise men did not report back to him (2.16), for example, could have easily been inferred by the reader on the basis of the resultant slaughter of the infants in

1 See Petersen, 'Point of View', p. 110.
2 Sayings such as these show what Chambers has labelled the 'involving function' wherein commentary serves to involve the reader. See 'Commentary', p. 329. Contra Petersen, 'Point of View', p. 110. The saying in the eschatological discourse (24.15) points out the significance of a story element.
3 Chatman, *Story and discourse*, p. 228.
4 *Ibid.*

Bethlehem! Because of its nature, however, this type of commentary usually takes the form of inside views of characters which evaluate their motives and feelings from some system of values. In Matthew the evaluation primarily takes place on the basis of a character's acceptance or rejection of Jesus—the one who reveals God's will. According to this evaluative standard, the Jewish leaders in particular fail since they lead the opposition to Jesus. Consequently, much of the judgment commentary in the Gospel is focused on the scribes and Pharisees. Negative judgment is expressed when the scribes' teaching is described as lacking authority (7.29), or when the imagery of helpless sheep without a shepherd is used to describe the crowds who follow Jesus (9.36). Both statements reflect an evaluation by the narrator that the Jewish leaders are neglecting or even misusing their responsibility to provide religious guidance for the Jewish nation. The statements of judgment against the Jewish leaders become more frequent as the Gospel moves toward its climax in the rejection and crucifixion of Jesus. Their rejection of Jesus is reflected in the narrator's descriptions of their indignation over Jesus' success (21.15) and their malice in trying to ensnare Jesus with trick questions (22.18). Once the Jewish leaders have succeeded in arresting Jesus, the narrator gives his opinion of the preceedings when he states that the leaders sought *false* testimony against Jesus (26.59), and that Pilate knew the Jewish leaders acted out of *envy* (27.18). Neither of these statements represents an objective and neutral reporting of events. Rather, both relect an evaluative bias against those who have rejected Jesus.[1]

Others besides the Jewish leaders are also judged because

---

1 Uspensky, *Poetics of Composition*, p. 14, argues that a specific means by which an author can express ideological point of view is to use a 'fixed epithet' which does not belong either to the speech characteristics of the speaker or depend upon its particular context, but rather 'manifests the evaluative position of the author'. While these statements by the narrator in the passion narratives are not composed of 'fixed epithets', they definitely reflect the evangelist's ideological point of view—the Jewish leaders would not have characterized the motivation for their actions as 'envy', nor would they have admitted to seeking 'false testimony' against Jesus!

they have rejected Jesus. The narrator makes it plain in an interpretive comment that unbelief is the reason Jesus chose not to perform miracles in his home town (13.58). In 19.22 the narrator describes the rich young ruler as 'sorrowful' when he is unable to respond positively to the call to follow Jesus. The disciples themselves are described as being indignant about something Jesus has taught or done in at least two places (20.24; 26.8). In both cases the resultant rebuke and clarification from Jesus shows that the disciples have misunderstood and not fully accepted Jesus' message and mission. The ambiguity of the narrator's evaluative judgment of the disciples, while not as strong as in Mark, is even present in the post-resurrection meeting with Jesus. The disciples are with Jesus, but the narrator describes some as still doubting (28.16). Thus whether it be the total rejection and unbelief of the town people, or the partial rejection represented by the disciples' misunderstanding, the narrator explains and interprets the actions of characters according to the standard of response to Jesus.

The narrator's evaluative judgments in the Gospel are not all negative, however: some characters respond positively and accept Jesus. The narrator characterizes Joseph as a just man (1.19), and this characterization is proven accurate by Joseph's acceptance of God's message through the angel. In other places the crowds or the disciples are portrayed as being in awe of Jesus and responding by worshipping him and glorifying God (9.8, 14.33; 17.6). The women in the Gospel do not desert Jesus as his twelve disciples did, but are at the cross and the tomb (27.55-56, 61; 28.7ff.). Their response to an encounter with the risen Jesus is to worship him (28.9). Generally, however, the narrator does not provide the implied reader with as much judgment-type commentary of a positive sort, wherein the character measures up to the standard of accepting Jesus and his message. Positive responses are for the most part plotted either in dialogue between Jesus and other characters or in the narration of events, rather than being cast in direct evaluative statements by the narrator. The role of Jesus as a spokesman for the implied author/narrator's evaluative point of view will be examined later in this chapter.

The narrative's ideological point of view, expressed in the fact that characters and events are evaluated on the basis of whether they accept or reject Jesus and his message of the Kingdom, dovetails with the plot theme of rejection and acceptance which was uncovered in the previous chapter. This correlation should not be surprising since Norman Petersen has argued that the plotting of actions by an author is a means of expressing point of view:

> in the plotting of incidents we can detect the formal manner in which the narrator successively discloses information to his reader, and sequentially relates items of information to one another, creating thereby a world of values as well as of events.[1]

Incidents are narrated in Matthew whereby characters are challenged and summoned to accept Jesus and his message. Jesus often meets with rejection rather than acceptance, however, and the story moves through progressive acts of rejection by the very people Jesus came to save, right up to the climax of his crucifixion. The total rejection of the Jewish nations and its leaders (27.20ff.) is contrasted with the acceptance—albeit at times imperfect and misconceived—of the disciples. The other plot theme discussed in the last chapter, promise and fulfillment, is related to the narrator's use of the Old Testament fulfillment quotations. These may be understood as generalizations, the third type of commentary found in Matthew.

2. *Generalization Commentary*

Generalization has already been defined as commentary which 'makes reference outward from the fictional to the real world, either to "universal truths" or actual historical facts'. A primary function of both factual and rhetorical generalization is to fulfill the need for verisimilitude.[2] By appealing either to some type of universal truth such as proverbial sayings, or to

1 Petersen, 'Point of View', p. 108. Petersen is of the opinion that with respect to Mark, it is 'only in the plotting of the episodes and the motivations imputed to the actions of characters that the full extent of Mark's ideological point of view can be seen'.
2 Chatman, *Story and Discourse*, pp. 228, 244.

historical facts known and recognized by one's readers, an author makes the narrative plausible. In Matthew both types of generalization are used. Factual generalization is used, for example, in 10.2ff. where the names of the twelve apostles are listed, and in 28.15ff. where the narrator reports that the story about Jesus' disciples stealing his body from the tomb is still circulated among the Jews. In the former case, the fact that historical persons are cited gives the mission specifically, and the Gospel generally, more credibility. The latter commentary presupposes and derives its forcefulness from the fact that the reader of the Gospel actually knows that this story is circulated. Its use not only supports the plausibility of Mathew's account of the events surrounding the crucifixion and resurrection of Jesus, but it also underlines the deceit of the Jewish leaders. It thus lends support to the evangelist's ideological point of view that judges the events narrated according to the standard of whether characters accept or reject Jesus, and reinforces the portrait of the Jewish leaders: they have rejected Jesus not only in life, but also now in his death!

The major use of generalization in Matthew, however, is found in the so-called fulfillment or formula quotations. While commentators have long considered these Old Testament quotations to be 'asides' from the evangelist which are not part of the story, the emphasis in Matthean studies has been placed on questions concerning the form and origin of the quotations rather than their rhetorical function in the narrative.[1] The fulfillment quotations have an important rhetorical function,

1 See Donald Senior, *What are They Saying about Matthew*? (New York: Paulist Press, 1983), pp. 37-46; Stanton, 'Origin and Purpose', pp. 1930-34; Frans Van Segbroech, 'Les citations d'accomplissement dans l'Évangile selon Matthieu d'après trois ouvrages récents', in *Matthieu*, ed. Didier, pp. 107-30, for surveys of recent scholarship. When the questions of the purpose or theology of the quotations has been raised, the debate has centered around whether the evangelist intended them in a polemical or apologetic sense to counter Jewish arguments against Jesus. Two scholars who have discussed the rhetorical function of the quotations are Hartman, 'Scriptural Exegesis', pp. 131-52, and Kingsbury, *Matthew as Story*, p. 33; cf. *idem*, 'Jesus in Matthew's Story', pp. 5ff.

however, in establishing the reliability and authority both of the narrator and of Jesus. Although the Old Testament quotations are concentrated in the opening chapters of the Gospel, they still highlight almost every aspect of Jesus and his mission: his birth (1.23; 2.6, 15, 28, 23), his entry into Galilee (4.15-16), his healings (8.17), his compassion and gentleness (12.18-21), his teaching in parables and the hardening of Israel (13.35), his entry into Jerusalem (21.5), and his passion and death (26.56; 27.9-10). The Old Testament and its authority as the word of God (1.22; 2.15) exist independently of the narrative world of the Gospel. When Matthew appeals to prophecies which lie outside of his Gospel's narrative world (prophecies whose authority is accepted by the implied reader), and when he shows how the events in Jesus' life which he is narrating fulfilled the Old Testament Messianic hopes, he thereby gives his narrative plausibility and reinforces the truthfulness of his claims about who Jesus is. Since the Old Testament formula quotations are cited by the narrator, his trustworthiness is also established for the implied reader.[1]

Jack Kingsbury has argued—on the basis of the evangelist's use of the formula quotations in particular, of other Old Testament references and allusions in general, and of Jesus' emphasis on doing the will of God—that God's point of view is normative in Matthew as the Gospel's ideological point of view.[2] Kingsbury is surely correct from a theological perspective to assert that God's evaluative point of view governs the narrative and controls the flow of history. Nonetheless, to say

---

1 Luz, *Matthäus*, pp. 140-41, suggests that Matthew's programmatic emphasis on Jesus' fulfillment of the law and the prophets is necessary for the evangelist because of the separation of his church from Israel. In this situation the demands of the whole Old Testament must be placed before the community in a way which was not necessary when the church was still within Judaism. If Luz's reconstruction of the community situation is accurate—and it is at least plausible—Matthew's church members would still need to consider the Old Testament as authoritative. Otherwise, the fulfillment quotations would not accomplish the rhetorical function for which we have argued.

2 Kingsbury, *Matthew as Story*, p. 33; *idem*, 'Figure of Jesus', pp. 5-7, 'A Rejoinder to David Hill', pp. 63-65.

simply that God's point of view governs the narrative fails both to explicate the content of that ideological point of view and to show how it structures the narrative world described in the Gospel. What the Old Testament quotations tell us is that the evangelist considered the events of Jesus' life to be the fulfillment of Old Testament Messianic expectations. In this capacity the formula quotations do not provide the implied reader with a system of values which govern the narrative. Rather, they serve as part of the text's strategy of meaningfulness by designating the supposed world which the narrative takes as its point of reference; the history of Israel as God's chosen people.[1] Jesus is a crucial part of this history and of the fulfillment of God's promises to his people.

The emphasis in the Old Testament fulfillment quotations is thus placed squarely on Jesus.[2] They function rhetorically to tell the implied reader the correct way to read the narrative, but not by establishing the normativeness of God's point of view. Instead, they bestow upon Jesus 'the badge of reliability'[3] as well as confirming the trustworthiness of the narrator. In the superscription and the genealogy, which are other examples of commentary, and in the frequent Old Testament quotations in the birth and infancy stories, the stage is set for reading the rest of the story by establishing the implied reader's initial understanding of Jesus' identity as the Son of God and promised Messiah.[4] As Son of God and as the central and consistently reliable character in the Gospel, Jesus' judgments are virtually identical to those of the implied

---

1 See Chambers, 'Commentary', pp. 334ff., for a discussion of this use of commentary in literary texts. Brown, *Birth*, p. 69, sees a similar function for the genealogy; Matthew uses the genealogy 'to stress Jesus' insertion into a history and a people'.

2 Luz, *Matthäus*, pp. 140ff., thus correctly argues that christology is the central subject matter of the OT quotations.

3 Booth, *Rhetoric of Fiction*, p. 18.

4 Luz, *Matthäus*, p. 139 argues that one of the reasons governing the evangelist's use of the fulfillment quotations is that he places them where he is not forced to alter his sources too drastically. Yet the concentration of quotations in the opening chapters also serves the rhetorical function of introducing Jesus and establishing his authority and trustworthiness for the implied reader.

author/narrator. Kingsbury is therefore correct when he argues that the Old Testament quotations contribute to Jesus' authority and help establish his teaching as the correct interpretation of the law and expression of God's will (cf. 5.17ff.).[1] In Matthew it is only through Jesus' way of looking at things that the implied reader is made aware of God's perspective (cf. 11.27).

By focusing on Jesus as the reliable interpreter of God's will, the Old Testament fulfillment quotations underline the gravity of the choice whether to accept or reject Jesus and his teaching. The theme of rejection is in fact the focus of some of the Old Testament citations themselves. The quotations in 13.14ff., 15.7ff. and 21.42ff. speak of rejection and obduracy on Israel's part, for example. It may also be significant that all four explicit citations of Isaiah are found grouped within chapters 4 to 13, if Hartman is correct that a quotation may be used because of the bundle of ideas it evokes.[2] Isaiah was the premier messenger of salvation to Israel even though the prophet underlined the failure of the nation to respond to his preaching. This prophet is therefore particularly well-suited for the evangelist to use in these chapters which present Jesus' mission to Israel and Israel's rejection of Jesus.[3] Finally, there is a clear convergence between Jesus and the narrator in the passion when Jesus says as his arrest that 'all of this has taken place so that the scriptures of the prophets might be fulfilled'

1   See Kingsbury, 'Jesus in Matthew's Story', p. 6, who describes Matthew as 'cloaking the life of Jesus and many of his words in the aura of Old Testament Scripture'. The debate between Kingsbury and David Hill on whether it is God's or Jesus' ideological point of view that is normative in Matthew thus appears inconsequential in one sense, because both men agree that Jesus reliably espouses God's point of view. Jesus is concerned that he does the will of his Father (3.14-15; 4.1-11; 26.39, 42) and he teaches his disciples to share the same concern (6.10; 7.21; 12.46ff.; 21.31). See *JSNT* 21 (1984), pp. 3-52, for Kingsbury's original essay and Hill's response. Kingsbury's rebuttal to Hill is found in 'Rejoinder', pp. 61-81.

2   Hartman, 'Scriptural Exegesis', p. 134.

3   Van Segbroeck, 'Les citations', p. 126. The thematic relations between the fulfillment quotations and Matthew's story speak against Strecker's view that the quotations are later 'pedantic additions' to the Gospel (*Weg*, p. 85).

(26.56; cf. 26.54), and this serves to highlight the motif of rejection in the Gospel.[1] Only here in the entire narrative does Jesus express on the phraseological plane with the same words what the narrator has been stating throughout the Gospel in the fulfillment quotations: the events in Jesus' life fulfill the Old Testament scriptures. The criterion of whether Jesus and his message are accepted or rejected is at the center of the author's overall ideological point of view in the Gospel, and it is by this standard that all characters and events in the story are judged.

The importance of the question of acceptance and rejection in Matthew's ideological point of view shows itself in the way that the fulfillment of other Old Testament predictions is predicated upon obedience to God's commands by characters in the narrative. Joseph thus marries Mary even though she is pregnant, names her son Jesus (1.20f.), flees to Egypt to escape Herod (2.13f.), and returns to Nazareth after Herod's death (2.19f.). In every case, events in Jesus' life would not have fulfilled the promises of the Old Testament if Joseph had not accepted the instructions of the angel.

In conclusion, the categories of promise and fulfillment derived from Matthew's use of the Old Testament formula quotations serve as generalizing commentary, commentary which gives the narrative verisimilitude and supports the ideological point of view of the narrator, to whom the issue of Jesus' acceptance and rejection is crucial. This support is achieved by appealing to beliefs and expectations which lie outside the narrative and by showing how they are fulfilled in the narrative. On one hand, some of the promises are fulfilled only through the acceptance and obedience of characters in the story, and on the other hand, the cloaking of Jesus with the aura of the Old Testament in general increases his sense of authority and reliability as the interpreter of God's will. If Jesus is a reliable spokesman for the ideological point of view of the narrator in Matthew, his responses to characters in the story become a means for the implied author/narrator to guide and control the implied reader. We must therefore

1 See Senior, *Passion of Jesus*, p. 88ff., who writes that 'the moment of the arrest condenses the entire passion of Jesus'.

examine the relationship between Jesus and the narrator.

D. *The Narrator, Jesus and Ideological Point of View*

Boris Uspensky writes that the simplest case with regard to point of view on the ideological plane is when the implied author carries out ideological evaluation from a 'single, dominating point of view' which subordinates all others to it.[1] We have argued that Matthew is an example of this type of narration and that the dominant ideological point of view is found in his conviction that Jesus is the Son of God whose mission and message are to be accepted and obeyed. All other points of view expressed by characters in the Gospel are evaluated according to whether or not Jesus is accepted or rejected. This ideological point of view, however, is not expressed solely by the narrator. Jesus is also a reliable spokesman for the system of values which structures the narrative world of Matthew. Jesus and the narrator thus function as reinforcing vehicles for the implied author's norms in Matthew by their alignment on the ideological plane.[2] The evangelist accomplishes this alignment through a number of different ways, some of which involve partial alignments between the narrator's and Jesus' points of view on the other planes which we have examined.

First, Jesus is simply the central character in the Gospel, and the plot of the whole Gospel is oriented toward him. As a result, all characters and all action in the narrative are viewed in relation to Jesus. On the spatial plane the narrator's point of view moves with Jesus. The reader is present with Jesus in scenes where Jesus is alone without other human contact (cf. 4.1-11; 14.23; 26.39ff.). When other characters are involved, incidents are plotted around Jesus: he teaches, he

---

1 Uspensky, *Poetics of Composition*, p. 8. Cf. Lotman, 'Point of View', pp. 341ff., who writes that the different and conflicting evaluative points of view which may be expressed in a narrative can be reduced to either 'true' or 'false' evaluations.

2 Matthew is not unique in this sense. David Hill, 'Response to Prof. Kingsbury', p. 38, raises the question as to whether 'this transparency to Jesus' point of view' by the narrator 'is not a feature common to at least all three canonical versions of the Jesus-story'.

heals and performs other miracles, people approach him with questions or problems, he is challenged and rejected by the religious leaders and people he came to save. On the temporal plane, the narrator's point of view is synchronized with Jesus in places, particularly with respect to Jesus' speech. In short, nothing happens in the Gospel where the focus is not somehow directed toward Jesus.

Second, and concomitant with the general orientation toward Jesus, the narrator provides a more extensive internal point of view of Jesus on the psychological plane. Booth has observed that 'narrators who provide inside views differ in the depth and axis of their plunge'.[1] While the Matthean narrator in general shows no interest in providing psychological analysis of characters' thoughts, feelings and motives (for example, no reason is given for Judas' betrayal), internal views of Jesus' mind are both numerous and given in more depth than those of other characters in the story. The implied reader is told that Jesus marvelled at a Gentile's faith (8.10), that he acted out of compassion and pity (9.36; 14.14; 20.34), that he did not perform miracles because of unbelief (13.58), and that he was troubled and sorrowful at Gethsemane (26.37). A few inside views of other individual characters are given. For example, after Peter's denial the reader is told that he remembered Jesus' prediction (26.75). But the inside views that are provided of groups such as the crowds, the disciples, and the Jewish leaders—amazement (7.28; 8.27; 9.33; 19.25; 21.20), fear (9.8; 14.26; 21.46), indignation (20.24; 21.15)—would often have been obvious to an external observer through the characters' actions and speech.

More importantly, however, the inside views of other characters which are offered are frequently communicated through Jesus' consciousness. Like the narrator, Jesus is aware of private conversations (9.3; 12.15; 16.7-8; 26.10) and thoughts (9.21; 22.18) of other characters. Jesus' omniscience is also visible in his ability to predict future events accurately. In the last chapter we saw that prediction and fulfillment is one of the devices used to plot the story in Matthew. Events

---

1 Booth, *Rhetoric of Fiction*, p. 163, and *idem*, 'Distance and Point of View', p. 77.

that are both predicted and fulfilled within the temporal boundaries of Jesus' life are frequently predicted by Jesus. He thus predicts his arrest, crucifixion and resurrection (17.22ff.; 20.17ff.; 26.2), his betrayal by Judas (26.21ff.), Peter's denial and the flight of the disciples (26.31ff.). Other events which are not fulfilled within the temporal limits of Jesus' life but which would have occurred by the time of the implied reader, such as the destruction of Jerusalem and the Temple (22.2ff.; 24.2) or the gift of the Kingdom being taken from Israel as a result of its rejection of Jesus (21.43), also contribute to the reader's confidence in Jesus' reliability. The way Jesus shares the narrator's ability to read the minds of other characters is therefore the rhetorical technique which is perhaps most effective in merging the narrator's and Jesus' point of view on the psychological plane.

Third, there is also a convergence between the narrator and Jesus on the phraseological plane. This convergence is visible when the Matthean narrator serves as an authoritative interpreter of Jesus' words. In a number of places the narrator explicitly interprets Jesus' words lest the implied reader miss the point or meaning of the saying (cf. 16.12; 17.13; 21.45). It is also visible in a number of words, phrases and concepts used by the narrator that are also present in Jesus' speech. For example, the narrator describes Joseph as a just (δίκαιος) man (1.19), while δίκαιος is used frequently by Jesus (5.45; 9.13; 10.41; 13.17, 43, 49; 23.35; 25.37, 46) and δικαιοσύνη appears as an important term in Jesus' teaching that characterizes his own actions (3.15), those of his disciples (5.6, 10, 20, 6.33), and those of John the Baptist (21.32). Parallels exist between the narrator's summary descriptions of Jesus' and the disciples' missions (4.23ff.: 9.35; 10.1), and Jesus' instructions at the sending out of the disciples (10.7-8). Similarities can also be seen between Jesus' and the narrator's attitude toward the Jewish leaders and institutions. Both use the phrase 'their (your) synagogues' (4.23; 9.35; 10.17; 12.9; 13.54; 23.34). The scribes are described by the narrator as teachers without authority (7.29; cf. 9.36) who are full of malice (πονηρίαν) (22.18). Jesus likewise questions the teaching of the scribes and Pharisees (15.2ff; ch. 23), and castigates them for being evil (πονηρός) (9.7; 12.34).[1] Finally, Jesus and the narrator agree that Jesus' life and death should be seen as the fulfillment of Old Testament prophecies (compare the Old Testament formula quotations with 26.54, 56). Moreover, the narrator and Jesus are the primary voices in the narrative who cite the Old Testament. It should be stressed that the convergence in phraseology between Jesus and the Matthean narrator is merely a literary impression. The point of view of both is ultimately controlled by the author.[2] The effect of this convergence between narrator and Jesus in Matthew, however, is that both can be trusted as reliable guides to the events which are narrated. They express the same system of values as the implied author.

Perhaps one of the more instructive examples of the evangelist's craft in merging the ideological point of view of the narrator with that of Jesus is to be found in the parable discourse of chapter 13. This chapter is presented as one of Jesus' great teaching discourses through the use of an introduction and the evangelist's characteristic concluding formula (13.1-3a, 53).[3] Yet, the implied reader does not find continuous direct speech from Jesus in this third major discourse, as might have been expected after the first two teaching discourses (5.3-7.27; 10.5b-42). Rather, chapter 13 contains a curious mixture of speakers and listeners. There are a number of different voices and types of speech—parables and interpretive commentary by Jesus, the citation of Old Testament Scripture, commentary by the narrator—as well as a rapid movement in the audience between crowds and disciples (vv. 10, 24, 36). As the discursive partner of the narrator, the implied reader is allowed to witness this movement and listen to these different

---

1 See J.D. Kingsbury, 'The Developing Conflict between Jesus and the Jewish Leaders in Matthew's Gospel: A Literary-Critical Study', *CBGQ* 49 (1987), pp. 60-64, who argues that 'evil' is the root character trait of the Jewish leaders in Matthew.

2 See Culpepper, *Anatomy*, pp. 42ff., and Petersen, 'Point of View', p. 109. Cf. Walhout, 'Text and Actions', pp. 63ff., and Wolterstorff, *Art in Action*, pp. 139-42, for discussions of the way in which an author is 'present' in a literary text.

3 See Terence J. Keggan, 'Introductory Formulae for Matthean Discourses', *CBQ* 44 (1982), pp. 415-30.

types of speaking in a way in which the crowds and disciples are unable to experience. Since it is all presented under the rubric of one of Jesus' discourses, however, the narrator's evaluative point of view which is operative in the discourse is communicated through the medium of Jesus' voice.[1]

The manner in which the implied reader is manipulated by the narrator deserves to be examined more closely. After the narrator introduces Jesus' speech, by describing him as telling the crowds 'many things in parables', the narrated character Jesus himself narrates, telling the parable of the Sower (vv. 3b-9). In verse 10 the narrator introduces a new element in the discourse when the disciples approach Jesus to ask not about the previous parable, but about his practice of speaking in parables to the crowd. Their question refers back to the narrator's description of Jesus' teaching activity (v. 3a) with the result that Jesus' explanation operates on two different levels; inside the story Jesus' explanation (vv. 10-17) is directed to the disciples' question, but it is also operative in the narrative as commentary to the implied reader.[2] The quotation from Isaiah thus functions on one level to interpret Jesus' speaking in parables, but the story also interprets Isaiah since Jesus' parable speaking is presented as the fulfillment of Scripture in a way not unlike the narrator's use of the Old Testament formula quotations. The explanation functions as a blessing upon the disciples but as a curse upon the crowds, and reflects the evaluative point of view that Jesus and his message should be accepted. Both the disciples and the crowds live in the unique time of revelation, but the disciples have the right kind of knowledge which has led to repentance, whereas the crowds are unable to appropriate the mysteries of the Kingdom because they have already proven themselves to be hardened to Jesus' mission and message.[3]

---

1 See Gary A. Phillips, 'History and Text: The Reader in Context in Matthew's Parables Discourse', *Semeia* 31 (1985), pp. 119-32, for a discussion of the overlapping and interpenetration between different levels of speaking in this discourse.

2 *Ibid.*, p. 122.

3 Kingsbury, *Parables of Jesus*, pp. 42-49; Patte, *Matthew*, pp. 186-89. Patte distinguishes between a basic knowledge of the Kingdom and a surplus knowledge of the mysteries of the Kingdom. The basic

Jesus returns to the parable of the Sower in 13.18-23 with an allegorical interpretation for the disciples. The story is retold, but as a narrated discussion of the parable rather than as a narrated story (cf. 13.3b-9). The point of the parable is made explicit and given a pragmatic emphasis which reflects the same evaluative point of view—that Jesus and his message should be accepted. The difference between those who bear fruit and those who do not is based upon what they do with the word; 'seeing and hearing' implies 'knowing and doing' the will of God. This ideological point of view is still expressed through Jesus' voice.

The narrator overtly asserts his presence again in 13.24 (cf. vv. 31, 33) following the allegory with the connecting comment 'another parable he put before them'. Although the implied reader is told later that the parables were addressed to the crowds (13.34), the ambiguity of the pronoun αὐτοῖς in these comments by the narrator serves to engage the implied reader.[1] Since there is no explicit change of audience, the implied reader might assume that the disciples are the ones being referred to by the pronoun, and thus they continue as the recipients of the parabolic teaching. After overhearing Jesus' discussions with his disciples in the preceding pericopae, the implied reader would have identified himself or herself with these who hear, understand, and act upon Jesus' proclamation. Upon discovering in 13.34, however, that Jesus has returned to his original discursive situation with the crowds as the audience, the implied reader is confronted with a question: Have I received the parables as the disciples or as the crowds? The crowds go away with exactly the same knowledge with

knowledge leads to repentance and a positive response to Jesus. Because the disciples have been given this knowledge, the mysteries of the Kingdom are available to them. The crowd, on the other hand, has rejected Jesus so that even what they do have will be taken from them. Cf. O. Lamar Cope, *Matthew: A Scribe Trained for the Kingdom of Heaven*, (CBQMS 5; Washington, DC: Catholic Biblical Association of America, 1976), pp. 18ff., 30, who points out that the evangelist uses Isa. 6.9-10, which speaks only of the blindness of the people, to make a contrast between the blindness of the people and the insight of the disciples.

1 See Edwards, *Matthew's Story*, p. 48; Patte, *Matthew*, pp. 192ff.

which they began the discourse, and thus unsuccessfully receive Jesus' teaching, but the implied reader has considerably more information through the benefit of Jesus' instruction.

The narrator enters into Jesus' discourse once again in 13.34-36a with an Old Testament fulfillment quotation and with commentary which summarizes and interprets the whole of the first half of the discourse.[1] Like the quotation from Isaiah in 13.14-15, Jesus' speaking in parables interprets Ps. 78.2 since Jesus' actions are portrayed as the fulfillment of Scripture. The narrator's comments and citation of the Old Testament also interpret the story, however, because they characterize Jesus' discussion with the crowds as parable-speaking. For those like the disciples who have been given the gift of understanding, the parables are revelatory. But for the crowds the parables are incomprehensible speech (cf. 13.11-13).[2] The narrator no longer speaks through Jesus to express this ideological point of view as he did in 13.10-17, but he speaks in his own voice.

There is an unambiguous change of audience for the second half of the discourse (13.36), with Jesus turning solely to the disciples. The narrator's presence here is not as obtrusive. Jesus moves directly from allegory and parable to other parables and allegory. The emphasis is on praxis in this half of the discourse: doing the will of God is the object of understanding about the Kingdom. The narrator does not intervene until the scribe parable (13.51-52), a parable which functions as a conclusion for the entire discourse by reflecting on what it means to interpret parabolic speech.[3] While Jesus' question is directed

1 See Kingsbury, *Matthew 13*, pp. 16, 89ff., 130ff., for a discussion of how 13.34-36 divides the parable discourse in half and represents Jesus' turning away from the Jews to his disciples. Contra Patte, *Matthew*, p. 195, who argues that 'all' in verse 34 only refers back to the previous 3 parables. The correlation between the functions of the OT quotations in 13.35 and 13.14-15 argues against such an interpretation. See Cope, *Matthew*, pp. 15-24, who argues that both OT passages serve as midpoint texts in the construction of the discourse.

2 Kingsbury, *Matthew 13*, p. 90.

3 According to Kingsbury (*Matthew 13*, p. 125), the parable serves as

to the disciples on the story level, the implied reader is also addressed on the level of the narrative: Has the implied reader understood what it means for the crowds to be unable to hear and understand the parables while the disciples succeed in understanding and doing the will of God? The rhetorical effect of this question on the implied reader in interpreting the whole discourse is visible in Jesus' response to the disciples' answer. In the parable of the scribe, the subject of the parable is no longer the Kingdom of Heaven, as it has been for the parables throughout the discourse, but 'a scribe trained for the Kingdom of Heaven'. The focus of the discourse is now upon what someone is like who follows and understands the Kingdom, and the implied reader who has followed the action of the discourse is addressed as well as the disciples.[1] If the disciples and the implied reader have truly understood, they too will be able to proclaim and do God's will.[2]

The discourse thus ends with the narrated Jesus telling a narrative which is addressed to the implied reader. Although portrayed as one of Jesus' major discourses, it has not simply contained uninterrupted direct speech by Jesus, but has consisted of a narrated character telling stories and becoming

the conclusion only for the second half of the discourse. Phillips points out, however, that the antecedent of 'all these things' in 13.51 is not only the allegorical interpretation of the Wheat and Tares (vv. 37-43), but also the Sower allegory in 13.18-23 ('History and Text', p. 131). This has the effect of uniting the two halves of the chapter.

1 Although it is true that the original audience of the parables, the crowd, has been left behind in the second half of the discourse, it is not the case that the crowds are 'only incidental to Matthew's purpose' as O. Lamar Cope claims (*Matthew*, p. 25). The contrast between the inability of the crowds to understand and the disciples' comprehension is a crucial element in the narrative strategy of the discourse whereby the implied author seeks to educate the implied reader in how to hear, understand, and enact Jesus' teaching.

2 See Phillips, 'History and Text', pp. 131-32; Edwards, *Matthew's Story*, p. 50. Edwards describes the ending of the discourse in the following way: 'It is appropriate that a "collection" of parables should end with a parable that implied that the reader must become like the disciples in order to understand the kingdom of heaven. The reader is drawn into the story, as a result, and is required to supply his own meaning'.

engaged in conversations with different audiences.[1] The narrator's evaluative perspective has been visible in commentary which stitches together and interprets the interaction between Jesus and his audience, but the parallels between this and Jesus' ideological point of view show how Jesus' speech mediates the implied author/narrator's point of view. It is therefore appropriate that the discourse concludes with a parable in Jesus' voice which seeks to engage the implied reader.

Because the narrator and Jesus share the same ideological point of view, the implied reader stands with Jesus as well as with the narrator in evaluating characters and events. The same evaluative system, expressed by the narrator, in which characters and actions are judged according to the criterion of acceptance or rejection of Jesus, should also be visible on the phraseological level of Jesus' speech.[2] Jesus thus joins John the Baptist (3.7ff.)[3] in condemning the intransigence, lack of

---

1 See Robert Kellogg, 'Oral Narrative, Written Books', *Genre* 10 (1977), pp. 655-65, for a good discussion of the ways in which an author can utilize a well-defined 'oral persona' in a written narrative to communicate a specific system of values.

2 See Anderson, 'Gender and Reading', pp. 10ff., 23ff. who notes that the various character groups in Matthew are primarily characterized in terms of their relationship to Jesus. Cf. Kingsbury's comments on the characterization of the disciples in Matthew (*Matthew as Story*, p. 13): 'Because the disciples possess conflicting traits, the reader is invited, depending on the attitude Matthew as narrator or Jesus takes toward them on any given occasion, to identify with them or to distance himself or herself from them. It is through such granting or withholding of appproval on cue, therefore, that the reader becomes schooled in the values that govern the life of discipleship in Matthew's story'. This schooling is not limited to the character traits of the disciples alone, however, but extends to the relationship of all the characters towards Jesus. Even Jesus' opponents can portray, in negative terms, 'the meaning of authentic discipleship' (Senior, *Passion of Jesus*, p. 36), and minor or marginal characters may possess exemplary character traits and values.

3 John's evaluation of the Jewish leaders is also in alignment with that of Jesus and the narrator/implied author, not only because Jesus and John share the same message (3.2; 4.17), but also because John is the precursor of Jesus. See Kingsbury, 'Jesus and the Jewish Leaders', pp. 65ff.

repentance and unbelief of the Jewish leaders and of his Jewish contemporaries (9.12f.; 11.20f.; 12.3ff.; 12.33f.; 12.38-45; 15.3ff.; 17.17f.; 23.13ff.). The people are judged to be an evil and adulterous (12.39) or faithless and perverse (17.17) generation, and 'hypocrite' appears as a favorite appellation for the scribes and Pharisees on the lips of the Matthean Jesus (23.13ff. for example). In the series of parables in 21.28-22.14 Jesus speaks of the judgment which awaits Israel for rejecting its Messiah.[1]

On an individual level, people are warned that they will be judged on the basis of whether they have done the will of Father (7.21ff.; cf. 25.31ff.)—a will which Jesus reveals (11.25ff.). If they are to enter the Kingdom of Heaven the righteousness of Jesus' disciples must exceed that of the scribes and Pharisees, the very people who bear the brunt of the negative evaluation by the Matthean Jesus because of their rejection of him (5.20). Even Jesus' disciples are not exempt from negative judgments. Peter is rebuked by Jesus because he did not accept the teaching about suffering Messiahship (16.22ff.), and all the disciples are reproached for their lack of understanding (16.11; 26.10f.) and faith (8.26; 17.20; cf. 14.31 where Peter alone is reprimanded).

Although we found few ideological comments which displayed a positive evaluation on the part of the narrator himself, positive responses to Jesus and character traits which are commended by the implied author/narrator are often cast in Jesus' direct speech. Thus, those who hear and practice Jesus' teachings are compared to a wise man (7.24ff.). The faith of the woman who had suffered twelve years with a hemorrhage is also praised (9.22), as is the Roman centurion whose faith is contrasted with a lack of response by Israel (8.10ff.).[2] In the instructions given to the disciples for their mission, they

1 See Schweizer, *Matthäus und seine Gemeinde*, pp. 116-25, and *idem*, *Matthew*, pp. 401-403, who argues that this parable trilogy, and chapters 21-25 in general, represent a trial schema in which Israel is tried for its rejection of Jesus.

2 See Kingsbury, *Matthew as Story*, pp. 26-27, and Anderson, 'Gender and Reading', pp. 11-21, for discussions of the way minor and marginal characters function in Matthew (they often serve as foils for the commendation of specific character traits and virtues).

are told that people who receive them are receiving Jesus and will therefore not lose their reward (10.40ff.). Jesus praises John the Baptist and his ministry (11.7ff.) which has the added effect of confirming John's ideological point of view, such as his evaluation of the Jewish leaders (cf. 3.7ff.). Jesus positively identifies those who do the will of the Father as his disciples and family (12.49ff.). The disciples are called blessed because they have understood Jesus' teachings (13.16ff.), and Peter is specifically blessed for his confession (16.17ff.). The disciples are also promised a future reward for the sacrifices made when they left all to follow Jesus (19.28ff.). In a series of parables Jesus teaches that those who are prepared for the coming of the Son of Man and those who have performed the deeds demanded of disciples will be rewarded (25.14ff., 31ff.). These are compared with good, faithful and wise servants (24.45ff.; 25.14ff.) and with wise maidens (25.1ff.).

Jesus' speech thus shares the ideological point of view of the narrator, and is, in fact, the primary vehicle by which the author expresses his ideological point of view. Both Jesus and the narrator evaluate characters and events according to the standard of whether Jesus and his message are accepted or rejected. Those who accept Jesus are praised, and those who reject him are reproached and warned about judgment. A number of Jesus' sayings have a dual thrust, which reflects this ideological point of view by posing the alternatives assumed in it—acceptance or rejection, reward or condemnation. In 5.20, for example, the righteousness of the scribes and Pharisees is judged deficient in some way for entry into the Kingdom, whereas the greater righteousness of the disciples will be rewarded. Similarly, in the parable of the two sons (21.28ff.) sinners are praised for believing John the Baptist, but the Jewish leaders are condemned for their lack of belief and repentance.[1]

Other characters express their evaluative points of view in the Gospel, but these are also emplotted by the author and evaluated ultimately according to the point of view of Jesus and the narrator. One way of examining the different points

---

1 Cf. Also 13.18ff., 36ff., 47ff.; 25.1ff., 31ff.—parables or interpretations of parables which all have a double perspective in their paraenesis.

of view towards Jesus among characters in the Gospel is to study the different appellations used by them to refer to Jesus. Boris Uspensky has suggested that the different appellations used to name a character are 'directly conditioned by the attitude towards the person referred to'.[1] Through the exposition and commentary at the beginning of the Gospel (especially in the genealogy and Old Testament fulfillment quotations), the implied reader knows Jesus' identity and is thereby able to evaluate with the narrator the names attributed to him by characters in the unfolding story. For example, the wise men in the infancy story call Jesus 'King of the Jews' (2.2), and their response is positively described by the narrator as rejoicing and worshipping Jesus (2.10ff.). On the other hand, both Satan and demons correctly identify Jesus by calling him 'Son of God' (4.3, 6; 8.29), but their confessions function ironically in the Gospel because they do not accept him. Instead, Satan and his overtures to Jesus are repulsed by the quotation of scripture, and the demons are cast out of the demoniac. In a similar manner the high priest calls Jesus 'Son of God' during Jesus' trial without accepting him, since he immediately accuses Jesus of blasphemy (26.63).[2]

The ideological point of view of the implied author/narrator

1 Uspensky, *Poetics of Composition*, p. 21. See pp. 25-32 for a discussion of 'Naming as a Problem of Point of View in Literature', Cf. Bruce J. Malina and Jerome H. Neyrey, *Calling Jesus Names: The Social Value of Labels in Matthew* (Sonoma, CA: Polebridge, 1988), pp. 35-38, for their discussion of labelling theory, and Petersen, 'Point of View', p. 111.

2 The title 'Son of God' here and 'King of the Jews' in 27.11 and 27.29 are also used ironically by the implied author. The characters who voice these confessions do not mean them, yet the narrator and the reader both know that these titles accurately describe who Jesus is. Uspensky, *Poetics of Composition*, p. 103, has written that irony occurs 'when we speak from one point of view, but make an evaluation from another point of view'. In these instances in Matthew, the confession is spoken from the point of view of characters who do not think that Jesus is 'Son of God' or 'King of the Jews', but they are evaluated from the point of view of the narrator and implied reader who recognize them as valid and true confessions. Cf. 22.16ff. where the same use of irony is present. See Senior, *The Passion of Jesus*, for a discussion of irony in Matthew's passion story.

is therefore not only expressed through the medium of Jesus in Matthew, but it is also used to evaluate all the other points of view in the narrative. Characters who voice points of view that are in harmony with the criterion of acceptance of Jesus are treated favorably, while those who reject Jesus are judged negatively. Names or points of view which by themselves are correct but which are voiced by characters who do not accept Jesus are placed in a context which evaluates them according to the overall perspective of acceptance or rejection of Jesus.

E. *Conclusion*

In summary, the implied author/narrator of Matthew is able to shape the role of the implied reader by the manner in which he tells his story. Despite the impression of pure reference created by an undramatized, third person, omniscient personality who tells the story retrospectively, the narrator tells the story from a particular ideological point of view which seeks to persuade the implied reader to accept Jesus and his message. From the very beginning of the story the implied reader is informed of Jesus' identity and his significance. The narrator provides the implied reader with information which is not available to characters in the story. By commentary, by the superscription and genealogy, by Old Testament fulfillment quotations, and by the emplotment of events and characters' responses to Jesus, the narrator portrays Jesus favorably. Character traits of those who accept Jesus and who obey God's will are commended, while negative responses and rejection of Jesus are correspondingly judged negatively.[1]

---

1 The ideological point of view which judges characters and events according to the criterion of whether Jesus is accepted or rejected helps explain the didactic nature of the Gospel with its concomitant emphasis on the sayings of Jesus. Cf. Theissen, *Miracles*, p. 233, who has written that Matthew can be described as a 'didactic gospel life'. It is still a Gospel, however, in which the focus is placed on Jesus. Care must therefore be taken that the so-called 'catechetical' interest is not over-emphasized. Contra Ernst von Dobschütz, 'Matthew as Rabbi and Catechist', in *Matthew*, ed. Stanton, pp. 24ff., and Krister Stendahl, 'Matthew', *Peake's Commentary on the Bible*, ed. M. Black and H.H. Rowley (London: Nelson, 1967),

The narrator, however, is not the sole spokesman for the implied author's values and norm in Matthew. The focus of the Gospel is placed squarely on Jesus, and the narrator tells the story in such a way as to align himself closely with Jesus. Spatially, the action follows Jesus. Phraseologically, the narrator and Jesus share much of the same speech. Psychologically, the inside view of Jesus are given in more depth and presented more sympathetically than those of other characters in the story. Temporally, the narrator is often synchronized with Jesus as he speaks. The upshot of this method of narration is that the ideological point of view of Jesus and the narrator come to be aligned. An emphasis is placed on Jesus' speech, which is also a medium for the implied author's value system, so Jesus addresses the implied reader together with the characters. The implied reader thus stands both with Jesus and the narrator, and receives the call to evaluate events and characters as they evaluate them. It now remains to examine in more depth the identity and role of the implied reader in Matthew's inclusive story, and to this task we turn in the next chapter.

p. 769. Stendahl has written that the nature of Matthew 'is a handbook for teaching and administration within the Church, and we have compared its form with the Manual of Discipline from Qumran'.

Chapter 5

THE IMPLIED READER IN
MATTHEW'S INCLUSIVE STORY

A. *Introduction*

The other participant in the communicative transaction—the audience who receives the Gospel—should figure prominently in any discussion of Matthew's inclusive story, since it is their experience as post-Easter Christians which is said to be 'included' in the story of Jesus' earthly ministry.[1] The tendency in Matthean scholarship when treating this aspect of Matthew's story has been to identify or equate character groups in the Gospel with persons beyond its narrative world. In this type of interpretation the disciples are often understood as representing the evangelist's audience. It has become almost axiomatic to argue that behind Matthew's portrayal of the disciples stands the experiences of his Christian community,[2] whereas the Jewish leaders in the narrative represent

---

[1] See Lampe and Luz, 'Diskussionsüberblick', in *Evangelium*, ed. Stuhlmacher, p. 413, who write that 'Mt erzählt eine "inclusive story", eine Geschichte in der die Gegenwart in Gestalt der Jünger in das Geschick irdischen Jesu eingeschlossen ist'.

[2] See Luz, 'Disciples', pp. 105, 110, Kingsbury, *Matthew 13*, p. 42, Jean Zumstein, *La Condition du croyant dans l'évangile selon Matthieu* (Göttingen: Vandenhoeck & Ruprecht, 1977), p. 81, for example. According to Zumstein Matthew underlines 'la valeur typologique' of the disciples, Jesus' opponents, and even the forgiven sinners in the Gospel, who prefigure the Gentiles that are welcomed into the church. Kingsbury writes that 'the correlation in the first Gospel between the disciples of Jesus and Christians of Matthew's day is so close that the disciples of the text simply become the representatives of the Christians, or Church, of this later age'. A variation of this type of interpretation is found in the work of Paul Minear (*Matthew*,

the Jewish rivals of the evangelist.[1]

One danger with this type of exegetical approach, however, is that the exegete may move too easily or directly from text to life-setting in the evangelist's community. Some scholars have recently cautioned that the Gospels are not 'allegories'[2] or 'cryptograms'[3] directed to the contemporaries of the evangelists, in which the relationship between text and reality can 'be clarified by a direct mapping of textual contents onto recon-

pp. 10-12, and *idem*, 'The Disciples and the Crowds in the Gospel of Matthew', *ATR Supplementary Series* 3 (1974), pp. 28-44). He believes that the disciples and crowds represent the ministers and laity of the evangelist's community. According to Minear Matthew portrays the disciples as those 'ordained and trained by Jesus to continue his several ministries' to the crowds ('Disciples and Crowds', p. 31). As readers of the Gospel, we should therefore assume that when Jesus is speaking to the crowds he was addressing Matthew's 'contemporary laymen', and when he is speaking to the disciples, Matthew has in mind 'the vocation of contemporary leaders' (*ibid.*, p. 41). Cf. the interpretation of the Sermon on the Mount by Oscar S. Brooks (*The Sermon on the Mount: Authentic Human Values* (Washington, DC: University Press of America, 1985), p. 95), who argues that the 'crowds' of Matthew's literary world are identified with the readers of the text. Brooks suggests that both are 'outsiders' who, 'overhearing' Jesus' instructions to the disciples, are prompted to ask, 'What is this saying to me?'.

1   Comber, 'The Verb *Therapeuo*', pp. 433-34, argues that the Jewish leaders represent Pharisees who were 'leading a vigorous reform movement' in Matthew's day. Cf. Minear, *Matthew*, pp. 11-12. Comber, however, interprets the crowds in Matthew in a manner different from Minear. They are a 'cipher' for Jewish people who, although wavering about joining the church, were still the objects of 'Jesus' beneficence' and the church's mission.

2   Elizabeth Struthers Malbon, 'Disciples/Crowds/Whoever: Markan Characters and Readers', *NovT* 28 (1986), p. 123. Malbon is reacting to a tendency in recent Markan scholarship to equate the disciples in Mark with either the evangelist's 'supposed opponents' or 'imagined hearers/readers'.

3   Luke T. Johnson, 'On Finding the Lukan Community: A Cautious Cautionary Essay', in *SBL 1979 Seminar Papers*, Vol 1, ed. Paul J. Achtemeier (Missoula, MT: Scholars Press, 1979), p. 93. Cf. Senior, *Passion of Jesus*, p. 181, who describes all of the characters in Matthew as 'anachronistic' in the sense that none of them are 'contemporaries of the reader'.

structed situations of origin'.[1] An exegete who makes this move may be neglecting the clear difference which Walter Ong has shown to exist between a person speaking to an audience which is present, with all the mutual and non-verbal communication such a face-to-face encounter offers, and an author writing to an absent audience which has been created in his or her imagination. The extent to which this imagined audience corresponds to the author's real audience is dependent both upon the author's knowledge of the actual circumstances of the readers, and upon the conformity of the imagined reader's fictional role to the actual audience's reality.[2] The narrative alone may not be able to reveal the identity of the actual audience or readers for whom Matthew wrote and whose experiences are said to be included in the Gospel. Many contemporary reconstructions of the community behind Matthew may in fact extend only as far as the audience which the written narrative implies.[3] Caution should therefore be exercised when speculating about an evangelist's actual community and the ways they are included in the Gospel.

Moreover, our discussion of the Matthean narrator/implied author in the previous chapter suggests that an audience which is included in the narrative will be a more nuanced figure than could be derived from a simple equation of textual characters with extratextual persona. We argued there that although the narrator/implied author's values are embedded

1 Bernard C. Lategan, 'Structure and Reference in Mt 23', *Neotestamentica* 16 (1982), p. 76.
2 See Walter J. Ong, 'The Writer's Audience is Always Fiction', *PLMA* 90 (1976), pp. 9-12.
3 See Robert A. Fowler, *Loaves and Fishes: The Fiction of the Feeding Stories in the Gospel of Mark* (SBLDS 54; Chico, CA: Scholars, 1981), pp. 149-53, who also cautions against equating the implied reader with real communities. He writes that 'what often passes for reflections of a palpable, historical, flesh-and-blood audience is in fact an aspect of the fictionalized audience created in the evangelist's imagination' (p. 228, n. 16). Cf. Kingsbury, 'Reflections on "The Reader"', pp. 454-59, who also differentiates between audiences in Matthew. The approach Kingsbury takes in this essay represents a change from his earlier redaction-critical work which we referred to above.

in Jesus, the implied author and narrator are not characters in the story. They have specific spatial, temporal, and ideological relationships to both the Gospel's narrative world which they have constructed and to the characters who populate this world. As the narrator/implied author's interlocutor, the implied or included audience also has corresponding relationships to Matthew's narrative world. An important aspect of this group's relationship to the Gospel's narrative world is that they know more than any character group in the story. With this knowledge, they are ultimately called upon to stand with Jesus and the narrator and judge events and characters according to the ideological point of view of the implied author. When discipleship is viewed from this perspective, it should not be defined as membership in a given narrative character group (e.g. the disciples) but as the attitudes, values, and behavior which the implied author wishes the implied audience to accept and display.[1]

A proper consideration of narrative characteristics such as these makes it problematic for one to identify or equate the experiences of the evangelist's Christian community which are said to be included or implied in the narrative with those of any single character group, even though this audience will no doubt identify with different characters and points of view in the Gospel. We have touched upon the function of the included or implied audience in previous discussions of Matthew's story and story-teller, but it is now appropriate to examine the identity and role of the implied reader in Matthew in a more systematic manner. In this chapter we will be especially interested in the implied reader's contribution to the pragmatic or appellative dimensions of the narrative—that is, how the story is meant to influence actual readers.

Since the different types of readers who populate a narrative text have proliferated in recent years as literary theorists have become interested in the role of an audience in the production of textual meaning, some clarification in terminology may be helpful before we begin.[2] Most literary theorists have

1 See Anderson, 'Gender and Reading', pp. 22-24.
2 See B.C. Lategan: 'Current Issues in the Hermeneutical Debate', *Neotestametica* 18 (1984), pp. 1-4, for an overview of the shifts in

paired an audience or reader-figure with each of the different voices operative in the telling of a story. Corresponding to the real author of the narrative are the actual flesh-and-blood readers of the Gospel. Encoded in the text and functioning as the counterpart to the implied author is the implied reader. The interlocutor of the narrator is the narratee who, like his or her partner in dialogue, may be overt or covert.[1]

The distinctions between a narrative's encoded interlocutors are helpful when the implied author has distanced him or herself from an unreliable narrator, or when it is clear that the implied reader should distance him—or herself from a gullible narratee. In narratives like the Gospels, however, in which the narrator is a reliable spokesman for the values and norms of the implied author, the distance between the implied reader and narratee is also negligible.[2] The narratee in effect stands in for the implied reader. We will therefore simplify matters by construing the addressee of the narrator/implied author as the implied reader while recognizing the distinction on the theoretical level.

Further refinements of these basic concepts are often found clustered around the idea of an 'ideal reader' who would fully understand and accept the implied author's words and point of view.[3] Steven Mailloux has pointed out, however, that the

focus in theological hermeneutics. Cf. also Eagleton, *Literary Theory*, p. 74. See the literature cited in the introduction for a discussion of the variety of readers in the different types of audience-oriented literary criticism.

1 The term 'narratee' is used by Chatman, *Story and Discourse*, pp. 150-51, 253-61; and Gerald Prince, 'Notes Toward a Categorization of Fictional "Narratees",' *Genre* 4 (1971), pp. 100-105, *idem*, 'Introduction to the Study of the Narratee', in *Reader-Response Criticism*, ed. Tompkins, pp. 7-25 and *Narratology: The Form and Functioning of Narrative* (Berlin: Mouton, 1982), pp. 18-21. The 'narratee' corresponds to Rabinowitz's 'narrative audience' ('Truth in Fiction', p. 127) in his typology of readers.

2 James M. Dawsey *The Lukan Voice: Confusion and Irony In Luke* (Macon, GA: Mercer, 1986), is an exception to the tendency to view the Gospel narrators as reliable. He argues that the Lukan narrator is unreliable.

3 Rabinowitz, 'Truth in Fiction', p. 134, speaks of an 'ideal narrative audience', and Prince, 'Introduction', in *Reader-Response Criti-*

'ideal reader' is 'merely an abstracted version of the "implied reader"'.[1] It is therefore unnecessary to assume that qualities attributed to the ideal reader are not already contained in the concept of an implied reader. For the sake of simplicity, we will also not use this term in our study.

Wolfgang Iser's definition of the implied reader as both textual structure to be realized and structured act of realization will be sufficient for our purposes.[2] As a textual structure, the implied reader is the audience presupposed by the narrative—'a sort of fictional inhabitant of the text' who 'embodies all the predispositions necessary for a literary work to exercise its effect'.[3] Being made up of all the directions for reading the text, and being present throughout the narrative listening to every word, the implied reader stands as the recipient of all the various textual strategies and rhetorical devices used to communicate. Thus, to speak of the implied reader is in a sense, to speak of the embodiment of the response Matthew was aiming at when he composed his Gospel.[4] As a structured

---

    cism, p. 8, speaks of the 'ideal reader'. See Iser, *Act of Reading*, pp. 27-38, for a discussion of several versions of the 'ideal reader'.

1 Mailloux, *Interpretive Conventions*, p. 203. Cf. Chatman, *Story and Discourse*, p. 253, n. 41. Fowler ('Who is "The Reader"?', p. 16) points out that the 'ideal reader' is primarily a fictive role or pose 'created and assumed by a critic as he or she presumes to address the critical community'.

2 For Iser, the concept of the implied reader 'incorporates both the prestructuring of the potential meaning by the text, and the reader's actualization of this potential through the reading process' (*Implied Reader*, p. xii). Cf. Perry, 'Literary Dynamics', p. 43, who defines this reader as 'a "maximal" concretization of the text that can be justified from the text itself while taking into account the norms (social, linguistic, literary, etc.) relevant for its period and the possible intentions of the author'.

3 Iser, *Act of Reading*, pp. 33-34.

4 Cf. Ong, 'Writer's Audience', p. 12, who argues that authors always construct a role for their audiences to play when they write, and Lategan, 'Reception, Redescription, Reality', p. 70. See also Kingsbury, *Matthew as Story*, p. 36, who has defined the implied reader as 'that imaginary person in whom the intention of the text is to be thought of as always reaching its fulfillment'. Stanley Fish, 'Interpreting the *Variorum*', in *Reader-Response Criticism*, p. 174,

act, the implied reader is also the stance readers take when they read, and the actions they perform in processing the textual structures. In the words of Walter Ong, the implied reader is the reader who 'must play the role in which the author has cast him'.[1]

In this chapter we will attempt to keep both aspects of the implied reader in focus. First, we will sketch a portrait of Matthew's implied reader, who can be defined in terms of a relationship both to the narrator/implied author and to the characters in the Gospel's story. By defining the implied reader in this way, we hope to avoid the confusion which often exists between considering the disciples as characters in the plotted story on the one hand, and the response which the evangelist was trying to elicit from his readers on the other. Secondly, factors which enter into the reading experience and the processing of the Gospel's narrative will be considered, for actual readers respond to the role of the implied reader when they read. It should be noted that the set of instructions for concretizing a text has gaps and indeterminacies.[2] This means that actual readers do not create identical readings since they fill in the gaps and actualize the narrative in different historical contexts. Our profile of the implied reader in Matthew and description of the reading process must therefore be recognized as nothing other than our own interpretation. It is hoped, however, that by taking into consideration the historical and cultural context in which the Gospel was written and the subsequent responses of the interpretive community of the church, the responses we attribute to the implied reader will not seem too idiosyncratic.[3]

has argued that 'intention and understanding are two ends of a conventional act, each of which necessarily stipulates (includes, defines, specifies) the other' so that to construct a profile of the implied reader is 'at the same time to characterize the author's intention'.

1 'Writer's Audience', p. 12.

2 Iser, *Implied Reader*, pp. 38-40, and *Act of Reading*, pp. 59-67, 167ff.

3 As an interpretive construct, the implied reader participates in the circularity of all interpretation. A portrait of the reader is constructed while one reads, but this portrait is then used to confirm and validate the reading experience. Cf. Suleiman, 'Introduction',

B. *Evidence of Matthew's Implied Reader*

1. *The Implied Reader and the Narrator / Implied Author*

Literary theorists have argued that in general, a given type of narrator tends to evoke a parallel type of encoded audience.[1] Because the implied reader and implied author are interdependent, many of the issues and evidence concerning the identity and poetics of the implied reader have already been studied from the angle of the narrator/implied author in earlier chapters, and so need only be summarized here. Like the implied author/narrator, the implied reader/narratee in Matthew is not evident as a specific individual or character in the story, even though there are signs of an intended audience in the Gospel.[2]

The most obvious way in which the implied reader can be detected and his or her role shaped by the implied author is through direct or explicit commentary. In the eschatological discourse Jesus' speech is interrupted by the narrator with a direct reference to the implied reader, 'Let the reader understand' (24.15).[3] References to extratextual knowledge in 27.8

---

in *The Reader in the Text*, p. 11. Fowler, 'Who is the "Reader"?' p. 21, sums up the intertwining of the different dimensions of the reader in reader-response criticism when he writes 'the reader has an individual persona (mine), a communal persona (the abstracted total experience of my critical community), and a textual persona (the reader implied in the text)'.

1 See Chatman, *Story and Discourse*, p. 255.

2 Gerald Prince ('Introduction', pp. 12-15) and Mary Ann Piwowarczyk ('The Narratee and the Situation of Enunciation: A Reconsideration of Prince's Theory', *Genre* 9 [1976], pp. 167-77) have identified seven signs which indicate the presence of a narratee: direct references, inclusive and indefinite pronouns or expressions, questions and pseudo-questions, negations, demonstrative comparisons and analogies, and 'over justifications' by the narrator. It is not necessary for all these signs to be present in every narrative, and they are not all used in Matthew. Prince's theory will provide us, however, with a structure to examine the implied reader in Matthew.

3 Although this reference to the reader is probably taken from Mark, it can still be used as evidence for the Matthean implied reader. The concept of implied author and reader are constructed on the basis of

and 28.15 by the phrase 'to this day' are also signs of the implied reader. These signs place the implied reader in the same spatio-temporal position as the implied author: in the indeterminate period between the resurrection and the parousia of the Son of Man.[1] From this vantage point the implied reader follows the narrator throughout all the events which are retrospectively narrated in the story of Jesus' life and ministry.

As the implied reader follows the narrator in his telling of the story of Jesus' life, the narrator also uses commentary to establish a close relationship of confidence with his interlocutor. The identity of Jesus and the significance of his mission is revealed to the implied reader from the beginning in the heading (1.1), the genealogy (1.2-17), a translation of Jesus' name (1.23), and a number of Old Testament fulfillment quotations (1.22-23; 2.15, 17-18, 23). The use of Old Testament fulfillment quotations continues throughout the Gospel illuminating and interpreting almost every aspect of Jesus' life and ministry. As references to extratextual texts, these play a major part in the narrative rhetoric so characteristic of Matthew. By means of these texts, the narrator specifies the supposed real world which the narrative takes as its reference—the history of Israel as God's chosen people—and the implied reader is told in an unambiguous way that Jesus should be understood as the fulfillment of God's promises to his people. The use of the Old Testament and its rhetorical effectiveness to persuade presuppose that the implied reader has some knowledge of this literature and its importance.[2]

---

textual evidence no matter what the source of this material. The same actual author could thus write a number of different works, each with a different implied author.

1 For other evidence in Matthew which places the implied reader in the time after the conclusion of the plotted story of Jesus' death and resurrection, see our discussion of prolepses in chapter 3.

2 See Terence J. Keegan, *Interpreting the Bible: A Popular Introduction to Biblical Hermeneutics* (New York: Paulist, 1985), p. 111. Luz, *Matthäus*, pp. 140ff., argues that Matthew's programmatic emphasis on the fulfillment of the Law and the Prophets in Jesus is necessary since he writes after the separation of the church from Judaism. This reconstruction of the Matthean *Sitz im Leben* does

Explanatory glosses similar to the translation of Jesus' name are also found elsewhere in the Gospel. The name Golgotha (27.33) and Jesus' Aramaic cry from the cross (27.46) are both translated for the implied reader. Cultural explanations are also used, as in 22.23 when the Sadducees are described as those who do not believe in resurrection, or as in 27.15 when the custom of releasing a prisoner during the feast is explained. This type of commentary either assumes that the implied reader is not competent in the linguistic and cultural codes used, thus standing in need of explanations,[1] or it is a means of supplying information from more than one source so as to help the implied reader interpret the text properly.[2]

The effect of this commentary on the role of the implied reader is an increased dependency upon the narrator for pointing out the correct way to interpret the story, and the Matthean narrator appears willing to assume this role of guide and interpreter for the implied reader. Old Testament fulfillment quotations are one of the more prominent means of the narrator's voice providing interpretive directions for reading the Gospel, but they are not the only devices utilized to mould the reader's response. For example, after the Sermon on the Mount the implied reader is informed that Jesus' teaching is authoritative (7.29). Twice the narrator explicitly

not invalidate our observation, however, that the authority of the Old Testament must be accepted by the Gospel's implied reader to be rhetorically effective.

1 In other instances, however, Matthew does not translate Semitic words. For example see ῥακά(5.22), μαμωνᾶι (6.24), βεελζεβούλ (10.25), and κορβᾶν (27.6). See Kingsbury, *Matthew as Story*, pp. 121-22.

2 By applying information theory to literary study and criticism, some recent literary theorists have emphasized the role of redundancy or repetition in teaching a reader how to read a text. In this paradigm redundancy is simply the repetition of information in the narrative and does not have the negative connotation it has in ordinary language. It is the element of predictability in communication that provides the means whereby 'plural meanings and ambiguities are eliminated and a single "correct" reading is imposed' (Susan R. Suleiman, 'Redundancy and the "Readable Text"', *Poetics Today* 1 (1980), p. 120). The role of repetition in the processing of Matthew will be discussed later in the chapter.

states what it is the disciples understood after Jesus' teaching, lest the implied reader miss the point (16.12; 17.13). In a similar manner, the narrator specifies in 21.45 that Jesus' parables are polemically directed against the Jewish leaders. Moreover, the narrator uses evaluative commentary to describe the perversity, malice and deceit of the Jewish leaders who reject Jesus (cf. 16.1; 19.3; 26.59ff.; 27.18), so indirectly emphasizing the positive action of acceptence.[1]

Concerning the implied readers' presence in Matthew and the implied author's use of commentary to educate them in how to read the story, the important point to note for our purposes is that information communicated in this way is not available to characters in the story. The implied readers thus have a distinct advantage over every character group in the Gospel. They are privy not only to information on the levels of both plotted story and the narrator's comments, but they can also observe the interaction among different characters and between characters and the narrator.[2]

Some of the evidence which is cited to support the transparency of the disciples' experiences for Matthew's post-Easter church should thus be recognized as being shared with, if not exclusively directed toward, the implied reader. The understanding of Jesus' teachings which the disciples achieve during Jesus' ministry, for example, is shared with the implied reader (cf. 16.12; 17.13).[3] Likewise, the echoes of the eucharist in Matthew's accounts of the feeding miracles (14.15-21; 15.32-38) are verbalized through the narrator's voice.[4] Finally, words usually understood as tranferring Jesus'

---

1 Matthew's use of evaluative commentary in conjunction with his conviction that Jesus and his teaching should be accepted rather than rejected is discussed in more detail in the previous chapter. Cf. Kingsbury, *Matthew as Story*, pp. 17-23, and *idem*, 'Jesus and the Jewish Leaders', for a discussion of the evangelist's general characterization of the Jewish leaders.

2 See, for example, our discussion of chapter 13 in the previous chapter.

3 See Barth, *TIM*, pp. 106ff., and Luz, 'Disciples', pp. 102-105, for a discussion of Matthew's use of the motif of understanding and the transparency of the disciples.

4 See Held, pp. 181-87, for a discussion of Matthew's alterations of the

authority to forgive sins to the Christian community are found in the narrator's conclusion to the healing of a paralytic (9.8).[1]

The significance of differentiating between the Gospel's different discourse levels in this manner has not always been fully appreciated by interpreters when they discuss the inclusive nature of Matthew's story. Ulrich Luz has pointed out, for example, that the feeding stories are not completely transformed into a eucharist story since Matthew retains details which do not fit into the eucharistic practices of his church. Luz argues instead that the 'historical residual' in the miracles means that 'it is precisely as past historical events that these two feeding stories become transparent for the present life of the community'.[2] Is it not the case, however, that many elements Luz identifies as 'historical residue' are story elements similar to those he identifes as transparent for the church's experience of the eucharist, but simply without the narrator's interpretive commentary? Without this 'historical residue' there would be no story to be transparent! If the experiences of the disciples are to be understood as transparent for the later Christian church, it is not simply because of what the disciples do in the story, but because of the fact that the narrator's manner of narrating, plotting and interpreting events points beyond the plotted story of Jesus' ministry to the implied reader in the time between the resurrection and parousia.

No character group in the Gospel can thus be simply equated with the readers of the evangelist's community who are said to be included in the story. The Christian in Matthew's church would probably correspond more closely to the implied reader.[3] It is to this figure that Matthew as narra-

two feeding stories in Mark alterations, which align them more closely with the Lord's Supper.
1 See Held, *TIM*, p. 273ff., Luz, 'Disciples', p. 108, *idem*, *Matthäus*, p. 23, and Leopold Sabourin, *The Gospel According to St. Matthew*, Vol. 2 (Bombay: St. Paul Publications, 1982), pp. 482ff., for a representative interpretations.
2 Luz, 'Disciples', pp. 105-106.
3 J.D. Kingsbury, 'The Place, Structure, and meaning of the Sermon on the Mount Within Matthew', *Int* 41 (1987), pp. 135-36; *idem*, *Matthew as Story*, pp. 120. We will not be using the notion of the

tor speaks and conveys information not available to any character in the story world of the Gospel, some of which is based in part upon the experiences of the post-Easter church. Because the implied reader is present with the narrator throughout the Gospel—silently observing every word spoken, every thought considered, and every interaction among characters,—the impression is created that the implied reader is included in the plotted story. With the information which the implied reader thus gains, an interpretive framework is provided which enables actual readers to recognize post-Easter experiences in Matthew's story world of Jesus' pre-Easter ministry.

Although the disciples are the character group in Matthew which is on the whole portrayed most favorably vis-à-vis Jesus, and although it is they who are to assume leadership and teaching positions in the post-Easter church (16.18-19; 18.15-20; 28.19-20), the implied readers should not be solely identified with them. The disciples are also at times inconsistent in following Jesus (cf. 8.26; 14.31; 15.16; 16.8, 23; 19.13; 20.20-28; 26.8, 40, 43, 56, 69ff.; 28.17 for example), whereas other characters display character traits in the Gospel and espouse viewpoints which are commended by the implied author (cf. 8.10ff.; 15.28 for example). An actual reader can thus learn about discipleship by observing all the characters in the Gospel and the stance they take in relationship to Jesus.[1]

implied reader, however, as an 'index' to Matthew's community in the second half of the first century. Cf. Culpepper, *Anatomy*, pp. 205-27, whose discussion of John's implied reader is also concerned with reconstructing the evangelist's first century intended audience. Our concern in this chapter is focused more narrowly on the appeal structure of the Gospel by which Matthew is able to involve and include readers in the telling of his story.

1 Contra Keegan, who argues in a chapter on 'The Reader in Matthew', that the purpose of Matthew is to challenge the reader to assume the role of the disciples (*Interpreting the Bible*, pp. 110-30). He writes that 'what the implied reader is challenged to do is to identify with the disciples, and to take up the challenge that is laid out to the disciples in becoming people, in becoming better Christians' (p. 127). Cf. Anderson, 'Gender and Reading', pp. 3-27, and Senior, *Passion of Jesus*, pp. 36ff., 181ff., for discussions of the way Matthew's portrayal of marginal characters and Jesus' opponents

The superiority of the implied reader to every character group in the Gospel will become evident as we turn to examine the implied reader in relationship to characters in Matthew's story.

2. *The Implied Reader and Characters in the Story*

a. *Jesus*. Jesus makes a greater contribution to defining the role of the implied reader in Matthew than any other character in the story. He is obviously the dominant character in the Gospel. More importantly, he also shares with the narrator the role of mouthpiece for the implied author's ideological point of view as we saw in the previous chapter. Frequent temporal synchronization between Jesus and narrator, which creates a sense of contemporaneity between narrator, characters, and implied reader, is one of the ways this is achieved. The result of this type of narration, however, is that Jesus often addresses the implied reader together with the characters in the story. Signs of the implied reader should therefore be found in Jesus' speech.

One easily recognizable sign of the implied reader can be seen in references to extratextual institutions, experiences and events which simply do not fit in the picture painted of Jesus' ministry in Matthew's narrative world.[1] For example, Jesus anachronistically promises his presence where two or three of his disciples are gathered (18.19-20), and the teaching in chapter 18 on discipline presupposes the existence of a community with defined boundaries and a shared life (18.15ff.). This community will face problems in the time between the resurrection and parousia. False prophets and Messiahs will arise to threaten them (7.15ff.; cf. 24.5, 11, 24), and they will face hardship and persecution. The predicted persecution of

can also inculcate norms and values of discipleship for the implied reader.

1 See our discussion in Chapter 3 of the different types of prolepses in Matthew. References to extratextual events in predictions which clearly look beyond the plotted story world of the Gospel (as e.g. in the eschatological discourse) do not function to address the implied reader in the same way as do comments which are ostensibly directed to the situation of the disciples during Jesus' ministry but whose reference is obviously outside the plotted story.

the disciples by both Jews and Gentiles (5.11-12; 10.17ff; cf. 23.34; 24.9) or the reference to the Gospel being proclaimed in the whole world (26.14) have no place in Jesus' earthly ministry. Finally, Jesus alludes to the destruction of Jerusalem (22.7; 23.37ff.).[1] Although these references may be puzzling to characters in the plotted story, they are perfectly intelligible to the implied reader who shares the vantage point of the Matthean implied author in the period following the resurrection.

A second rhetorical device which may point to the implied reader is found in 'questions' or 'pseudo-questions' from characters in the plotted story.[2] Questions demand a response, and rhetorical questions in particular can be utilized to involve the implied reader in the story. According to George Kennedy, rhetorical questions functioned in ancient rhetoric to maintain audience contact.[3] In written texts this audience should include the implied reader as well as those who are listening to Jesus teaching in the plotted story.[4] Jesus' teaching frequently contains rhetorical questions which are so tendentious that they compel either the acceptance or rejection of their premises. Since many of these questions are

---

1 K. Rengstorf, 'Die Stadt der Mörder (Mt. 22,7)', in *Judentum, Urchristentum, Kirche* (Berlin: Töpelmann, 1960), pp. 106-29, argues against any necessary reference to AD 70 in the parable of the wedding feast, pointing to the theme of military expeditions and the destruction of cities in the Old Testament. He is unable to explain, however, why Matthew interrupts the coherent flow of the narrative with a theme which is out of place. Most commentators see a reference to the destruction of Jerusalem in this parable. Cf. Meier, *Vision*, pp. 13, 153; Thiselton, 'Reader-Response Hermeneutics', p. 86.

2 Prince, 'Introduction', pp. 13-14.

3 George A. Kennedy, *New Testament Interpretation through Rhetorical Criticism* (Chapel Hill, NC: The University of North Carolina Press, 1984), pp. 29, 57. Cf. Tannehill, *Sword of His Mouth*, p. 115.

4 Rhetorical questions are an effective means of accomplishing reader participation because the 'force of the interrogative draws us into its rhythm and creates in us the expectation of an answer' (Stanley Fish, *Self-Consuming Artifacts: The Experience of Seventeenth-Century Literature* [Berkeley, CA: University of California Press, 1971], p. 60).

based on a common experience of the world of nature or of
human relationships, the implied reader and actual readers
would be engaged by them as much as the characters in the
plotted story to whom they are addressed (see 5.13, 46-47;
6.25-31; 7.3-4, 9-12, 16; 9.15; 10.29, 12.26, 27, 29, 34; 16.26;
18.12; 23.17, 19 for examples).

Besides rhetorical questions which generally serve to
involve the implied reader in the story and personally
confront him or her with the demands of Jesus' teaching,
there are other questions which also appear to be derived from
or to refer to the implied reader. Jesus' rhetorical question in
26.54, in which he asks how the scriptures are to be fulfilled by
the events of the passion, belongs to this second category of
questions. On the level of the plotted story in Matthew, Jesus
has not been seen specifically teaching his disciples how the
events of his life and ministry lead to his arrest and crucifixion
in Jerusalem in fulfillment of the Old Testament, as the
Lukan Jesus does for example (cf. Lk. 4.18-19, 21; 18.31;
24.25ff., 44ff.). Rather, the extensive citation of the Old
Testament in the fulfillment quotations is addressed to the
implied reader in the Matthean narrator's voice. Jesus'
question in 26.54 is thus directed not so much to characters in
the story as to the implied reader, who has been the recipient
of the numerous Old Testament fulfillment quotations, and
whose real counterpart would have benefitted from the
church's post-Easter reflection on scripture vis-à-vis Jesus'
ministry and death. In this way the implied reader alone
would be in a position to answer Jesus' question.

Characters besides Jesus also voice questions which are
directed to the implied reader and serve to test both knowledge
and appropriation of assertions made by Matthew in the narration of his story. The perceptive implied reader would have
no difficulty answering the disciples' question 'what sort of
man is this?' at the conclusion of the account of the calming of
the story (8.27). The disciples may not know, but the implied
reader will certainly recognize Jesus as Son of God, having
followed and understood the commentary at the beginning of
the Gospel in the genealogy, the Old Testament fulfillment
quotations, and the birth, infancy and temptation stories. The
questions of the crowds in 12.23 and 13.54ff. serve a similar

function. From what the narrator/implied author has communicated through commentary, the implied reader will know that Jesus is the Son of David and that God is the source of his wisdom and power to perform miracles.

The questions of the Gadarene demoniacs in the pericope following the calming of the storm, 'What have you to do with us, O Son of God? Have you come here to torment us before the time?' (8.29), not only answer the disciples' earlier question, but they too refer to the implied reader. They function differently from the above examples, however, by appealing to the reader's extratextual knowledge instead of being based upon commentary directed to the implied reader. While the questions are not answered for the characters in the plotted story, at the same time the reference to Jesus tormenting the demons, which is the presupposition for the second question, would be intelligible to the implied reader, who is situated in the time following Jesus' death and resurrection. Matthew's use of both types of questions—those which refer to and those which derived from the implied reader—highlights the superiority of the implied reader to any character group in the Gospel.

Another sign of the implied reader is visible in the use of impersonal, indefinite or inclusive pronouns and expressions in Jesus' teaching. By means of this technique, Matthew is able to extend the invitation and demands of discipleship beyond characters in the story.[1] The movement from characters in the plotted story to the implied reader is especially suggested by the use of (1) 'Whoever' type statements, and (2) statements about 'many' and 'all'. Jesus' teaching is generalized by these expressions so that the implied reader is also challenged to adopt the attitudes and behavior which are being urged upon Jesus' listeners.

The 'whoever' type of statement is the more prevalent form of these addresses to the implied reader in Matthew.[2] Such

1 See Malbon, 'Disciples/Crowds/Whoever', pp. 124-26. Prince, 'Introduction', p. 13, lists this as one of the signs of a narratee.
2 'Whoever' statements are formed by a variety of different grammatical constructions: (1) by substantival participles (frequently used in conjunction with πας), (2) by the definite relative pronoun ὅς or the

statements occur frequently throughout the entirety of Jesus' ministry, challenging the hearers to obedience and action. The following sayings are only a sample: 'Whoever relaxes the least of these commandments' (5.19), 'no one is able to serve two masters' (6.24), 'every one who hears these words of mine' (7.24, 26), 'he who does not take up his cross and follow me' (10.38), 'whoever gives to one of these little ones a cup of cold water' (10.42), 'he who has ears to hear' (11.15; 13.9, 43), 'whoever does the will of the Father' (12.50), 'if any man would come after me' (16.24), 'whoever humbles himself like this child' (18.4), 'whoever would be great among you' (20.26), 'all who take the sword' (26.52).[1] Characters in the story are certainly included in the 'whoever' of Jesus' teaching, but so is the implied reader. Jesus' promise in 19.29 that every one who has left house and family will receive a hundredfold thus echoes Peter's earlier statement 'we have left everything and followed you' (19.27), for example, but the implied reader will recognize that others besides the disciples have also made similar sacrifices for the sake of Jesus' name.

Statements by Jesus to characters in the story that center on the words 'many' (πολλοί) and 'all' (πᾶς) are not as numerous, but they too point to the implied reader: Jesus has come to give his life as a ransom and pour out his blood for many (20.28; 26.28), many will come from east and west in the Kingdom of Heaven (8.11), many that are first will be last, and the last first (19.30), many are called (22.14), the Son of Man will gather all nations for judgment (25.32), the disciples are to make disciples of all nations (28.19).[2] Statements such as

---

indefinite relative ὅστις (both often appear with ἄν or ἐάν transforming a relative clause into a conditional clause which makes a general assertion: see Blass, DeBrunner and Funk, *Grammar*, §380), (3) by indefinite pronominal adjectives such as οὐδείς, and 4) by the use of τίς as a relative pronoun. According to Gundry, *Matthew*, pp. 81, 85, 133, 646, πᾶς and the expression ὅσ/ὅστις ἀνεάν are characteristic of Matthew's diction. Cf. Goulder, *Midrash*, p. 482, who also lists ὅστις as characteristic of Matthew's vocabulary.

1 Other examples not cited are 5.21, 22, 28, 32, 39, 41; 7.8, 21; 9.12, 10.22, 31f., 37f., 40f.; 11.6, 11, 27f.; 12.30, 32; 13.12, 52; 16.25; 18.5, 6; 19.9, 12, 29; 23.11; 24.13, 36; 25.29.

2 We have failed to mention the numerous occurrences of πᾶς with

Jesus' invitation for 'all who labor and are heavy-laden' (11.28) open up the story for a larger group than the disciples (i.e. the implied readers) to learn from Jesus and obey him as he interprets God's will through his teaching.

The internal organization of Jesus' teaching in Matthew further contributes to the narrative's structure of appeal for the implied reader. Not only does the arrangement of Jesus' teaching in five great discourses help create a sense of immediacy and presentness as we saw in the previous chapter, but the teaching is also arranged in such a way that the final part of each discourse generically points beyond the discourse's immediate narrative setting to address 'whoever' would be a disciple.[1] The Sermon on the Mount thus concludes with the description of a judgment (7.21-23) on people who have been prophesying and performing miracles in Jesus' name—activities which suggest the post-Easter development of the church and its worship—and with a parable (7.24-27). These pericopae function to exhort 'everyone' to act upon what Jesus has just finished teaching in the Sermon.

The last half of the mission discourse (10.26-42) likewise sets out conditions of discipleship in more general terms than are found in the first half.[2] Included in this part of the discourse are many of the 'whoever' type statements which point

participles or pronouns, although many of the references have been cited above, which assign a generic meaning to the participle or pronoun.

1 Patte, *Matthew*, pp. 153-54, points this out in connection with the so-called mission discourse, but this phenomenon is not limited to this one discourse. See Patte's comments on the Sermon on the Mount (p. 63), where he argues that 5.3-10 and 7.21-27 serve the function of establishing the 'I-you' relationship of the discourse so that readers will identify themselves as its addressees. Cf. James P. Martin, 'The Church in Matthew', *Int* 29 (1975), p. 43, who argues that 'we have access to the church of Matthew largely through the discourses'.

2 Cf. David L. Barr, *New Testament Story: An Introduction* (Belmont, CA: Wadworth, 1987), p. 190, who writes that the 'second half of the discourse is clearly "Christian"; it depends on the post Easter reflection on the meaning of Jesus for the church'. We must demur from Barr's outline of the discourse, however. The mid-point occurs at 10.24-25 rather than 10.26-31 as he suggests.

to the implied reader. The concluding series of logia (vv. 40-42) returns more specifically to the theme of mission, but the thrust of the sayings is different from the earlier section on receiving travelling missionaries (10.11-14). The instructions at the end of the discourse appear to be directed to those who will be offering hospitality to the itinerant missionaries and thus also point beyond the twelve disciples as the sole recipients of the discourse.[1] Furthermore, the open-ended nature of this discourse serves to engage the implied reader. Matthew shows no apparent interest in the disciples' mission as an event in Jesus' ministry, since he does not record their departure or return. His interest lies rather in Jesus' instructions with a view to the on-going mission of the church.[2]

In the parable discourse of chapter 13 the implied reader is not only the recipient of Jesus' parables, but also observes both the movement between different audiences in the discourse and the narrator's comments in stitching the various parts together. When Jesus asks his final question (13.51), 'Have you understood all these things?', he addresses it to both the disciples and the implied reader as the final parable shows (v. 52). The subject for this parable is no longer the Kingdom of Heaven but 'a scribe trained for the Kingdom of Heaven'. The

---

1	This shift in perspective does not necessitate a change of audience to the crowd in 10.42, as some have proposed (contra Edwards, *Matthew's Story*, p. 36). First, there is no textual basis for such a shift. Second, the narrator does not place the reader in the crowd throughout the Gospel as Edwards suggests. Third, the tendency to open up the conclusion of the discourses to include the implied reader in addresses to characters in the plotted story—without a corresponding shift in audience—is consistently carried out throughout the Gospel. Patte, *Matthew*, pp. 156-57, handles the shift in perspective by proposing the presence of two types of disciples in the story: ideal disciples who are described in Jesus' teaching and actual disciples who both carry out the mission and receive the 'little ones'. Patte's interpretation will be discussed in more depth when we discuss the implied reader and the disciples.

2	The open-ended nature of the mission discourse is widely recognized. See Brown, 'Mission to Israel', pp. 75ff.; F.W. Beare, 'The Mission of the Disciples and the Mission Charge: Mt. 10 and Parallels', *JBL* 89 (1970), p. 1-13; Luz, 'Disciples', pp. 99-101.

discourse thus concludes by focusing on what someone is like who follows and understands the Kingdom, and it is directed to the implied reader who has followed the action of the discourse as well as to the disciples.[1]

The fourth discourse is often referred to as the community or ecclesiastical discourse because of the way in which many of the sayings point beyond Jesus' ministry to the life of the post-Easter Christian community.[2] Matthew closes this discourse with a saying congruent both with its theme and with his method of structuring the discourses generally. A conclusion is appended to the parable of the unforgiving servant which makes the story an allegory that warns how God will deal with 'every one' who does not forgive (18.35).[3]

Finally, Matthew concludes the eschatological discourse with a series of sayings and parables which highlight the indeterminacy of the period before the parousia and exhort the hearers to be ready for the End (24.32-25.46). Since the disciples and the implied reader share the same indeterminate period between the resurrection and parousia, the exhortations for watchfulness are relevant for both. The fact that the scene of the last judgment (25.31-46) includes 'all the nations' emphasizes the comprehensiveness of Jesus' teaching. It now becomes clear that the referent of the servants and maidens in the preceding parables should not be limited to a small and closed group of disciples but widened to include all who hear the Gospel, that is to say, the implied readers (cf. 24.14 and the inclusive language used).[4]

The rhetorical stragtegy of using inclusive terms in the final sections of Jesus' great teaching discourses is also found in Matthew's conclusion to the Gospel. The final scene (28.16-20) points beyond the characters in the plotted story and opens up

1 See the previous chapter for a more thorough discussion of the ways in which the implied reader is involved by the rhetoric of this discourse.
2 See Thompson, *Matthew's Advice*, for a detailed study of chapter 18.
3 See Bernard Brandon Scott, 'The King's Accounting: Matthew 18.23-34', *JBL* 104 (1985), pp. 429-31.
4 Patte, *Matthew*, p. 348. See chapter 3 for a more thorough discussion of the way Matthew's eschatological discourse entangles the implied reader.

the whole Gospel to the implied reader by serving as a beginning as well as an ending. As the narrator relates the final
scene to the implied reader, the Gospel closes with dialogue
between Jesus and the disciples. In the Great Commission the
narrator and implied reader are placed in the same temporal
position as the disciples; the time of mission following the resurrection and prior to the comsummation of the age. The
promise of Jesus' presence with the disciples, 'always, until the
close of the age', is thus equally applicable to the implied
reader. Moreover, the inclusive scope of Jesus' commission,
'make disciples of all nations', appeals to the implied reader.
This command is interpreted, however, with reference to the
teaching of the earthly Jesus, as the phrase 'teaching them to
observe all that I have commanded you' (28.20) plainly
shows.[1]

With this backward glance at all Jesus has taught, the disciples and the implied reader are challenged to accept Jesus'
call and be obedient to his teaching as it has been narrated in
the Gospel.[2] Matthew 28.16-20 thus serves as an ending by
achieving literary closure for the Gospel.[3] Jesus' obedience as

1 The aorist ἐνετειλάμην unambiguously looks back at the teaching of
   the earthly Jesus. See Günther Bornkamm, 'The Risen Lord and
   the Earthly Jesus: Matthew 28.16-20', in *The Future of our Religious Past*, ed. J.M. Robinson (London: SCM, 1971), pp. 223-24, and
   Luz, 'Disciples', pp. 109, 112-13.
2 The primary affective response that the conclusion of Matthew's
   narrative seeks to produce in actual readers is therefore obedience
   to Jesus—rather than 'worship' (28.17) and 'confidence' (28.20) as
   Frank Matera argues ('Plot of Matthew's Gospel', p. 242). This is
   not intended to deny, however, that worship and confidence are
   proper responses for Matthew. Rather, the emphasis does not seem
   to be placed on these responses in our reading of the narrative. The
   commission should also not be narrowly conceived of as a mere
   mission command. It is directed to the overall life of the church as
   others have pointed out, and thus shares in the wider appeal to the
   implied reader for which we have been arguing. See the discussions
   of Bornkamm, 'Risen Lord', p. 222f.; Donaldson, *Jesus on the
   Mountain*, p. 182.
3 Closure is not simply the way a narrative ends. Norman Petersen
   defines it as 'the sense of a literary ending derived from the satisfaction of textually generated expectation' ('When is an End not the

Son, which led him to the cross, is vindicated by God the Father in resurrection and exaltation. The universal authority with which Jesus was tempted in the wilderness (4.1-11) is given him by God. The world-wide mission which had been foreshadowed and alluded to throughout the Gospel (2.1-11; 4.15-16; 5.14; 8.11; 10.18; 13.38; 15.21-28; 24.14; 26.13) is now explicitly commanded. Jesus' promise of his presence repeats what the narrator has told the implied reader at the outset of the story—Jesus is God with us (1.23)—and forms an inclusion which encompasses the Gospel.

The convergence of the narrator's and Jesus' speech that is accomplished by this inclusio indicates that the implied reader is the recipient of Jesus' words on the mountain as well as the eleven disciples.[1] This address is a challenge for the implied reader to obey Jesus' teaching, and so the final scene also functions as a beginning; the beginning of the unnarrated story of the church's life in the time between the resurrection and parousia, lived in the presence of the resurrected Jesus and in obedience to his teaching.[2] Instead of framing the nar-

---

End?', p. 152). See Otto Michel, 'The Conclusion of Matthew's Gospel', in *Matthew*, ed. Stanton, pp. 35ff.; Bauer, *Structure of Matthew's Gospel*, pp. 115-27; Donaldson, *Jesus on the Mountain*, pp. 188-90; Goulder, *Midrash*, p. 449; Matera, 'Plot', pp. 241ff.; Lohr, 'Oral Techniques', p. 410, for discussions of the way this final scene serves as a summary and climax for the Gospel. Michel even writes that 'it is sufficient to say that the whole Gospel was written under this theological premise of Matt. 28.18-20'.

1 Cf. Burnett, 'Prolegomenon', p. 102.

2 J.L. Magness, *Sense and Absence: Structure and Suspension in the Ending of Mark's Gospel* (Semeia Studies; Atlanta: Scholars Press, 1986), p. 19, has written that 'the endings we read or sense are both endings and beginnings of the on-going but narrated story or of our re-reading of the fore-going story'. See pp. 81-82 for Magness's interpretation of Matthew's ending. He treats Matthew's conclusion as an omitted ending by focusing on the non-narration of Jesus' ascension. If one emphasizes Jesus' words on the other hand, as we have done, Matthew's final scene can be seen as an open-ended conclusion which draws together the plot themes of the Gospel and implies the on-going life of the church. Matera, 'Plot', p. 252 also describes the great commission as a beginning. Cf. White, *Metahistory*, pp. 6-7, for a discussion of how the same event can serve as a

rative with a conclusion which adopts a position external to the narrative in order to facilitate the reader's departure from the narrative world, Matthew closes his Gospel with open-ended dialogue which also challenges the implied reader.[1] Although the story of the church's mission is not narrated in the Gospel, the open-ended nature of the ending with the Great Commission and the promise of Jesus' presence carries actual readers forward from the text's conclusion into their own present. Here they must try to complete this story from their own experiences, but in a way which is in harmony with the textual structures and ideological point of view of the plotted story. In Matthew this means that actual readers are challenged to accept Jesus and be obedient to his teaching as the expression and interpretation of God's will. In short, actual readers are to assume the role of the implied reader.[2]

If, as we have argued, obedience to Jesus' teaching is one of the attitudes which the Matthean implied author seeks to

different element in many different historical stories. For example, the ascension can serve as the conclusion to the story of Jesus' ministry in Luke 24 while at the same time functioning as the beginning of the story of the church's mission in Acts 1. See Tannehill, *Unity of Luke-Acts*, pp. 298-301, Mikeal C. Parsons, *The Departure of Jesus in Luke-Acts. The Ascension Narratives in Context* (JSNT Supplement Series 21; Sheffield: JSOT Press, 1987), pp. 72-113, 191-99, for discussions of closure and openness in the conclusion of Luke.

1 See Uspensky, *Poetics*, pp. 137-40, 146-51, for a discussion of the literary technique of framing. He argues that by adopting a point of view which is external to the narrated events, an author can assist a reader to make the transitions back and fourth from real world to represented narrated world. Some of the literary techniques or conventions frequently used to frame narrative are found in the conclusion to other Gospels. John, for example, refers to the narrator in the first person and the reader in the second person (Jn 20.31; 21.24-25; cf. 1.14, 16), and Luke uses a silent scene in the ascension which creates the impression that the narrator is an observer (Lk. 24.50-52; cf. Lk. 1.1-4, where first and second person pronouns are also used). Cf. Culpepper, *Anatomy*, p. 46, Tannehill, *Unity of Luke-Acts*, p. 300. Matthew's conclusion using dialogue thus contributes to the 'inclusive' nature of the Gospel.

2 Cf. Anderson, 'Gender and Reading', pp. 23-24.

inculcate in actual readers, then those characters in the Gospel who hear Jesus' teaching should contribute to the portrait of the implied reader, for they are the ones who have the opportunity to respond in a positive way to Jesus in the narrative world. Actual readers who try to assume the role of the implied reader in the Gospel can learn from, and perhaps even imitate, those who are obedient to Jesus in the plotted story. Since the disciples are the primary character group in Matthew who respond positively to Jesus and receive his teaching, we turn now to examine their contribution in defining and shaping the role of the implied reader.

b. *Disciples*. What Robert Tannehill has pointed out in a study of Mark is also true of Matthew; readers would identify more easily and readily with characters who not only embody positive attributes, but who also share the readers' position.[1] Assuming the intended audience of the Gospel were Christians, actual readers would identify with the disciples as the primary characters in the Gospel who respond to Jesus' call to follow him and receive his teaching. The disciples have thus often been understood to be the means whereby the readers of Matthew's community come to be included in the plotted story of the earthly Jesus. Features such as the portrayal of the disciples with post-Easter attributes like understanding, or such as their post-Easter type of confessions of Jesus as Lord and Son of God have been noted to support this interpretation.[2]

---

1 Tannehill, 'Disciples in Mark', p. 392. Cf. Augustine Stock, *Call to Discipleship: A Literary Study of Mark's Gospel* (Wilmington, Del: Michael Glazier, 1982), p. 108, who also describes the disciples' contribution to the inclusive nature of Mark's story. This tendency might even be greater in Matthew than in Mark because of the way Matthew concludes his Gospel with the disciples reconciled to Jesus.

2 See Barth, *TIM*, pp. 105-25, for example, for the evidence of how Matthew's portrayal of the disciples is more sympathetic than Mark's, and Held. *TIM*, pp. 265-75, who has similarly described Matthew's adaptation of the miracle stories in order to fit the experiences of the post-Easter church. Luz's essay 'Disciples', pp. 98-128, is probably the best and most thorough statement for interpreting the disciples in Matthew as 'transparent' for the Matthean

Although there can be little doubt that Matthew's portrayal of the disciples in this manner has helped actual readers to identify with the disciples and to respond to Jesus' call for discipleship, it remains true that discussions of whether 'the disciples' are limited to the Twelve and of how they are transparent for the later church have not always clearly distinguished between the disciples as a character group in the plotted story and the reader responses elicited by the Gospel.[1] It seems to be assumed that if actual readers are to respond to the demands of the Gospel and take on the role of the implied reader, they must do so by assuming the role of the disciples in Matthew. This assumption overlooks the fact, however, that the implied reader rather than the character group 'the disciples' represents the embodiment of the response which the implied author was seeking, and the implied reader is distinct from the disciples as characters in the plotted story, as we shall see.

Jack Kingsbury has argued, for example, that Matthew points beyond the experiences of the disciples in the plotted story to the experiences of the post-Easter church by highlighting Jesus' close association with the disciples. The evangelist accomplishes this by his use of the preposition μετά which, when used with the genitive case, denotes accompaniment. In contrast to Mark, Matthew uses this preposition to restrict the association of Jesus almost exlusively to the circle of the disciples. Kingsbury argues that those who have the

community. Cf. Mark Sheridan, 'Disciples and Discipleship in Matthew and Luke', *BThB* 3 (1973), pp. 241-51, Kingsbury, *Matthew 13*, pp. 40-42, *idem*, 'Verb *Akolouthein*', pp. 56-73, for similar views. The opposing viewpoint is expressed by Strecker, *Weg*, pp. 191ff., and van Tilborg, *Jewish Leaders*, pp. 112ff., who is of the opinion that 'according to Matthew the Christian is not a μαθητὴς Ἰησοῦ' because his 'concept οἱ μαθηταὶ Ἰησοῦ embraces only the historical group of the δώδεκα'.

1 Anderson, 'Gender and Reading', pp. 20ff., perceptively notes that the answer to the question of whether women and other marginal characters in Matthew should be considered disciples is strongly influenced by whether different interpreters 'define discipleship as membership in the character group or the proper relationship to Jesus'. Senior, *Passion of Jesus*, p. 177, for example, describes some of the minor characters in the passion story as '"unexpected" disciples' because they respond positively to Jesus.

privilege of Jesus' company after the resurrection comprise the church (cf. 16.18; 18.20; 28.20). He thus concludes that Matthew uses the concept of 'being with Jesus' to assert theologically 'the truth that the church worships and carries out its ministry to the close of the age in the presence and on the authority of the exalted Son of God, through whom God exercises his gracious, saving rule' (cf. 1.23).[1]

We do not wish to dispute Kingsbury's emphasis on the importance for Matthew of the resurrected Jesus' presence in the ongoing life and ministry of the church, but his exegesis of Matthew's use of μετά to arrive at this conclusion appears to be an example of a tendency in redaction criticism to build theological edifices on the relatively small foundation of single words or minor editorial activity by an evangelist. Kingsbury is correct to note Matthew's redactional changes in Mark's use of μετά, but the occurrences of μετά in conjunction with Jesus and his disciples are not that numerous, and the majority of them are found in the latter chapters of the Gospel.[2] It seems odd that Matthew would have waited until the passion narrative to use μετά with the disciples, had it been his intention to stress their accompaniment with Jesus by means of this preposition.[3] If the preposition had been used more frequently throughout the entirety of the Gospel, particularly in those sections when Jesus is teaching, then Kingsbury's claim that this literary device is the bearer of a theological truth might be

---

1 Kingsbury, *Matthew*, pp. 30ff. and *idem Matthew as Story*, pp. 105-106. Kingsbury is drawing upon the work of Frankemölle (*Jawhebund*, ch. 1), who highlights Matthew's use of the concept of 'being with Jesus' in conjunction with his own thesis that Matthew is developing a 'covenant theology' on the basis of the Deuteronomist and Chronicler.

2 The disciples are referred to in 10 of the 14 cases cited by Kingsbury as examples of Matthew's use of μετά to denote accompaniment with Jesus. Yet none of these references is found before the passion narratives (26.18, 20, 29, 36, 38, 40, 51, 69, 71; 28.20). In other passages cited by Kingsbury to support his claims about the disciples the preposition is not even used (cf. 16.21; 18.20; 20.17-19).

3 This is especially true if Luz is correct that the disciples function as 'ear-witnesses' in Matthew ('Disciples', pp. 102-105). It would therefore be important that the disciples are 'with' Jesus so they can hear and understand Jesus' teaching.

more convincing.

Moreover, a narrative analysis of Matthew clearly reveals the presence of information and teaching which the evangelist communicates to his readers/church but which is not available to the disciples even though they are 'with' Jesus. For example, the implied reader rather than the disciples is the recipient of the commentary and exposition at the beginning of the Gospel that reveals Jesus' identity and provides the interpretive framework necessary for correctly understanding the Gospel. The implied reader is also the beneficiary of the numerous Old Testament fulfillment quotations from the narrator. In other cases, the disciples are absent from plotted events in the story and so miss out on the information communicated in these incidents. In the baptism and temptation stories (3.13-4.11) as well as in Gethsemane (26.39ff.), Matthew establishes Jesus as the Son who is completely obedient to God's will, and yet the disciples are not privy to the struggle Jesus faces as he seeks to fulfill God's will: in these situations, it is the implied reader alone who has privileged access to Jesus.[1] Likewise, the disciples are apparently absent from the scene in chapter 11 when Jesus responds to the questions of the messengers from John the Baptist, pronounces his woes on the unrepentant cities, offers his hymn of jubilation to God (vv. 25-27) and holds out an invitation to the heavy-laden (vv. 28-30).[2] The superiority of

---

1 See Bauer, *Structure of Matthew's Gospel*, pp. 60-62, for a discussion of how Matthew emphasizes Jesus' obedience to God in these incidents.

2 Stanton ('Matthew 11.28-30', pp. 6-7) believes that Jesus' invitation is addressed to the disciples rather than the crowds because of the costly nature of discipleship which is portrayed in chapter 10. Celia Deutsch, *Hidden Wisdom and the Easy Yoke: Wisdom, Torah and Discipleship in Matthew 11.25-30* (JSNT Supplement Series 18; Sheffield: JSOT Press, 1987), pp. 40ff., and Patte, *Matthew*, pp. 165-66, argue on the other hand that the invitation is issued to the crowds who are heavy-laden because of the religious leaders of Israel. The addressees are in fact not specified, but the inclusive language used in the invitation points beyond any single character group in the narrative to the implied reader who is also challenged by Jesus' call. One is thus not reduced to identifying 'the weary and heavy-laden' with the alternatives of either disciples or crowds.

the implied reader to the disciples because of this knowledge militates against a simple identification of implied reader and disciple. The implied reader is 'with' Jesus and becomes the recipient of all the rhetoric of the Gospel—which is aimed at influencing actual readers—in a way that is simply not available to the disciples as characters in the plotted story.

The assertion that the disciples disclose for the church the proper response to Jesus because they are 'with Jesus' during his earthly ministry as it is recounted in the Gospel is thus inadequate, because it ultimately reduces both the narrative rhetoric meant to influence readers and the range of values and attitudes that the evangelist wishes his readers to adopt. If the implied reader is identified with the character group the disciples, only those values and attitudes which are displayed by the disciples in the plotted story become exemplary for the actual readers.[1] While the disciples are the primary character group who generally interact positively with Jesus, others also display traits which are approved by the implied author and Jesus. Joseph is obedient to God throughout the birth and infancy stories, for example, and minor characters such as a Roman centurion (8.5f.) or Canaanite woman (15.21f.) display faith.[2] Although these characters and others like them never become members of the character group 'the disciples', the stance they take in relationship to Jesus is instructive for

Stanton's interpretation is an example of the tendency to confuse the disciples as a character group with the way in which a reader or listener responds to the Gospel. The disciples, as a character group in the plotted story, are absent from the scene when Jesus offers this invitation, but it is certainly directed to those who respond positively in obedience to Jesus. Cf. Keegan, *Interpreting the Bible*, pp. 124-25, who discusses this passage from the perspective of the implied reader.

1 Anderson, 'Gender and Reading', p. 24 writes that 'the superiority of the implied reader to all character groups also gives the lie to any interpretation which insists certain readers must identify with certain character groups'.

2 See Anderson, 'Gender and Reading', and Kingsbury, *Matthew as Story*, pp. 25-27. Kingsbury notes that most of the minor characters in Matthew are exemplary figures displaying 'traits that reflect the system of values which both Jesus and Matthew as narrator advocate'.

the implied reader insofar as they embody aspects of discipleship when they respond positively to God or to Jesus. The positive responses of these minor charcters are in fact often contrasted with the shortcomings of the disciples. The implied
reader is therefore called to stand with the implied author and
Jesus and evaluate all characters, even the disciples,
according to the implied author's ideological criterion of
whether they accept Jesus and his teaching.[1]

The necessity for distinguishing the implied reader from the
disciples as a character group becomes visible in the
conflicting character traits with which the disciples are
portrayed. They respond to Jesus' call to follow, but they are
also inconsistent in their obedience, and they frequently fail to
live up to Jesus' standards.[2] Daniel Patte has proposed that we
deal with the imperfections of the disciples as a character
group in Matthew by making a distinction between the
'actual' disciples and the 'ideal' disciples described in Jesus'
teaching.[3] It is thus the 'less-than-perfect' actual disciples who
receive the responsibility to 'make disciples of all nations'
(28.19), but they are to discharge this commission by calling
people to become the 'ideal' disciples of Jesus' teaching.
Although Patte's concept of an 'ideal disciple' handles the
inability of those Jesus calls to live up to his standards, there is
no textual basis for distinguishing between two 'types' of
disciples.[4] The 'ideal disciple' should therefore be seen as a

1 Kingsbury, *Matthew as Story*, p. 13, recognizes this as he writes that
'because the disciples possess conflicting traits, the reader is
invited, depending on the attitude Matthew as narrator or Jesus
takes towards them on any given occasion, to identify with them or
to distance himself or herself from them'. At other times, however,
Kingsbury seems to disregard the difficulties in judging character
traits when the reader is too closely identified with the disciples as a
character group in the plotted story.

2 Despite the fact that Matthew has generally improved Mark's portrayal of the disciples, he also describes them negatively, as has
been frequently noted. See Richard Edwards' essay 'Uncertain
Faith' for a summary of the ambiguities in Matthew's description of
the disciples from a reader-response perspective.

3 See Patte, *Matthew*, pp. 119, 136, 391ff., and 397, for example.

4 Patte is also ambiguous in his use of the concept of ideal disciples—
which leads to other problems. On the one hand, he defines them as

version of the implied reader. The implied reader fully accepts and understands the implied author's ideological point of view, which in Matthew—as we earlier argued—is tantamount to accepting Jesus' teaching. But the implied reader is furthermore able to understand and appreciate all the narrative rhetoric which is used in the Gospel, and is thus a more encompassing concept than an 'ideal disciple' who is merely extrapolated from Jesus' teaching.

The disciples as a character group in the plotted story of the Gospel must therefore not be seen as a cipher for the members of Matthew's church, for the Matthean implied reader is an entity distinct from the disciples. The disciples neither embody all the values and norms commended by the implied author, nor do they know everything about Jesus which would help the Matthean church members and other actual readers respond properly to Jesus.[1] The positive role of the disciples in the narrative rhetoric of Matthew will be explored later in the

the disciples described in Jesus' teaching, and contrasts them with the shortcomings of actual disciples who answer Jesus' call. On the other hand, the women who minister to Jesus at his crucifixion are identified as ideal disciples because of their actions (*Matthew*, pp. 391ff.). If one operates by the latter definition, however, many of the minor characters in Matthew should also be seen as 'ideal disciples' because they too exhibit character traits commended by the implied author. Kingsbury (*Matthew as Story*, pp. 25-27) has pointed out that these characters usually possess only one character trait, and this single trait hardly qualifies a character for discipleship. If one postulates an implied reader, however, the positive function of these minor characters can be accounted for in the Gospel's narrative rhetoric. The implied reader will recognize the character trait which is being commended and incorporate it into the composite system of values being advocated. Cf. Senior, *Passion of Jesus*, p. 177, who describes Matthew's use of minor characters as examples—often in contrast to the flawed response or rejection of more major characters such as the disciples—as 'an effective dramatic ploy'.

1 Anderson, 'Gender and Reading', pp. 23-24, has an excellent discussion of this point in relationship to gender issues. When discipleship is not equated with membership in a character group in the plotted story of the Gospel, women can judge some of 'the partriarchal assumptions implicit in their ideological viewpoints'.

chapter when we consider the implied reader from the perspective of the stance and actions readers take when reading
Matthew. We will now examine the implied reader's relationship to one final character group in Matthew: the Jewish leaders.[1]

c. *The Jewish leaders.* The Jewish leaders in Matthew comprise a monolothic front opposed to Jesus and uniformly characterized in negative terms.[2] They reject Jesus and his teaching, and thus the implied author's ideological point of view, as

1 *Ibid.*, pp. 10-11. She has identified 5 major character groups in
  Matthew: the Jewish leaders, the disciples, the crowds, the suppli-
  cants, and the Gentiles. We have treated here categories of the sup-
  plicants and Gentiles in our discussion of minor characters who
  exhibit positive character traits. The characterization of the crowds
  is not completely negative as it is with the Jewish leaders, even
  though the crowds eventually side with the leaders at Jesus' crucifixion. Neither are they followers of Jesus with positive traits, however. Like all the character groups, their response to Jesus is compared and contrasted with that of others, and the implied reader is
  invited to judge them accordingly. The contrast between the crowds
  and the Jewish leaders highlights the perversity and opposition of
  the leaders to Jesus.

2 The character group 'Jewish leaders' is composed of the scribes,
  Pharisees, Sadducess, elders and chief priests. The homogeneity of
  this group in Matthew does not accurately reflect the historical situation of Jesus' day, as many have pointed out. See Tilborg, *Jewish
  Leaders*, pp. 1-6, and Walker, *Heilsgeschichte*, pp. 11-33, for example. One must also be careful about seeing the Jewish leaders as
  representatives of the Judaism of Matthew's own day. Their portrayal in Matthew is a good example of the way narratives may
  require readers willingly to suspend their disbelief in order to
  accept the story on its own terms and enter into its narrative world.
  For the implied reader of Matthew, the various sects of Judaism
  exist in the way described in the Gospel. Cf. Rabinowitz, 'Truth in
  Fiction', pp. 127-33, for a discussion of the theoretical basis of such
  an audience in narrative. See Lategan, 'Unresolved Methodological
  Issues', pp. 18-25, and Keegan, *Interpreting the Bible*, pp. 113-15,
  127-29, for its application when interpreting Matthew. Cf. Kingsbury, *Matthew as Story*, pp. 17-24, *idem*, 'The Developing Conflict
  between Jesus and the Jewish Leaders', for a discussion of the Jewish leaders' characterization in Matthew.

we have seen in earlier chapters. By their words and deeds, and by the narrator's commentary, the implied reader is led to turn away from the Jewish leaders and the value system they espouse. The repudiation of the Jewish leaders and their point of view, however, still contributes to the formation and education of the implied reader. First, their rejection of Jesus is instructive insofar as their opposition provides the implied reader with a negative example.[1] Many of the character traits they exhibit are antithetical to the value system and virtues which Jesus calls his followers to display and which fully characterize his own life. The woes against the scribes and Pharisees in Mt. 23 are representative of the contrasts between the Jewish leaders and Jesus' ideological point of view. The Jewish leaders do not practice what they preach, and they perform acts of piety ostentatiously in order to be praised by others (23.3-5; cf. 6.1-6; 16-18). As religious leaders of Israel, they shut entry into the Kingdom instead of providing access to it (23.13-15). They display blindness about the Law (cf. 15.1-10), their teaching on oaths distorts the meaning of sacred things (23.16-22), and the weightier matters of the Law are neglected while their observance of insignificant things is scrupulous (23.23-24; cf. 12.1-8). The Jewish leaders may thus appear outwardly righteous, but inwardly they are full of hypocrisy and lawlessness (23.27-28). In short, they fail to do the will of God.[2]

Jesus, on the other hand, is fully obedient to the will of God, and Matthew is at pains to show that Jesus lives what he preaches. He does not have divided loyalty to God like the hypocritical Jewish leaders, but is single-hearted in his devotion. This single-heartedness is seen in the baptism, temptation,

---

1 Senior, *Passion of Jesus*, p. 36, writes that 'one of the functions of the opponents is to portray, in negative terms, the meaning of authentic discipleship'. Cf. Bauer, *Structure of Matthew's Gospel*, pp. 65-71.

2 David Hill, 'False Prophets and Charismatics: Structure and Interpretation in Matthew 7.15-23', *Bib* 57 (1976), pp. 337-38, argues that the nomistic significance of ἀνομία in Mathew has been 'greatly exaggerated'. It simply denotes not doing the will of God (cf. 7.21ff.; 13.41). Cf. Kingsbury, *Matthew as Story*, p. 19.

and Gethsemane stories.[1] Entry into the Kingdom is not
barred by Jesus as it is by the Jewish leaders, but rather its
arrival is tied up with Jesus' ministry (4.17; 12.28). He does not
neglect mercy and justice in his ministry (12.1-12; 15-21), but
epitomizes what it means to love God with heart, soul and
mind, and to love neighbor as oneself (22.37-40).[2] Jesus
moreover demands the same virtues of his followers. They too
are to be perfect (5.48) and obedient to God's will (cf. 7.21f.;
12.46-50). In contrast to behavior of the Jewish leaders, Jesus'
disciples are warned against abusing oaths (5.33-37) and
exhorted to practice their acts of piety secretly before God (6.1-
6; 16.18).[3]

This rather selective sampling of the antithetical pairing
between the value systems espoused by Jesus and the Jewish
leaders demonstrates how the Jewish leaders can instruct the
implied reader by way of negative example. Since so many of
their vices are the polar opposites of the virtues enacted and
taught by Jesus, his positive voicing of the implied author's
ideological point of view is reinforced by the negative example
of his opponents. Their opposition to Jesus and his teaching
furthermore alerts the implied reader to the opposition and
costs he or she may face in following Jesus (cf. 5.11-12; 10.16-
25, 34-39; 16.24-27).[4]

Another way in which the Jewish leaders contribute to the
formation and education of the Matthean implied reader is

1 Guelich (*Sermon on the Mount*, pp. 278ff.) argues that
'righteousness' is the opposite of hypocrisy in Matthew, whereas
Kingsbury (*Matthew as Story*, p. 19) argues that it is 'perfection'. In
both interpretations, however, Jesus still exemplifies the virtue
which is opposite to the Jewish leaders and demands the same attitude and behavior of his followers.

2 See Birger Gerhardsson, 'The Hermeneutic Program In Matthew
22.37-40', in *Jews, Greeks and Christians: Religious Cultures in
Late Antiquity*, ed. Hamerton-Kelly and R. Scroggs (Leiden: Brill,
1976), pp. 145-49.

3 Garland, *Matthew 23*, p. 123, argues that Matthew's use of the concept of hypocrisy portrays the Jewish leaders as the antithesis of the
disciples (cf. 24.51). Our interest lies not so much in the two groups
as characters in the plotted story, as in the different ideological
point of view they voice.

4 Senior, *Passion of Jesus*, pp. 36-37.

suggested by Matthew's use of irony.[1] Gail O'Day offers a simple working definition of irony as 'that specific rhetorical figure or more encompassing general literary mode in which two contradictory or conflicting meanings are held together in one image or expression'.[2] Irony is thus a 'two-story' phenomenon, in which an apparent meaning below is held in tension with another perspective above which is somehow incongruous or contradictory to the lower level.[3] The victim of the irony is usually unaware of the higher meaning, and an intimacy is created between implied reader and implied author when they share in the irony. The ironies in Matthew are 'stable' because they are based on a vision of the truth that can be retrieved,[4] and 'corrective' because the higher perspective exposes and invalidates the lower.[5]

The Jewish leaders are the primary victims of irony in Matthew and therefore the spokesmen for the lower level point of view that is rejected. Their inability to recognize Jesus sets up much of the irony of the Gospel. The implied reader, on the other hand, is informed of Jesus' identity through the genealogy, the birth and infancy stories, the Old Testament fulfillment quotations, and the baptismal story,[6] and this

1 Irony is widely recognized as a trait in John. See Paul D. Duke, *Irony in the Fourth Gospel* (Atlanta: John Knox, 1985); Gail R. O'Day, *Revelation in the Fourth Gospel: Narrative Mode and Theological Claim* (Philadelphia: Fortress, 1986); Culpepper, *Anatomy*, pp. 165-80, for recent discussions of the use of irony in the fourth Gospel. In the Synoptic Gospels irony figures most prominently in the passion narratives. See Senior, *Passion of Jesus*, for comments on Matthew's use of irony.

2 Gail R. O'Day, 'Narrative Mode and Theological Claim: A Study in the Fourth Gospel', *JBL* 105 (1986), p. 663. See D.C. Muecke, *The Compass of Irony* (London: Methuen, 1969), and Wayne Booth, *A Rhetoric of Irony* (Chicago: University of Chicago Press, 1974), for the most thorough recent discussions of irony.

3 Booth, *Irony*, pp. 36-39. Cf. Uspensky, *Poetics*, p. 103, who writes that 'irony occurs when we speak from one point of view, but make an evaluation from another point of view'.

4 Booth, *Irony*, pp. 5-6.

5 Muecke, *Irony*, p. 23.

6 J.D. Kingsbury, 'The Parable of the Wicked husbandmen and the Secret of Jesus' Divine Sonship in Matthew', *JBL* 105 (1986), pp. 647-

knowledge at the outset provides the foundation for the implied author to communicate his point of view over the heads of the characters in the plotted story.[1] Irony is thus already present in the story of the magi in chapter 2. Gentiles must go to the Jewish leaders to learn where the Messiah is to be born because the Jewish leaders have the Scriptures, but the Jewish leaders are unable to understand, respond properly, and to worship Jesus even though they have read the Scriptures (2.5-6).[2]

It is in the passion story that irony is used most frequently in Matthew, however, as the Jewish leaders reject the one who according to Scripture is their eschatological King. They enlist Judas to help them in their plot to kill Jesus, and he looks for an 'opportunity' to betray him (εὐκαιρίαν, 26.16). Jesus, however, seeks the same καιρός (26.18), so that the implied reader can recognize Judas unwittingly helping Jesus accomplish God's will.[3] When Jesus is arrested and his passion moves toward its climax, the words and deeds of the Jewish leaders and those who help them crucify Jesus constantly show themselves to be full of irony as their ignorance and rejection of Jesus is made plain to the implied reader. The accusation that Jesus is able to destroy the temple (26.61-62) is framed in such a way that it asserts Jesus' Messianic power, and yet in his arrest he had chosen to remain powerless, refusing to use power and violence (26.52ff.). For the implied reader, who is

49, argues that despite the form of the saying, Jesus is the only human character in the plotted story to hear the voice from heaven at his baptism. His identity as Son of God is thus revealed only to Jesus and the implied reader.

1 Cf. Culpepper, *Anatomy*, p. 168, who points out that the Johannine prologue serves a similar function. He quotes with approval a classicist's comment that 'the omniscient prologue was almost indispensable in plays which exploited dramatic irony on hidden identity' (Philip W. Harsh, *A Handbook of Classical Drama* (Stanford, CA: Stanford University Press, 1944), p. 316).

2 See Brown, *Messiah*, pp. 182ff., Kingsbury, 'Jewish Leaders', pp. 61, 65. Cf. Mt. 17.10-11, where the scribes are similarly described as knowing that Elijah must first come, but as refusing to repent when Elijah does come in the form of John the Baptist (3.7-10; 17.12-13; 21.31-32).

3 Senior, *Passion of Jesus*, p. 57.

situated in the time following the destruction of the temple and Jerusalem, there is the added irony that Matthew apparently links this tragedy with Jesus' death (cf. 21.41; 22.6ff.).[1] The powerlessness of Jesus in dying on the cross leads to the destruction of the temple and thus ironically fulfills the accusation made against Jesus (cf. 27.40).

Throughout the passion narrative Jesus is mocked, but true characteristics of Jesus are unwittingly voiced in these mockeries for the implied reader to recognize. Caiaphas' question of Jesus (26.62) takes up the language of Peter's confession (16.16), but Caiaphas utters it in disbelief rather than the faith which characterized Peter's declaration. The irony of the trial is that Jesus is condemned for blasphemy when he has in fact spoken the truth. The Jewish leaders have tried to turn the truth into a lie.[2] The subsequent taunting of Jesus by the Jewish leaders to prophesy (26.68) is perceived as ironic by the implied reader who has seen Jesus accurately predict approaching events throughout the Gospel, especially since the incident is followed immediately by Peter's denial (26.69-75), which fulfills Jesus' earlier prophecy (26.34).[3]

Pilate unwittingly stumbles on to the truth when Jesus is addressed 'King of the Jews' (27.11), and his mock coronation (27.27ff.) by the soldiers ironically portrays the manner of his rule. His royal status is not to be found in the usual power of royalty, but in the self-giving service of the Son of Man (20.28). The parody continues at the crucifixion when Jesus' royal court consists of two robbers, the type of people he had earlier been criticized for associating with by the Jewish leaders (cf. 9.11; 11.19). The implied reader would recognize the irony in the challenges for Jesus to save himself by coming down from the cross (27.39, 42), because it is in dying that he is saved and saves the lives of others (cf. 16.25; 26.28). The implied reader would likewise recognize the contradictions in

---

1 *Ibid.*, p. 94, Patte, *Matthew*, p. 373.
2 Cf. Frank J. Matera, *Passion Narratives and Gospel Theologies: Interpreting the Synoptics Through Their Passion Stories* (New York: Paulist, 1986), pp. 100ff., Kingsbury, *Matthew as Story*, p. 88, *idem* 'Developing Conflict', p. 63.
3 Senior, *Passion of Jesus*, p. 99, Patte, *Matthew*, pp. 374ff.

the Jewish leaders' request for a sign so they may believe (27.41), because twice before they have asked for signs (12.38; 16.1). Jesus' dying and rising is in fact the one sign he has given them, but they cannot comprehend it. Finally, the behavior of the Jewish leaders after the resurrection is ironical. They remember Jesus' predictions about his resurrection and fear that the second 'fraud will be worse than the first' (27.64). Their statement, however, anticipates the post-Easter mission of the church while they themselves perpetuate the fraud concerning Jesus' resurrection (28.11-15)![1]

Matthew's use of irony has a twofold effect on the reader. First, it invites the implied reader to become involved and reconstruct the implied author's meaning. An ostensible structure of meaning must be rejected and a different point of view accepted. By being forced to make decisions about the different perspectives, the implied reader is drawn into the implied author's vision of truth. A community between author and reader is thus formed, so that inclusion is a primary effect of Matthew's irony.[2] Irony also functions as a weapon, however, and the Jewish leaders are the primary victims of Matthean irony. They do not recognize the higher meaning of their words and actions, and the implied reader is led to reject the system of values they espouse.[3]

All character groups in the Gospel thus contribute to the portrait of the implied reader, but none should be identified with this portrait. The implied reader is superior to every character who interacts with Jesus. As the implied author's interlocutor the implied reader has access to knowledge inac-

---

1 See Senior, *Passion of Jesus*, pp. 131-35, 154, and Patte, *Matthew*, pp. 394ff., for a fuller discussion of Matthew's use of irony in Jesus' passion.

2 Booth, *Irony*, p. 28, writes that 'every irony inevitably builds a community of believers even as it excludes'. Cf. Culpepper, *Anatomy*, p. 180, who writes that John's use of irony 'sweetens and spices the fellowship between readers and narrator'.

3 Duke, *Irony*, p. 40, writes that 'while irony is a witness to those who will see, it is a weapon against those who will not see'. See pp. 29-42 of Duke's study for a more thorough discussion of the functions of irony.

cessible to characters in the plotted story. He or she also fully accepts the ideological point of view of the implied author and either identifies with or rejects traits and points of view which are commended or criticized. This process of identifying with or backing away from different characters and points of view brings us to consider how readers experience and respond to the story.

C. *The Implied Reader and the Act of Reading*

Literary theorists who use the concept of an implied reader point out that this fictional person is not only the role implied or projected by the narrative, but also includes the processes and actions performed by actual readers in assuming the role required by the text. Some of the processes necessary for readers to actualize the text have already been noted in our previous discussions of the implied reader. For the implied reader to grasp the implied author's use of irony in connection with the Jewish leaders, for example, the literal meaning of their words must be rejected and a new cluster of meanings reconstructed based on inferences about the implied author's knowledge and beliefs. Matthew's use of rhetorical questions likewise requires the implied reader to respond and look at matters from a new perspective, even when they are stated in such a way that a particular conclusion is inevitable. Other aspects of how the meaning potential of Matthew may be actualized and of how actual readers are manipulated by the text will now be discussed, but first we will briefly summarize some critical moves and strategies utilized in the reading process as identified by reader-response critics.

The temporal dimension of reading is perhaps the most important aspect of the interaction between reader and text. Information is communicated and experienced sequentially, and in the linear unfolding of the narrative a reader constructs a narrative world. The processes of anticipation and retrospection are key elements in the successive reading activities. Hypotheses about what will happen are formed, confirmed, or altered in the time flow of reading as new information and events become available. Iser describes this temporal reading process in the following way:

> We look forward, we look back, we decide, we change our
> decisions, we form expectations, we are shocked by the non-
> fulfillment, we question, we muse, we accept, we reject; this
> is the dynamic process of recreation.[1]

The initial information communicated in the narrative
sequence is influential in educating a reader how to read the
story, because this material is read with an open mind. Early
information is retained and conditions the process and interpretation of later information in the narrative, that is, unless
and until it is undermined by new material.[2] The initial
information thus becomes the base that can be manipulated as
the story progresses to achieve certain effects in actual readers. In the dynamic process of reading one expects the literary
text to be as coherent as possible, and readers will try to form a
consistent interpretation of the diverse elements in the unfolding narrative. Iser labels this reading activity 'consistency-
building' and defines it as

> the process of grouping together all the different aspects of
> a text to form the consistency that the reader will always be
> in search of. While expectations may be continually
> modified, and images continually expanded, the reader will
> strive, even if unconsciously, to fit everything together in a
> consistent pattern.[3]

The formation of coherent interpretations may be
facilitated by an author's use of redundancy. This is the
repetition of information from more than one source in a
narrative. Its use increases predictability and thus the
probability of one interpretation by reducing the alternatives.

1 Iser, *Implied Reader*, p. 288. Cf. Perry, 'Literary Dynamics', pp. 47-
58. Mailloux, 'Learning to Read', pp. 95-96, *idem, Interpretive Conventions*, pp. 67-90, for other discussions and applications of a temporal based model reading.
2 See Sternberg, *Expositional Modes*, pp. 93ff., and Perry, 'Literary
Dynamics', pp. 49-53, for discussions of the 'primacy-recency' effect
in reading. Cf. Moore, 'Stories of Reading', pp. 144-52, who argues
that while the 'virgin reader' typical of temporalizing reader-
response exegesis is anachronistic for Gospel research, it may
paradoxically more closely approximate the primitive 'oral-aural
experience' of the Gospel's first century recipients.
3 Iser, *Implied Reader*, p. 283.

Redundancies also have a persuasive function. By allowing one to predict what will happen, they reinforce the narrative world which a reader will have constructed. If one can predict correctly the next item in a sequence, one is more likely to accept it.[1]

If these critical strategies are applied to Matthew, they help describe how the implied reader is educated to read the Gospel. The temporal, sequential nature of reading suggests that the order of incidents, characters and teaching in Matthew is not a matter of indifference as if the Gospel were 'an essay in story form' in which each occurrence of a word or concept were to be given equal weight by an interpreter.[2] At the beginning of Matthew the focus is on Jesus, and he is presented as the obedient Son of God, the fulfillment of God's plan, and the Messiah of Israel who will save his people. Unlike characters in the story, the implied reader is thus given an orientation and frame of reference for interpreting subsequent events. The abruptness with which Jesus' first disciples respond to his call and leave their families and livelihood (4.18-22) is therefore not surprising for the implied reader who knows Jesus' identity and authority—even though no explanation for their unusual decision is given in the plotted story. The extensive exposition about Jesus at the beginning of the Gospel does not mean, however, that curiosity and suspense is shifted away from Jesus' actions to the disciples and Jesus' opponents in Matthew, as Richard Edwards has suggested.[3] The exposition has not specified what type of Messiah Jesus will be and how he will save his people.

One consequnce of this positive initial characterization of Jesus is that the implied reader will view Jesus as a reliable

1 See Suleiman, 'Redundancy', pp. 119-42, for a discussion of redundancy in narrative. Cf. Anderson, 'Double and Triple Stories', and Burnett, 'Prolegomenon', who use the concept of redundancy to interpret Matthew.
2 Edwards ('Uncertain Faith', p. 47) points out that redaction critics frequently appear to operate on this assumption so that an evangelist's theology of discipleship, for example, may be constructed by systematically compiling every reference to the disciples in the Gospel.
3 *Ibid.*, p. 50.

spokesman for the implied author's ideological point of view. Other characters will be judged according to their responses to Jesus' words and deeds and his response to them. Positive characterizations and responses will attract the implied reader, create sympathy for these characters, and encourage identification between the two.[1] The first impression of the disciples for the implied reader is therefore favorable when they follow Jesus (4.18-22). The importance of the disciples for Matthew is underlined in the next narrative action of Jesus, when he sits on the mountain to 'teach' his disciples (5.1). Since Jesus is a well-defined 'oral narrative persona' in the Gospel, the narrative audience to whom he is speaking assumes an important function.[2] As the primary recipients of Jesus' teaching, especially of the five great discourses, the disciples indicate the kind of audience for which such teaching may be appropriate. Jesus invites people to follow him, and his teaching is directed to those who, like the disciples, are obedient to his interpretation of God's will. The initial favorable impression of the disciples and reader identification with them thus plays a crucial part in the rhetoric of the Gospel for the readers must accomodate themselves to the world of Jesus the oral performer and his audience by being sympathetic to their values and responses. The disciples as Jesus' audience become the link whereby the readers become connected to the teaching of the earthly Jesus (cf. 28.16-20).[3]

1 See Mailloux, 'Learning to Read', pp. 103ff., for a discussion of the place of reader identification and self-evaluation in the critical strategies of reader-response critics. Cf. Tannehill, 'Disciples in Mark', and Edwards, 'Uncertain Faith', who use this strategy in their interpretations of discipleship in Mark and Matthew.

2 Kellogg, 'Oral Narrative', p. 660. Kellogg uses Chaucer's *Canterbury Tales* to illustrate his discussion of oral narrative story-tellers and their audiences. One obviously does not find in Matthew the variety of narrated narrators which there is in Caterbury Tales, but Jesus functions in a similar way as does an oral person within a written narrative because of his great blocks of uninterrupted teaching. Instead of expanding the universe of a tellable story as in Chaucer, however, Matthew's portrayal of Jesus serves to narrow and focus more sharply on a restricted value system.

3 Cf. Brown, 'Mission to Israel', p. 77, and Luz, 'Disciples', p. 105. Luz thus correctly stresses that in Matthew the disciples primarily

The portrait of the disciples is not uniformly positive, however, and the conflicting behavior of the disciples frustrates the readers' ability to construct a consistent pattern. On the one hand, the ambivalence of the disciples in their obedience and following of Jesus leads the implied reader to judge the disciples' behavior negatively when they fail to live up to Jesus' standards.[1] On the other hand, the parallels between Jesus and his disciples in Matthew drive the implied reader to look to Jesus and his behavior rather than to the disciples to learn what it means to live a life obedient to God. Jesus becomes a model of righteousness.[2]

Having the implied reader judge and/or identify with the characters is only one step on the way to having the real readers judge themselves. Whereas actual readers can judge both themselves and characters in the narrative, they can correct only themselves. The disciples are reconciled to Jesus in the conclusion of Matthew, but the ambivalence with which they portrayed challenges actual readers to assume the role of the implied reader, and in doing so, to be fully obedient to Jesus in ways in which the disciples have failed.[3]

function as 'ear-witnesses'. The disciples are the ones who have heard and understood the teachings of Jesus in his lifetime, and it is through their witness and experiences that these teachings are preserved. It is in this sense that Peter and the other disciples can be spoken of as the foundation of the church (cf. 16.18ff.; 18.18), as J.D. Kingsbury ('The Figure of Peter in Matthew's Gospel as a Theological Problem', *JBL* 98 [1979], pp. 81-82) and P. Hoffmann ('Der Petrus-Primat im Matthäusevangelium', in *Neues Testament und Kirche*, ed. J. Gnilka [Freiburg; Herder, 1974], pp. 108-10) have pointed out.

1 See Edwards, 'Uncertain Faith', and Kingsbury, *Matthew as Story*, pp. 13-17, 103-19, for descriptions of Matthew's ambivalent portrayal of the disciples.

2 See Bauer, *Structure of Matthew's Gospel*, pp. 57-63 and chapter 6 of my Oxford D. Phil. dissertation, which was not published in this book, for a tracing of the parallels between Jesus and the disciples and a defense of this interpretation.

3 Cf. Tannehill, 'Disciples in Mark', p. 393, who argues that the tension between attraction and repulsion im Mark's portrayal of the disciples 'can lead the sensitive reader beyond a naively positive view of himself to self-criticism and repentance'. Although

D. *Conclusion*

By using the literary concept of the implied reader, we have tried to show the inadequacy of explaining the inclusive nature of Matthew's Gospel through an identification of the evangelist's community, whose experiences are said to be included in the story of Jesus' earthly ministry, with the experiences of the disciples. The disciples provide the link for the implied reader to the teaching of the earthly Jesus which is to be obeyed, but the implied reader is superior to them and every other character group in the Gospel which responds to Jesus, having access to not only the information communicated to characters on the level of the plotted story, but also the narrator's commentary.

The challenge to accept Jesus' call is extended beyond the characters of the plotted story to the 'whoever' of the readers/hearers of the Gospel by means of commentary, rhetorical questions, inclusive language, and irony. The affective response which the implied reader embodies should thus not be confused with the role of any of the characters in the plotted story, for no one group serves as the sole role model in its response to Jesus. The implied reader learns what it means to accept Jesus and his interpretation of God's will from the various character groups, because they are all ultimately judged by this ideological point of view which the narrator and Jesus express.[1] Jesus, on the other hand, exemplifies and embodies the life of obedient trust in God the Father and love for all humanity to which he calls his followers. He can function as a model for the implied reader.

Matthew has modified the portrait of the disciples which he took over from Mark so that the sense of repulsion may be less pronounced, the disciples are still inconsistent in their obedience to Jesus in Matthew, and actual readers should learn from their shortcomings.

1 See Anderson, 'Gender and Reading', pp. 22-24.

Chapter 6

CONCLUSION: JESUS AS EXEMPLARY
FOR DISCIPLESHIP

A. *Summary*

Even though the historical processes which led up to the writing of Matthew may have been long and complex, the final work is a unified narrative which tells a dynamic story and seeks to influence its readers. Given the gospel genre's interest in influencing and evoking a response from readers, the pragmatic or rhetorical dimensions of the narrative are important topics for discussion. We therefore set out in this study to investigate the narrative rhetoric of Matthew by paying particular attention to the way in which the reader who is included or implied in the Gospel helps structure the response of actual readers and invites them to inhabit imaginatively Matthew's narrative world. By using a type of literary or narrative criticism that seeks to describe the shaping of a reader's experience of a text, we have been able to consider aspects of the Gospel's narrative which more traditional historical critical methods may not have explored adequately.

The different aspects of the Matthean narrative which we have considered separately—plot, characters, point of view, commentary, and so on—all elucidate the role of the implied reader and contribute to the appellative strategies of the Gospel. A literary world is created whose temporal boundaries stretch from Abraham in the history of Israel to the indefinite future of the coming of the Son of Man. Within this world, the narrator retrospectively narrates the story of Jesus' life and ministry and leads the reader to view each character and event from his point of view. Jesus is portrayed as God's Son, the Messiah fulfilling God's promises to Israel, the one who has come to save his people from their sins. It is the unity of Jesus' life and ministry as portrayed in the narrative which gives the Gospel its sense of completeness rather than a theological concept of salvation history. The focus is on Jesus throughout the Gospel. Spatially, the action follows Jesus. Phraseologically, the narrator and Jesus share much of the same speech. Psychologically, the inside views of Jesus are both given in more depth and presented more sympathetically than are those of other characters. Temporally, the narrator is often synchronized with Jesus when he speaks. This mode of narration aligns the narrator's ideological point of view with Jesus so that he becomes the medium for the implied author's system of values.[1] Characters are judged according to their response to Jesus and the story is plotted so that they are challenged either to accept or to reject Jesus and his interpretation of God's will.

While the disciples are the major character group in the Gospel portrayed most favorably vis-à-vis Jesus, one should not identify them with the evangelist's audience that is included or implied in the narrative, as has often been done. The concept of transparency in Matthew's portrayal of the disciples cannot be used to support the equation of textual characters with extratextual persons (e.g. Matthew's church). Our study of the narrative rhetoric of Matthew has shown that the implied reader, as the narrator's encoded interlocutor, lives in the period between the resurrection and the indefinite future of the coming of the Son of Man, sharing with the characters plotted in the story a world with the same temporal boundaries. The implied reader has the benefit of the narrator's commentary throughout the gospel, however, and is told Jesus' identity from the beginning. In this way the implied reader knows more than every character in the story, and with this knowledge is called both to stand with Jesus and the implied author, and to judge characters according to their response to Jesus. Discipleship does not mean membership in a character group, but concerns the values that Jesus and the implied author commend to their hearers/readers. The implied reader is thus able to learn from all the characters,

1 Cf. Anderson, 'Gender and Reading', pp. 22-25.

both negatively and positively, what it means to follow Jesus.

Through such narrative techniques as the use of indefinite and inclusive language in Jesus' teaching and an open-ended conclusion to the Gospel, the invitation and demands of discipleship are extended beyond characters in the story to the implied reader. He or she also is challenged with the disciples in the Great Commission to be obedient to Jesus' teaching. The disciples, as the narrative persons who receive most of Jesus' teaching, provide the link whereby the implied reader is connected to Jesus' teaching, but they also fail at times to live up to Jesus' standards. Jesus, however, exemplifies in his own life the virtues demanded of the disciples so that he can be seen as a model for discipleship for the implied reader.

B. *Jesus as Model*

How does Matthew's portrayal of Jesus make him exemplary for discipleship?[1] In its broadest terms, Jesus' function as a model for discipleship in Matthew can be seen in the evangelist's portrait of Jesus as a righteous person who knows and obediently does the will of God.[2] The concepts of 'doing the will of God' and 'righteousness' figure prominently in the charac-

---

1 The idea that Jesus is exemplary for the disciples in Matthew is one of the theses developed in the studies of Meier (*Vision*), Strecker, (*Weg*), and Bauer (*Structure of Matthew's Gospel*, pp. 57-63). See also Matera, *Passion Narratives*, pp. 142-48, who discusses Jesus as a model in the Matthean passion account. This aspect of Matthew's portrayal of Jesus has on the whole been neglected, however, in studies of Matthew's theology. For example, Margaret Pamment ('The Kingdom of Heaven in the Gospel according to Matthew', *NTS* (1981), p. 214) has written that 'in the first Gospel, Jesus is presented not only as Christ, Lord, Son of God and Son of Man, but also as model for discipleship', without offering any evidence to substantiate the claim that Jesus functions as a model.
2 Cf. Kingsbury, *Jesus Christ*, p. 75, who argues that Matthew places both 'the narrative line and the great discourses in the service of the image he projects of Jesus at his baptism and temptation as the authoritative Son who knows and does his Father's will'. The narrative line of the story portrays Jesus as the one who is obedient to God's will and the discourses project Jesus as one who knows and teaches this will.

terization of both Jesus and the disciples. Matthew establishes Jesus as one who is concerned to do God's will at the beginning of his public ministry when Jesus is baptized by John in order to 'fulfill all righteousness' (3.15).[1] His obedience to the will of God is further emphasized in the temptations, as he resists the devil by quoting Deuteronomy and stressing that humankind lives 'by every word that proceeds from the mouth of God' (4.4).[2] At the end of Jesus' ministry this characterization is reaffirmed when Jesus prays in Gethsamene that God's 'will be done' (26.39, 42), and when Pilate's wife identifies him as 'righteous' (27.19). Moreover, Jesus' concern for the will of God can be seen throughout the Gospel when Jesus interprets the Law and the prophets and uses them to support his actions against the criticism of the Jewish leaders. The evangelist's use of 'righteousness' and 'doing the will of God' as the conditions in two different sayings about entering the Kingdom (5.20; 7.21) highlights the importance of these concepts for discipleship in his Gospel. In 12.49ff. Matthew gives probably his best thumb-nail definition of a disciple as one who 'does the will of my Father in heaven'. Jesus can thus be seen in very broad terms as the prototype of a righteous person who does the will of God in Matthew.

A prominent aspect of Jesus' obedience to the will of God in Matthew is his acceptance of the role of the meek and lowly Servant of God.[3] He fulfills Isaianic Servant prophecies (8.17; 12.18-21) both in his healing ministry and in the way he withdraws from Pharisaic opposition and avoids Messianic self-advertisement. He has come to serve others (20.28) and this way of service means a suffering which culminates on the cross. Matthew has taken over traditional sayings which con-

---

1 Cf. Strecker, *Weg*, pp. 179ff., Schweizer, *Matthäus und seine Gemeinde*, p. 19.
2 See Gerhardsson, *The Testing of God's Son*, Thompson, 'Called-Proved-Obedient', Gundry, *Matthew*, p. 56. Cf. also Luz, *Matthäus*, p. 162, who argues that the exemplary or paraenetic thrust of the temptations in Matthew are secondary to their Christological meaning.
3 See David Hill, 'Son and Servant: An Essay on Matthean Christology', *JSNT* (1980), pp. 2-16, who argues that Matthew uses the Servant theme to give content to his Son of God Christology.

nect Jesus with the disciples, who are also called upon to serve others (20.28) and to take up their crosses and suffer (16.24). He has highlighted the exemplary character of Jesus' actions present in such sayings, however, both by strengthening the parallels between Jesus and the disciples, and by underlining Jesus' role as the Servant of God. The parallels in the mission discourse between Jesus and the disciples (who share in his rejection and persecution) are therefore strengthened,[1] and persecution for the sake of righteousness (another Matthean concept) is equated with persecution for the sake of Jesus in the beatitudes (5.10-12). The virtue of meekness is blessed in one of the beatitudes (5.5), and childlike humility is demanded of the disciples in another of Matthew's sayings about entering the Kingdom (18.4). Both characteristics are attributed to Jesus in 11.28-30 when he issues an invitation to learn from him, the meek and lowly Servant of God.[2] The virtue of being a peace-maker (5.9) and the demand not to resist evil (5.38ff.) are also realized by Jesus when he refuses to use violence at his arrest (26.52ff.). The attitudes of the meek and lowly Servant of God which find expression in Jesus' life and ministry are thus exemplary for the disciples of whom the same attitudes are demanded.

Jesus is also a model for the piety which is demanded of the disciples. The public ostentation of the Pharisees (6.1ff.; 23.5ff.) is condemned, and the disciples are exhorted to let their good deeds cause people to glorify God rather than bring honor to themselves (5.13ff.; 23.5ff.). Jesus' deeds have a similar witness character to them (15.31), and although Jesus is the disciples' master, he is still servant (23.10ff.). Jesus is also a model as a person of prayer. He teaches the disciples to pray (6.9ff.) and prays or realizes many of the petitions himself (4.1ff.; 26.36ff.). In his praying at Gethsamene, as earlier in the wilderness, Jesus is exemplary in the way he resists temptation.[3]

---

1 See Brown, 'Mission to Israel', p. 78ff.
2 Cf. Meier, *Vision*, p. 129, who writes that 'the disciple who humbles himself (*tapeinosei*) imitates what is for Matthew the essential attitude of Jesus, the meek and humble (*tapeinos*) (cf. 11.29)'.
3 See Goulder, *Midrash*, pp. 298-300, Schweizer, *Matthew*, pp. 493-94.

Finally, 'the greater righteousness' demanded of the disciples can be summed up with the command to love and be perfect as their heavenly Father is perfect (22.40; 5.43ff.; cf. 7.12). Jesus makes this command concrete in his interaction with the people to whom he ministers. He exhibits impartiality when he receives children (19.13ff.) and shares table fellowship with the sinners and outcasts of society (8.10ff.; 26.6ff.). Matthew prefaces some of his summaries of Jesus' healings and acts of ministry with the observation that Jesus acted out of compassion for the people (9.36; 14.14; 15.32; cf. 20.34). The scribes and Pharisees are criticized for neglecting the weightier matters of the law—justice, mercy, and faith (23.23)—but Jesus interprets and fulfills the Law with acts of love and mercy (9.13; 12.7), and it is this ethical side of righteousness rather than its cultic side which seems to be emphasized by Jesus (cf. 15.1ff.). The attitude of mercifulness that is blessed in one of the beatitudes (5.7) is thus actualized in the evangelist's portrayal of Jesus.

The exemplary character of Jesus for the disciples would not be immediately self-evident to the reader, however, since the Gospel is a narrative about Jesus' life and ministry. The link between Jesus and disciples are uncovered only in the linear unfolding of the story, and the manner in which the evangelist forces the reader to make many of the connections is masterful. The initial scenes of Jesus' baptism and temptation play a crucial role in setting the tone of Matthew's entire portrayal of Jesus because of the so-called 'primacy-recency' effect in narrative.[1] Although the evangelist has already disclosed Jesus' identity and mission to the implied reader in the birth and infancy stories, the baptism and temptation establish Jesus as the righteous Son of God, the Servant of God, who is obedient to his Father's will. This first impression of the adult Jesus will figure prominently in the evangelist's later portrayal of Jesus the model for discipleship, because it establishes the way in which Jesus—who has already been identified as

1 See Sternberg, *Expositional Modes*, pp. 93ff., Perry, 'Literary Dynamics', pp. 49-53. According to Sternberg, this effect is basically 'the proverbial tenacity and enduring influence of first impressions' (p. 93).

the Son of God—will actualize his sonship.

The contribution of the baptism and temptation stories to the exemplary characterization of Jesus in Matthew would not be obviated by a nullification of the primacy-recency effect through an actual reader's familiarity with the Gospel. Paul Ricoeur has observed that as soon as a story is well-known, as the Gospel must have been if it was used in Matthew's church,

> retelling takes the place of telling. Then following the story is less important than apprehending the well-known end as implied in the beginning and the well-known episodes as leading to the end.[1]

If readers were therefore acquainted with the Gospel before-hand, the exemplary character of Jesus in the baptism and temptation would be immediately transparent. Such readers would know the importance of righteousness and doing the will of God in the teaching of Jesus in Matthew, so that in these events they would recognize Jesus' obedience and see him actualizing these demands in his own life.

These stories also provide a link between Jesus and the disciples in Matthew's first great block of Jesus' teaching. After the disciples' destiny is linked with Jesus in the traditional account of the call of the first disciples, Matthew provides his readers with a systematic presentation of Jesus' teaching in the Sermon on the Mount. This teaching discourse contains many of the specific ethical responsibilities of the disciples, and it may not be accidental that all but one of the occurrences of the term δικαιοσύνη are found either before or in the Sermon (21.32 is the exception). Matthew uses this concept to connect the disciples with Jesus. The exemplary nature of Jesus the one who fulfills righteousness is further underlined in the Sermon by 5.17-20 which in a sense legitimates Jesus' role as a model for discipleship in the Gospel. It is because Jesus is the eschatological fulfiller of the Law and the prophets and the revealer of God's will that he is exemplary for the disciples. Jesus' teaching and actions provide the center and norm of the disciples' obedience to the will of God.[2]

1 Ricoeur, 'Narrative Time', p. 179.
2 Cf. Kingsbury, 'Sermon on the Mount', p. 143, who writes that Jesus Son of God 'stands before the disciples as the one who realizes in his

Once the evangelist has made the intitial connection and established the solidarity between Jesus and the disciples, the specific content of Jesus as a model is explicated throughout the Gospel. This is accomplished by specifying, first in the Sermon, and later in other teaching material, some of the virtues and ethical responses required of the disciples, and then by showing the way Jesus exemplifies these virtues and attitudes in his own life as the story of his ministry unfolds. The interrelationship between Jesus and the disciples continues throughout the Gospel as Matthew uses the same terms to describe both Jesus' life and ministry on the one hand, and the disciple's life and mission on the other. Verbal and thematic redundancy or repetition reinforces the links and educates the implied reader. In the double stories of the healing of the demoniac for example (9.32-34; 12.22-37), the words 'ruler of demons' (9.34; 12.24) and 'Beelzeboul' (10.25; 12.24) are combined to link the destiny of the disciples with that of Jesus.

Repetition is also used, however, to underline not only Jesus' obedience, but also the disciples' failure to live up to the standards set by Jesus in his teaching and life. For example, Jesus is repeatedly portrayed as obedient to God's will (cf. 3.15; 6.10; 26.39, 42), but the disciples fall asleep and are unable to pray with Jesus in Gethsamene. The disciples are rebuked by Jesus for their little faith in both stories of the stilling of the storm (8.26; 14.31), but their wavering faith is highlighted in a third rebuke (16.8; cf. 17.20) when they still do not understand Jesus' teaching after two feeding incidents. In a similar way the disciples are instructed about the Kingdom with a child as an example (18.3), but they reject children almost immediately after the conclusion of Jesus' teaching discourse (19.13-15). The disciples are reconciled to Jesus after the resurrection (28.1-10, 16-20), but they are also still portrayed ambivalently as doubting.[1] When the disciples are given the commission to

life the ethic of greater righteousness' and thus serves as an 'example' for those who are unable to lead the life to which they are called.

1 There has been a debate recently on how to interpret the ambiguous οἱ δὲ in 28.17. Edwards ('Uncertain Faith', p. 59), C.H. Giblin ('A Note on Doubt and Reassurance in Mt 28.16-20', *CBQ* 37 [1975],

make disciples by teaching all nations to observe what Jesus has commanded, the implied reader is linked to the earthly Jesus—as we earlier argued—but does not look to the disciples for a model of what it means to observe all that Jesus commanded, because the disciples have not fully actualized this teaching in their lives. Instead, the implied reader of the Gospel remembers the connections between Jesus' life and the demands made on the disciples, and sees that Matthew portrays Jesus as a model of discipleship.

One might object that there is a strand of thought in Matthew's redaction which appears to challenge our thesis that Jesus serves as a model for the disciples in Matthew. In 18.6, for example, Matthew has added the prepositional phrase εἰς ἐμέ to his Markan source (9.42). Although many of the miracle stories in Matthew associate faith with Jesus, this is the only logion in any of the Synoptic Gospels to speak of having faith in Jesus. Sayings such as this one and others like it (e.g. 14.31, which speaks of the disciples worshipping Jesus, or 18.20, which promises the presence of Jesus when two or three are gathered in his name—all of these peculiar to Matthew) highlight the differences between Jesus and the disciples. There can thus be no question that Jesus Son of God is on a different level from the disciples in Matthew. He is the one in whom God is with his people saving them from their sins (1.21, 23). He is the one who issues summons to his disciples to follow him (4.18-20; 9.9). He is the one who is the eschatological fulfiller of the Law and prophets (5.17). He has

pp. 68-71) and K. Graystone ('The Translation of Matthew 28.17', *JSNT* 21 [1984], pp. 105-109) understand 28.17 as referring to all the disciples worshipping and doubting. On the other hand K.L. McKay ('The Use of *hoi de* in Matthew 28.17', *JSNT* 24 [1985], pp. 71-2) and P.W. van der Horst ('Once More: The Translation of οἱ δὲ in Matthew 28.17'. *JSNT* 27 [1986], pp. 27-30) argue that it is untenable to translate 28.17 as all worshipped and doubted. According to them, οἱ δε must be understood partitively, so that some disciples worshipped and other disciples doubted. The disciples are still portrayed ambivalently in both interpretations, however, thus making it problematic to equate them with the implied reader even though they are reconciled with Jesus. Cf. Matthew 14.31-33 where διστάξω is also used with προσκυνέω.

a priority and uniqueness which cannot merely be imitated by his disciples, and sayings such as 14.31, 18.6 and 18.19-20 reflect the perspective and idioms of the post-resurrection community who have experienced the presence of the risen Lord (28.20).

On the other hand, this perspective in Matthew should not be seen to invalidate our thesis that Jesus is portrayed in an exemplary manner in the Gospel. Matthew identifies the one who is active in the community with the earthly Jesus in his closing pericope (28.16-20).[1] This has the effect of stressing the continuing validity and binding character of the earthly Jesus' teaching and deeds for the Matthean community. The concept of solidarity between Jesus and the disciples—already found in sayings taken from the tradition (20.28; 16.24; cf. 10.38), which explicitly link the disciples' behavior and Jesus' actions—is therefore highlighted by Matthew by an increased emphasis on the teaching of Jesus. This helps give specific content to the moral and ethical expectations placed upon the disciples. The teaching is that of the earthly Jesus, however, who by his own life interprets these demands as they are realized in his actions. In Matthews' Jesus the implied reader and the disciples are therefore presented with a model of life and actions obedient to the will of God, albeit a perfect model to which the disciples will never attain.[2] The idea that Jesus can function as a model for the disciples while at the same time

1 See Luz, 'Disciples', pp. 112ff., who along with others has pointed out that Matthew makes no mention of the Spirit in this closing pericope. He concludes that 'the formulation "I am with you" probably means in effect the same as what is said with the catch-word "Spirit"'. It is significant that Matthew mentions the continuing presence of Jesus with his community rather than speaking of the Spirit, because this emphasizes the continuity of the risen Jesus with the earthly Jesus.

2 Cf. Schweizer, 'Matthew's Church', p. 145, who explains with the following analogy the way in which the disciple is both called and yet unable to imitate Christ: 'a little boy trots behind his father who cuts a path through the impenetrable jungle with his bush knife. By his own feeble powers the boy could not have done that himself, so he is doing something quite different from his father in front, but he nevertheless follows exactly in his footsteps. That is how followers walk in the way that Jesus has opened up for them'.

being Son of God in Matthew is further supported by the way the evangelist consciously parallels yet subordinates John the Baptist to Jesus.[1] Jesus is exemplary as a model for discipleship because what he experiences and does is also what the disciples must do.

C. *Conclusion*

The literary paradigm and methods used in this study should not be construed as rendering the methods of the historical critical paradigm obsolete. The different methods simply ask different types of questions. We have thus not considered historical questions about Jesus' ministry or the shape of Matthew's community in this study. The different methods of the paradigms can complement one another, however, and each should contribute to a responsible biblical interpretation. Further research needs to be done to find ways to wed fruitfully the two approaches, but it is hoped that this study has made way for an increased appreciation of how Matthew's narrative shapes one's experience of the story. With this understanding comes the awareness that there are other ways of perceiving the events of Jesus' life. But the evangelist surely also invites us, the actual readers, to share his vision and to respond in obedience along with the implied reader to Jesus' call in the Great Commission.

---

1 Cf. Meier, 'John the Baptist', pp. 388-400, for a good discussion of Matthew's use of 'parallelism-yet-subordination' in his treatment of the Baptist. John the Baptist and Jesus are both introduced with the same verb, they proclaim the same message, both face the same united front of Jewish leaders, both 'fulfill all righteousness', both are manifestations of the works of divine wisdom (11.19), and both are rejected and martyred by faithless Israel. Yet the Baptist is also presented as subordinate to Jesus.

SELECTED BIBLIOGRAPHY

I. *Literary Studies*

Abrams, M.H.
    1958   *The Mirror and the Lamp*. New York: W.W. Norton.
    1981   *A Glossary of Literary Terms*. 4th edn. London: Holt, Reinhart and Winston.

Auerbach, Erich
    1953   *Mimesis: The Representation of Reality in Western Literature*. Trans. by W.R. Trask. Princeton: Princeton University Press.

Booth, Wayne C.
    1961   'Distance and Point of View: An Essay in Clarification'. *Essays in Criticism* 11: 60-79.
    1974   *A Rhetoric of Irony*. Chicago: University of Chicago Press,
    1978   'Metaphor as Rhetoric: The Problem of Evaluation'. *Critical Inquiry* 5: 49-72.
    1983   *The Rhetoric of Fiction*. 2nd edn. Chicago: University of Chicago Press.

Bruns, Gerald L.
    1980   'Intention, Authority and Meaning'. *Critical Inquiry* 7: 297-309.

Casparis, C.P.
    1975   *Tense Without Time: The Present Tense in Narration*. Swiss Studies in English 84. Berne: Francke Verlag.

Chambers, Ross
    1978   'Commentary in Literary Texts'. *Critical Inquiry* 5: 323-37.

Chatman, Seymour
    1978   *Story and Discourse: Narrative Structure in Fiction and Film*. London: Cornell University Press.

Cohen, Ted
    1978   'Metaphor and the Cultivation of Intimacy'. *Critical Inquiry* 5: 3-12.

Crites, Stephen
    1971   'The Narrative Quality of Experience'. *JAAR* 39: 292-311.

Crossan, Robert
    1980   'Do Readers Make Meaning?'. In *The Reader in the Text*, pp. 149-64. Ed. Susan R. Suleiman and Inge Crosman. Princeton, NJ: Princeton University Press.

262   *Matthew's Inclusive Story*

Culler, Jonathan
  1975   *Structuralist Poetics: Structuralism, Linguistics and the Study of Literature*. London: Routledge & Kegan Paul.
Eagleton, Terry
  1983   *Literary Theory: An Introduction*. Oxford: Blackwell's.
Eco, Umberto
  1976   *A Theory of Semiotics*. London: Indiana University Press.
  1979   *The Role of the Reader: Explorations in the Semiotics of Texts*. London: Indiana University Press.
Fish, Stanley
  1980   'Interpreting the *Variorum*'. In *Reader-Response Criticism: From Formalism to Post-Structuralism*, pp. 164-84. Ed. J.P. Tompkins. London: Johns Hopkins University Press.
  1971   *Self-Consuming Artifacts: The Experience of Seventeenth-Century Literature*. Berkeley: University of California Press.
Fowler, Robert M.
  1985   'Who is "The Reader" in Reader Response Criticism?'. *Semeia* 31: 5-23.
Gardner, Helen
  1982   *In Defence of the Imagination*. Oxford: Clarendon.
Genette, Gerard
  1980   *Narrative Discourse: An Essay in Method*. Trans. by Jane E. Lewin. Oxford: Blackwell's.
Hirsch, E.D. Jr
  1967   *Validity in Interpretation*. New Haven, CT: Yale University Press.
  1976   *The Aims of Interpretation*. London.
Holub, Robert C.
  1984   *Reception Theory: A Critical Introduction*. London: Methuen.
Iser, Wolfgang
  1971   'Interminacy and the Reader's Response in Prose Fiction'. In *Aspects of Narrative*, pp. 1-45. Ed. J. Hillis Miller. New York: Columbia University Press.
  1974   *The Implied Reader: Patterns of Communication in Prose Fiction from Bunyan to Beckett*. Baltimore: Johns Hopkins University Press.
  1978   *The Act of Reading: A Theory of Aesthetic Response*. Baltimore: Johns Hopkins University Press.
Kellogg, Robert
  1977   'Oral Narrative, Written Books', *Genre* 10: 655-65.
Kermode, Frank
  1967   *The Sense of an Ending: Studies in the Theory of Fiction*. New York: OUP.
  1979   *The Genesis of Secrecy: On the Interpretation of Narrative*. Cambridge, MA: Harvard University Press.
Krieger, Murray
  1964   *A Window to Criticism: Shakespeare's Sonnets and Modern Poetics*. Princeton: Princeton University Press.

Lanser, Susan Snaider
   1981   *The Narrative Act: Point of View in Prose Fiction*. Princeton, NJ: Princeton University Press.
Lentricchia, Frank
   1980   *After the New Criticism*. London: Athlone.
Lotman, J.M.
   1975   'Point of View in a Text'. *New Literary History* 6: 339-52.
Lundin, Roger, Anthony C. Thiselton and Clarence Walhout
   1985   *The Responsibility of Hermeneutics*. Grand Rapids: Eerdmans.
Mailloux, Steven
   1977   'Reader-Response Criticism?'. *Genre* 10: 413-31.
   1979   'Learning to Read: Interpretation and Reader-Response Criticism'. *Studies in the Literary Imagination* 12: 93-108.
   1982   *Interpretive Conventions: The Reader in the Study of American Fiction*. London: Cornell University Press.
Mendilow, A.A.
   1965   *Time and the Novel*. New York: Humanities Press.
Muecke, D.C.
   1969   *The Compass of Irony*. London: Methuen.
Ong, Walter J.
   1975   'The Writer's Audience is Always Fiction'. *Publications of the Modern Language Association of America* 90: 9-21.
Pascal, Roy
   1977   'Narrative Fictions and Reality'. *Novel* 11: 40-50.
Piwowarczyk, Mary Ann
   1976   'The Narratee and the Situation of Enunciation: A Reconsideration of Prince's Theory'. *Genre* 9: 161-77.
Perry, Menakhem
   1979   'Literary Dynamics: How the Order of a Text Creates Its Meaning'. *Poetics Today* 1: 35-64, 311-61.
Prince, Gerald
   1971   'Notes Toward a Categorization of Fictional "Narratees"'. *Genre* 4: 100-105.
   1980   'Introduction to the Study of the Narratee'. In *Reader-Response Criticism: From Formalism to Post-Structualism*, pp. 7-25. Ed. J.P. Tompkins. London: Johns Hopkins University Press.
   1982   *Narratology: The Form and Functioning of Narrative*. Berlin: Mouton.
Rabinowitz, Peter J.
   1977   'Truth in Fiction: A Reexamination of Audiences'. *Critical Inquiry* 4: 121-41.
Ricoeur, Paul
   1980   'Narrative Time'. *Critical Inquiry* 7: 169-90.
Scholes, Robert and Robert Kellogg
   1966   *The Nature of Narrative*. London: OUP.
Steiner, George
   1979   'Critic'/'Reader'. *New Literary History* 10: 423-52.

Sternberg, Meir
   1978   *Expositional Modes and Temporal Ordering in Fiction*. London: Johns Hopkins University Press.
Suleiman, Susan R.
   1980   'Redundancy and the "Readable Text"'. *Poetics Today* 1: 119-42.
   1980   'Varieties of Audience-Oriented Criticism'. In *The Reader in the Text*, pp. 1-45. Ed. S.R. Suleiman and I. Crosman. Princeton: Princeton University Press.
Suleiman, Susan R., and Inge Crosman
   1980   ed. *The Reader in the Text*. Princeton: Princeton University Press.
Tompkins, Jane
   1980   ed. *Reader-Response Criticism: From Formalism to Post-Structuralism*. London: Johns Hopkins University Press.
Uspensky, Boris
   1973   *A Poetics of Composition: The Structure of the Artistic Text and Typology of a Compositional Form*. Trans. by V. Zavarin and S. Wittig. Berkeley: University of California Press.
Weimann, Robert
   1976   *Structure and Society in Literary History: Studies in the History and Theory of Historical Criticism*. Charlottesville, VA: University Press of Virginia.
Wellek, Rene
   1963   *Concepts of Criticism*. New Haven, CT: Yale University Press.
Wellek, Rene and Austin Warren
   1961   *Theory of Literature*. 2nd edn. London: Jonathan Cape.
White, Hayden
   1973   *Metahistory. The Historical Imagination in Nineteenth Century Europe*. London: Johns Hopkins University Press.
   1980   'The Value of Narrativity in the Representation of Reality'. *Critical Inquiry* 7: 5-27.
Wimsatt, William, and Monroe Beardsley
   1954   *The Verbal Icon*. Lexington, KY: University of Kentucky Press.
Wolterstorff, Nicholas
   1980   *Art in Action: Toward a Christian Aesthetic*. Grand Rapids: Eerdmanns.

II. *Biblical and Theological Studies*

Alter, Robert
1981   *The Art of Biblical Narrative*. New York: Basic Books.
1987   and Frank Kermode, ed. *The Literary Guide to the Bible*. London: Collins.

Anderson, Janice Capel
1983   'Matthew: Gender and Reading'. *Semeia* 28: 3-27.
1985   'Double and Triple Stories, The Implied Reader, and Redundancy in Matthew'. *Semeia* 31: 71-89.

Aune, David E.
1981   'The Problem of the Genre of the Gospels: A Critique of C.H. Talbert's What is a Gospel?'. In *Gospel Perspectives,* Vol. II, pp. 9-60. Ed. by R.T. France and D. Wenham. Sheffield: JSOT Press.

Bacon, B.W.
1930   *Studies in Matthew*. London: Constable.

Banks, Robert
1974   'Matthew's Understanding of the Law: Authenticity and Interpretation in Matthew 5.17-20'. *JBL* 93: 226-42.

Barr, David
1987   *New Testament Story: An Introduction*. Belmont, CA: Wadsworth.

Barr, James
1973   *The Bible in the Modern World*. London: SCM.
1973   'Reading the Bible as Literature'. *BJRL* 56: 10-33.
1976   'Story and History in Biblical Theology'. *JR* 56: 1-17.
1981   'Some Thoughts on Narrative, Myth and Incarnation'. In *God Incarnate: Story and Belief*, pp. 14-23. Ed. by A.E. Harvey. London: SPCK.

Barton, John
1984   *Reading the Old Testament. Method in Biblical Study*. London: Darton, Longman & Todd.

Barth, Gerhard
1963   'Matthew's Understanding of the Law'. In *Tradition and Interpretation in Matthew* pp. 58-164. By G. Bornkamm, G. Barth, H. Held. Trans. by Percy Scott. London: SCM.

Bassler, Jouette M.
1986   'The Parable of the Loaves'. *JR* 66: 157-72.

Bauer, David R.
1988   *The Structure of Matthew's Gospel. A Study in Literary Design*. JSNT Supplement Series 31. Sheffield: Almond.

Beardslee, W.A.
1970   *Literary Criticism of the New Testament*. Guides to Biblical Scholarship. Philadelphia: Fortress.

Beare, F.W.
1970   'The Mission of the Disciples and the Mission Charge. Matthew 10 and Parallels'. *JBL* 89: 1-13.
1981   *The Gospel According to Matthew*. Oxford: Blackwell.

Beavis, Mary Ann
    1987   'The Trial before the Sanhedrin (Mark 14.53-65): Reader Response
            and Greco-Roman Readers'. *CBQ* 49: 581-96.
Betz, Hans-Dieter
    1979   'The Sermon on the Mount: Its Literary Genre and Function'.
            Harvard Theological Review 59: 285-97.
    1985   *Essays on the Sermon on the Mount*. Philadelphia: Fortress.
Blass. F., A. Debrunner, and R. Funk
    1961   *A Greek Grammar of the New Testament and Other Early Chris-
            tian Literature*. Chicago: University of Chicago Press.
Boers, Hendrikus
    1980   'Language Usage and the Production of Matthew 1.18-2.23'. In
            *Orientation by Disorientation: Studies in Literary Criticism and
            Biblical Literary Criticism*, pp. 217-34. Ed. Richard A. Spencer.
            PTMS 35. Pittsburgh: Pickwick.
Bornkamm, Günther
    1963   'End-Expectation and Church in Matthew'. In *Tradition and
            Interpretation in Matthew* pp. 15-51. Trans. by Percy Scott. London:
            SCM.
    1963   'The Stilling of the Storm in Matthew'. In G. Bornkamm, G.
            Barth, and H. Held, pp. 52-57. Trans. by Percy Scott. London: SCM.
    1971   'The Risen Lord and the Earthly Jesus: Matthew 28.16-20'. In *The
            Future of our Religous Past*, pp. 203-229. Ed. by J. Robinson. Trans.
            by C.E. Carlston and R.P. Scharlemann. London: SCM.
    1983   'The Authority to "Bind" and "Loose", in the Church in Matthew's
            Gospel: The Problem of Sources in Matthew's Gospel'. In *The
            Interpretation of Matthew*, pp. 85-97. Ed. Granham N. Stanton.
            London: SPCK.
Brooks, Oscar S.
    1985   *The Sermon on the Mount: Authentic Human Values*. Washing-
            ton, DC: University Press of America.
Brown, Raymond
    1977   *The Birth of the Messiah*. London: Geoffrey Chapman.
Brown, Schluyer
    1977   'The Two-Fold Representation of the Mission in Matthew's
            Gospel'. *StT* 31: 21-32.
    1978   'The Mission to Israel in Matthew's Central Section (Mt. 9.35-
            11.1)'. *ZNW* 69: 73-90.
    1979   'Biblical Philology, Linguistics and the Problem of Method'.
            Heythrop Journal 20: 295-98.
    1980   'The Matthean Community and the Gentile Mission'. *NovT* 22: 193-
            221.
Bultmann, Rudolph
    1951-55 *Theology of the New Testament*. Trans. by K. Grobel. New York:
            Scribner's.
    1963   *The History of the Synoptic Tradition*. Trans. by J. Marsh. Oxford:
            Blackwell.

Burger, C.
1973 'Jesu Taten nach Matthäus 8 und 9'. *ZThK* 70: 272-87.
Burnett, Fred W.
1981 *The Testament of Jesus-Sophia: A Redaction-Critical Study of the Eschatological Discourse in Matthew*. Washington, D.C.: University Press of America.
1985 'Prolegomenon to Reading Matthew's Eschatological Discourse: Redundancy and the Education of the Reader in Matthew'. *Semeia* 31: 91-109.
Clark, K.W.
1947 'The Gentile Bias in Saint Matthew'. *JBL* 66: 165-72.
Comber, J.A.
1978 'The Verb *Therapeuo* in Matthew's Gospel'. *JBL* 97: 431-34.
Combrink, H.J. Bernard
1983 'The Structure of Matthew as Narrative'. *Tyndale Bulletin* 34: 61-90.
Comstock, Gary
1986 'Truth or Meaning: Ricoeur versus Frei on Biblical Meaning'. *JR*: 117-40.
Conzelmann, Hans
1959 'Geschichte und Eschaton nach Mc 13'. *ZNW* 50: 210-21.
Cope, O. Lamar
1976 *Matthew: A Scribe Trained for the Kingdom of Heaven*. CBQMS 5. Washington, D.C.: Catholic Biblical Association of America.
Cothenet, E.
1972 'Les Prophètes chrétiens dans l'Évangile selon saint Matthieu', In *L'Évangile selon Matthieu: Rédaction et Théologie*, pp. 281-308. Ed. M. Didier. Gembloux: Duculot.
Cullmann, Oscar
1967 *Salvation in History*. Trans. by S.G. Sowers. London: SCM.
Culpepper, R. Alan
1983 *Anatomy of the Fourth Gospel: A Study in Literary Design*. Philadelphia: Fortress.
1984 'Story and History in the Gospels'. *Review and Expositor* 81: 467-78.
Dahl, Nils A.
1983 'The Passion Narrative in Matthew'. In *The Interpretation of Matthew*, pp. 42-55. Ed. Graham N. Stanton. London: SPCK.
Davies, W.D.
1964 *The Setting of the Sermon on the Mount*. Cambridge: CUP.
Dawsey, James D.
1986 *The Lukan Voice: Confusion and Irony in Luke*. Macon, GA: Mercer.
Deutsch, Celia
1987 *Hidden Wisdom and the Easy Yoke: Wisdom, Torah and Discipleship in Matthew 11.25-30*. JSNT Supplement Series 18. Sheffield: JSOT Press.

Dewey, Joanna
    1980   *Markan Public Debate: Literary Technique, Concentric Structure,
            and Theology in Mark 2.1–3.6.* SBLDS 48. Chico, CA: Scholars
            Press.
Didier, M. ed.
    1972   *L'Évangile selon Matthieu: Rédaction et Théologie.* Gembloux:
            Duculot.
Dillon, R.J.
    1978   *From Eye-Witnesses to Ministers of the Word.* AnaBib 82. Rome:
            Biblical Institute Press.
Dobschütz, Ernst von
    1983   'Matthew as Rabbi and Catechist'. Trans. by Robert C. Morgan. In
            The Interpretation of Matthew, pp. 19-29. Ed. Graham N. Stanton.
            London: SPCK.
Donaldson, Terence L.
    1985   *Jesus on the Mountain: A Study in Matthean Theology.* JSNT
            Supplement Series 8. Sheffield: JSOT Press.
Duke, Paul D.
    1985   *Irony in the Fourth Gospel.* Atlanta: John Knox.
Dunn, James D.G.
    1970   *Baptism in the Holy Spirit.* London: SCM.
Edwards, O.C.
    1977   'Historical-critical Method's Failure of Nerve and a Prescription
            for a Tonic: A Review of Some Recent Literature'. *ATR* 59: 115-34.
Edwards, Richard A.
    1985   *Matthew's Story of Jesus.* Philadelphia: Fortress.
    1985   'Uncertain Faith: Matthew's Portrayal of the Disciples'. In *Disci-
            pleship in the New Testament*, pp. 47-61. Ed. Fernando F. Segovia.
            Philadelphia: Fortress.
Ellis, E. Earl
    1983   'Gospel Criticism: A Perspective on the State of the Art'. In *Das
            Evangelium und die Evangelien*, pp. 27-54. WUNT 28. Ed. Peter
            Stuhlmacher. Tübingen: Mohr.
Fenton, John C.
    1959   'Inclusio and Chiasmus in Matthew'. *Studia Evangelica I. Texte
            und Untersuchungen zur Geschichte der altchristlichen Literatur*
            73, pp. 174-79. Ed. by K. Aland and F.L. Cross. Berlin: Akademie-
            Verlag.
    1963   *The Gospel According to Matthew.* Pelican Gospel Commentaries.
            Harmondsworth: Penguin.
Fitzmyer, J.A.
    1981   *The Gospel According to Luke (I-X).* Anchor Bible, 28. New York:
            Doubleday.
Fowler, Robert A.
    1981   *Loaves and Fishes: The Function of the Feeding Stories in the
            Gospel of Mark.* SBLDS 54. Chico, CA: Scholars.

Frankemölle, Hubert
    1974   *Jahwebund und Kirche Christi: Studien zur Form- und Traditionsgeschichte des 'Evangeliums' nach Matthäus*. NTAbH 10 Münster: Aschendorff.

Frei, Hans W.
    1974   *The Eclipse of Biblical Narrative: A Study in Eighteenth and Nineteenth Century Hermeneutics*. New Haven: Yale University Press.
    1975   *The Identity of Jesus Christ: The Hermeneutical Bases of Dogmatic Theology*. Philadelphia: Fortress.

Frye, Roland M.
    1971   'A Literary Perspective for the Criticism of the Gospels'. In *Jesus and Man's Hope*, Vol. 2, pp. 193-221. Ed. D.G. Miller and D.Y. Hadidian. Pittsburgh: Pittsburgh Theological Seminary.
    1979   'The Jesus of the Gospels: Approaches Through Narrative Structure'. In *From Faith to Faith: Essays in Honor of Donald G. Miller on His Seventieth Birthday*. pp. 75-89. Ed. D.Y. Hadidian. PTMS 31. Pittsburgh: Pickwick.

Funk, Robert
    1966   *Language, Hermeneutic and the Word of God*. London: Harper & Row.

Garland, David
    1979   *The Intention of Matthew 23*. NovTSup. 52. Leiden: Brill.

Gaston, Lloyd
    1975   'The Messiah of Israel as Teacher of the Gentiles'. *Int* 29: 24-40.

Gerhardsson, Birger
    1966   *The Testing of God's Son (Mt 4.1-11): An Analysis of an Early Christian Midrash*. Trans. J. Toy. Lund: Gleerup.
    1973   'Gottes Sohn als Diener Gottes, Messias, Agape, und Himmelsherrschaft nach dem Matthäusevangelium'. *StT* 27: 73-106.
    1976   'The Hermeneutic Progress in Matthew 22.37-40'. In *Jews, Greeks and Christians: Religious Cultures in Late Antiquity*, pp. 129-50. Ed. R. Hamerton-Kelly and R. Scroggs. Leiden: Brill.

Giblin, Charles H.
    1968   'Theological Perspective and Matthew 10,23b'. *ThSt* 29: 637-61.
    1975   'A Note on Doubt and Reassurance in Mt 28.16-20'. *CBQ* 37: 68-75.

Goulder, M.D.
    1974   *Midrash and Lection in Matthew*. London: SPCK.

Grassi, Joseph
    1977   'The Last Testament-Succession Literary Background of Matthew 9.35–11.1 and its Significance'. *BThB* 7: 172-76.

Grayston, K.
    1984   'The Translation of Matthew 28.17'. *JSNT* 21: 105-109.

Green, H.B.
    1968   'The Structure of St. Matthew's Gospel'. In *Studia Evangelica IV. Texte und Untersuchungen zur Geschichte der altchristlichen Literatur* 102, pp. 47-59. Ed. K. Aland and F.L. Cross. Berlin: Akademie.

1975   *The Gospel According to Matthew.* The New Clarendon Bible. Oxford: OUP.

Grobel, Kendrick
     1962   'Biblical Criticism'. In *The Interpreter's Dictionary of the Bible*, Vol. 1, pp. 407-13. Nashville: Abingdon.

Guelich, Robert, A.
     1976   'The Matthean Beatitudes: Entrance-Requirements or Eschatological Blessing?'. *JBL* 95: 415-34.
     1982   *The Sermon on the Mount: A Foundation for Understanding.* Waco, TX: Word.
     1983   'The Gospel Genre'. In *Das Evangelium und die Evangelien*, pp. 183-219. Ed. Peter Stuhlmacher. WUNT 28. Tübingen: Mohr.

Güttgemanns, Erhardt
     1979   *Candid Questions concerning Gospel Form Criticism. A Methodological Sketch of the Fundamental Problematics of Form and Redaction Criticism.* Trans. by W.G. Doty. PTMS 26. Pittsburgh: Pickwick.

Gundry, Robert H.
     1967   *The Use of the Old Testament in St. Matthew's Gospel with Special Reference to the Messianic Hope.* NovTSup 18. Leiden: Brill.
     1982   *Matthew: A Commentary on His Literary and Theological Art.* Grand Rapids: Eerdmans.

Hare, Douglas R.A.
     1967   *The Theme of Jewish Persecution of Christians in the Gospel According to St. Matthew.* SNTSMS 6. Cambridge: CUP.

Hare, Douglas R.A. and Daniel J. Harrington
     1975   ' "Make Disciples of All the Gentiles" (Mt. 28.19)'. *CBQ*: 359-69.

Hartman, Lars
     1972   'Scriptural Exegesis in the Gospel of Matthew and the Problem of Communication'. In *L'Évangile selon Matthieu: Rédaction et Théologie*, pp. 31-52. Ed. M. Didier. Gembloux: Duculot.

Harvey, A.E.
     1981   'Christian Propositions and Christian Stories'. In *God Incarnate: Story and Belief*, pp. 1-13. Ed. A.E. Harvey. London: SPCK.

Hawkins, J.C.
     1899   *Horae Synopticae.* Oxford: Clarendon.

Held, Heinz Joachim
     1963   'Matthew as Interpreter of the Miracle Stories'. In *Tradition and Interpretation in Matthew*, pp. 165-299. Trans. by Percy Scott. London: SCM.

Hendrickx, Herman
     1984   *The Sermon on the Mount.* London: Geoffrey Chapman.

Hengel, Martin
     1973   'Historische Methoden und theologische Auslegung des Neuen Testaments'. *KuD* 19: 85-90.
     1981   *The Charismatic Leader and His Followers.* Trans. by James C.G. Greig. Edinburgh: T & T Clark.

Hill, David
1965   'Δίκαιοι as a Quasi-Technical Term'. *NTS* 11: 296-302.
1972   *The Gospel of Matthew*. The New Century Bible Commentary. London: Marshall, Morgan & Scott.
1976   'False Prophets and Charismatics: Structure and Interpretation in Matthew 7, 15-23'. *Bib* 18: 327-48.
1977   'On the Use and Meaning of Hosea VI, 6 in Matthew's Gospel'. *NTS* 24: 107-19.
1980   'Son and servant: An Essay on Matthean Christology'. *JSNT* 6: 2-16.
1984   'The Figure of Jesus in Matthew's Story: A Response to Professor Kingsbury's Literary Critical Probe'. *JSNT* 21: 37-52.

Hoffmann, P.
1974   'Der Petrus-Primat im Matthäusevangelium'. In *Neues Testament und Kirche*, pp. 94-114. Ed. J. Gnilka. Freiburg: Herder.

Hooker, Morna D.
1971   'The Prohibition of Foreign Missions (Mt. 10.5-6)'. *ExT* 82: 361-65.

Horst, P.W. van der
1986   'Once More: The Translation of οϱ όέ in Matthew 28.17'. *JSNT*: 27-30.

Jacobsen, A.D.
1982   'The Literary Unity of Q'. *JBL* 101: 365-89.
1982   'The Literary Unity of Q: Lk. 10.2-16 and Parallels as a Test Case'. In *Logia*, pp. 419-23. Ed. J. Delobel. Leuven: University Press.

Johnson, Luke T.
1979   'On Finding the Lukan Community: A Cautious Cautionary Essay'. In *SBL 1979 Seminar Papers*. Vol. 1, pp. 87-100. Ed. Paul Achtemeier. Missoula, MT: Scholars Press.

Johnson, Marshall D.
1969   The Purpose of the Biblical Genealogies. *SNTSMS* 8. Cambridge: CUP.
1974   'Reflections on a Wisdom Approach to Matthew's Christology'. *CBQ* 36: 44-64.

Käsemann, Ernst
1969   'Blind Alleys in the "Jesus of History" Controversy'. In *New Testament Questions of Today*, pp. 23-65. Trans. by W.J. Montague. London: SCM.

Karris, Robert J.
1985   *Luke: Artist and Theologian*. New York: Paulist.

Kea, Perry V.
1986   'The Sermon the Mount: Ethics and Eschatology'. *SBL* 1986 Seminar Papers, pp. 88-98. Ed. K.H. Richards. Atlanta: Scholars.

Keck, Leander E.
1980   'Will the Historical Method Survive? Some Observations'. In *Orientation by Disorientation: Studies in Literary Criticism and Biblical Literary Criticism*, pp. 115-28. Ed. Richard A. Spencer. PTMS 35. Pittsburgh: Pickwick.

Keegan, Terence J.
    1982   'Introductory Formulae for Matthean Discourses'. *CBQ* 44: 415-30.
    1985   *Interpreting the Bible: A Popular Introduction to Biblical Hermeneutics.* New York: Paulist.

Kelber, Werner
    1985   'Apostolic Tradition and the Form of the Gospel'. In *Discipleship in the New Testament*, pp. 24-46. Ed. Fernando F. Segovia. Philadelphia: Fortress.

Kennedy, George A.
    1984   *New Testament Interpretation through Rhetorical Criticism.* Chapel Hill, NC: University of North Carolina Press.

Kilpatrick, G.D.
    1946   *The Origins of the Gospel According to Matthew.* Oxford: Clarendon.

Kingsbury, Jack D.
    1969   *The Parables of Jesus in Matthew 13.* London: SPCK.
    1976   *Matthew: Structure, Christology, Kingdom.* London: SPCK.
    1978   *Matthew. A Commentary for Preachers and Others.* London: SPCK.
    1978   'Observations on the "Miracle Chapters" of Matthew 8-9'. CBQ 40: 559-73.
    1978   'The Verb *Akolouthein* ("To Follow") as an Index of Matthew's View of His Community'. *JBL* 97: 56-73.
    1979   'The Figure of Peter in Matthew's Gospel as a Theological Problem'. *JBL* 98 : 67-83.
    1981   *Jesus Christ in Matthew, Mark and Luke.* Philadelphia: Fortress.
    1983   'The Theology of St. Matthew's Gospel According to the Griesbach Hypothesis'. In *New Synoptic Studies*, pp. 331-61. Ed. W.R. Farmer. Macon, GA: Mercer University Press.
    1984   'The Figure of Jesus in Matthew's Story: A Literary-Critical Probe'. *JSNT* 21: 3-36.
    1985   'The Figure of Jesus in Matthew's Story: A Rejoinder to David Hill'. *JSNT* 25: 61-85.
    1986   *Matthew as Story.* Philadelphia: Fortress.
    1986   'The Parable of the Wicked Husbandmen and the Secret of Jesus' Divine Sonship in Matthew'. *JBL* 105: 643-55.
    1987   'The Developing Conflict between Jesus and the Jewish Leaders in Matthew's Gospel: A Literary-Critical Study'. *CBQ* 49: 57-73.
    1987   'The Place, Structure and Meaning of the Sermon on the Mount Within Matthew'. *Int* 41: 131-43.
    1988   'On Following Jesus: The "Eager" Scribe and the "Reluctant" Disciple'. *NTS* 34: 45-59.
    1988   'Reflections on "The Reader" of Matthew's Gospel'. *NTS* 34: 442-60.

Koch, Klaus
    1969   *The Growth of the Biblical Tradition. The Form Critical Method.* Trans. S.M. Cupitt. New York: Scribner's.

Kretzer, Armin
  1971 *Die Herrschaft der Himmel und die Söhne des Reiches*. Stuttgarter biblische Monographien 10. Stuttgart: KBW Verlag.
Krentz, Edgar
  1963 'The Extent of Matthew's Prologue'. *JBL* 83: 409-414.
Kümmel, W.G.
  1975 *Introduction to the New Testament*. Trans. by H.C. Kee. Rev. edn, London: SCM.
Kurz, William S.
  1987 'Narrative Approaches to Luke-Acts'. *Bib* 68: 195-220.
Lategan, B.C.
  1977 'Structural Interrelations in Matthew 11-12'. *Neotestamentica* 11: 115-29.
  1982 'Structure and Reference in Mt 23'. *Neotestamentica* 16: 74-87.
  1984 'Current Issues in the Hermeneutical Debate'. *Neotestamentica* 18: 1-17.
  1985 and Vorster, W.S. *Text and Reality: Aspects of Reference in Biblical Texts*. Semeia Series. Philadelphia: Fortress.
Linmans, A., and B. van Iersel
  1978 ' "The storm on the lake" Mk iv 35-41 and Mt viii 18-27 in the Light of Form Criticism, "Redaktionsgeschichte" and Structural Analysis'. In *Miscellanea Neotestamentica*, Vol. 2, pp. 17-48. Ed. T. Baarda, A.F.J. Klijn, and W.C. Van Unnik. NovTSup 48, Leiden: Brill.
Loader, W.R.G.
  1982 'Son of David, Blindness, Possession, and Duality in Matthew'. *CBQ* 44: 570-85.
Lohmeyer, Ernst
  1958 *Das Evangelium Matthäus*. Ed. by W. Schmauch. 2nd edn. Göttingen: Vandenhoeck & Ruprecht.
Lohr, Charles H.
  1961 'Oral Techniques in the Gospel of Matthew'. *CBQ* 23: 403-35.
Louw, J.P.
  1977 'The Structure of Mt. 8.1–9.35'. *Neotestamentica* 11: 91-97.
Luz, Ulrich
  1983 'The Disciples in the Gospel according to Matthew'. Trans. by Robert C. Morgan. In *The Interpretation of Matthew*, pp. 98-128. Ed. Graham N. Stanton. London: SPCK.
  1985 *Das Evangelium nach Matthäus (Mt. 1-7)*. EKK I/1. Neukirchen: Neukirchener Verlag.
Luz, Ulrich and Peter Lampe
  1983 'Diskussionsüberblick'. In *Das Evangelium und die Evangelien*, pp. 413-31. Ed. Peter Stuhlmacher. WUNT 28. Tübingen: Mohr.
McEleney, Neil J.
  1981 'The Beatitudes of the Sermon on the Mount/Plain'. *CBQ* 43: 1-13.
McKay, K.L.
  1985 'The Use of *hoi de* in Matthew 28.17d: A Response to K. Grayston'. *JSNT* 24: 71-72.

McKnight, Edgar V.

1980   'The Contours and Methods of Literary Criticism'. In *Orientation by Disorientation: Studies in Literary Criticism and Biblical Literary Criticism*, pp. 53-70. Ed. Richard A. Spencer. PTMS 35. Pittsburgh: Pickwick.

1985   *The Bible and the Reader: An Introduction to Literary Criticism.* Philadelphia: Fortress.

1988   *Post-Modern Use of the Bible: The Emergence of Reader-Oriented Criticism.* Nashville: Abingdon.

McNeile, A.H.

1911   '*Tote* in St Matthew'. *JTS* 12: 127-28.

Magness, J.L.

1986   *Sense and Absence: Structure and Suspension in the Ending of Mark's Gospel.* Semeia Studies. Atlanta: Scholars.

Malbon, Elizabeth Struthers

1986   'Disciples/Crowds/Whoever: Markan Characters and Readers'. *NovT* 28: 104-30.

Malina, Bruce and Neyrey, Jerome H.

1988   *Calling Jesus Names: The Social Value of Labels in Matthew.* Sonoma, CA: Polebridge.

Marshall, I. Howard, ed.

1977   *New Testament Interpretation: Essays on Principles and Methods.* Exeter: Paternoster.

1983   'Luke and His Gospel'. In *Das Evangelium und die Evangelien*, pp. 289-308. Ed. Peter Stuhlmacher. WUNT 28. Tübingen: Mohr.

Martin, James

1975   'The Church in Matthew'. *Int* 29: 41-56.

Marxsen, Willi

1968   *Introduction to the New Testament.* Trans. by G. Buswell. Oxford: Blackwell.

1969   *Mark the Evangelist: Studies on the Redaction History of the Gospel.* Trans. by Roy Harrisville *et al.* Nashville: Abingdon.

Matera, Frank J.

1986   *Passion Narratives and Gospel Theologies: Interpreting the Synoptics Through Their Passion Stories.* New York: Paulist.

1987   'The Plot of Matthew's Gospel'. *CBQ* 49: 233-53.

Michel, Otto

1983   'The Conclusion of Matthew's Gospel'. Trans. by Robert C. Morgan. In *The Interpretation of Matthew*, pp. 30-41. Ed. Graham N. Stanton. London: SPCK.

Meier, John P.

1980   'John the Baptist in Matthew's Gospel'. *JBL* 99: 383-405.

1976   *Law and History in Matthew's Gospel.* AnaBib 71. Rome: Biblical Institute Press.

1979   *The Vision of Matthew: Christ, Church and Morality in the First Gospel.* New York: Paulist.

Minear, Paul S.
 1974 'The Disciples and the Crowds in the Gospel of Matthew'. *ATR Supplementary Series* 3: 28-44.
 1984 *Matthew: The Teacher's Gospel*. London: Darton, Longman & Todd.

Moore, Stephen D.
 1987 'Are the Gospels Unified Narratives?' *SBL* 1987 Seminar Papers, pp. 443-58. Ed. K.H. Richards, Atlanta: Scholars.
 1988 'Stories of Reading: Doing Gospel Criticism As/With a "Reader"'. *SBL 1988 Seminar Papers*, pp. 141-59. Ed. David J. Lull. Atlanta: Scholars.

Moule, C.F.D.
 1967 'Fulfillment Words in the New Testament: Use and Abuse'. *NTS* 14: 293-320.

Nations, Archie L.
 1983 'Historical Criticism and the Current Methodological Crisis'. *ScJTh* 36: 59-71.

Neirynck, F.
 1988 'ΑΠΟ ΤΟΤΕ ΗΡΞΑΤΟ and the Structure of Matthew'. *ETL* 64: 21-59.

Nicol, W.
 1977 'The Structure of Matthew Seven'. *Neotestamentica* 11: 77-90.

Nolan, Brian M.
 1979 *The Royal Son of God: The Christology of Matthew 1-2 in the Setting of the Gospel*. Orbis Biblicus et Orientalis 23. Göttingen: Vandehoeck & Ruprecht.

O'Day, Gail R.
 1986 'Narrative Mode and Theological Claim: A Study in the Fourth Gospel'. *JBL* 105: 657-68.
 1986 *Revelation in the Fourth Gospel: Narrative Mode and Theological Claim*. Philadelphia: Fortress.

Pamment, Margaret
 1981 'The Kingdom of Heaven in the Gospel according to Matthew'. *NTS* 27: 211-32.

Parsons, Mikeal C.
 1987 *The Departure of Jesus in Luke–Acts. The Ascension Narratives in Context*. JSNT Supplement Series 21. Sheffield: JSOT Press.

Patte, Daniel
 1976 *What is Structural Exegesis? Guides to Biblical Scholarship*. Philadelphia: Fortress.
 1987 *The Gospel According to Matthew: A Structural Commentary on Matthew's Faith*. Philadelphia: Fortress.

Pesch, Rudolph
 1967 'Eine altestamentliche Ausführungsformel im Matthäusevangelium: Redaktionsgeschichtliche und exegetische Beobachtungen'. *BZ* 10 (1966): 220-45, and 11: 78-85.

Petersen, Norman
 1974 'On the Notion of Genre'. *Semeia* 1: 134-81.

1978   *Literary Criticism for New Testament Critics*. Guides to Biblical Scholarship. Philadelphia: Fortress.
1978   'Point of View in Mark's Narrative'. *Semeia* 12: 97-121.
1980   'Literary Criticism in Biblical Studies'. In *Orientation by Disorientation: Studies in Literary Criticism and Biblical Literary Criticism*, pp. 25-52. Ed. Richard A. Spencer. PTMS 35. Pittsburgh: Pickwick.
1980   'When is the end not the End? Literary Reflections of the Ending of Mark's Narrative'. *Int* 34: 151-66.
1984   'The Reader in the Gospel'. *Neotestamentica* 18: 38-51.
1985   *Rediscovering Paul. Philemon and the Sociology of Paul's Narrative World*. Philadelphia: Fortress.

Perrin, Norman
1972   'The Evangelist as Author: Reflection on Method in the Study and Interpretation of the Synoptic Gospels and Acts'. *Biblical Research* 17: 5-18.
1976   'The Interpretation of the Gospel of Mark'. *Int* 30: 115-24.

Phillips, Gary A.
1985   'History and Text: The Reader in Context in Matthew's Parables Discourse'. *Semeia* 31: 111-38.

Poland, Lynn M.
1985   *Literary Criticism and Biblical Hermeneutics: A Critique of Formalist Approaches*. AAR Academy Series 48. Chico, CA: Scholars Press.

Polzin, Robert A.
1980   'Literary and Historical Criticism of the Bible: A Crisis in Scholarship'. In *Orientation by Disorientation: Studies in Literary Criticism and Biblical Literary Criticism*, pp. 99-114. Ed. Richard A. Spencer. PTMS 35. Pittsburgh: Pickwick.

Przbylski, Benno
1974   'The Role of Mt. 3.12–4.11 in the Structure and Theology of the Gospel of Matthew'. *BThB* 4: 222-35.
1980   *Righteousness in Matthew and His World of Thought*. SNTSMS 41. Cambridge: CUP.

Radermakers, J.
1972   *Au fil de l'Évangile selon saint Matthieu*. Heverlee-Louvain: Institut d'Études Théologiques.

Rengstorf, K.
1960   'Die Stadt der Mörder (Mt 22, 7)'. In *Judentum, Urchristentum, Kirche*, pp. 106-29. Berlin: Töpelmann.

Resseguie, James L.
1984   'Reader-Response Criticism and the Synoptic Gospels'. *JAAR* 52: 307-24.

Reventlow, Henning Graf
1985   *Problems of Old Testament Theology in the Twentieth Century*. Trans. by John Bowden. London: SCM.

Rhoads, David and Donald Michie

    1982   *Mark as Story: An Introduction to the Narrative of a Gospel.* Philadelphia: Fortress.

Rhoads, David

    1982   'Narrative Criticism and the Gospel of Mark'. *JAAR* 50: 411-34.

Robbins, Vernon K.

    1984   *Jesus the Teacher: A Socio-Rhetorical Interpretation of Mark.* Philadelphia: Fortress.

Sabourin, Leopold

    1977   'The Coming of the Son of Man (Mt. 10.23b)'. *BThB* 7: 5-11.

    1982   *The Gospel According to St. Matthew.* 2 Vols. Bombay: St. Paul.

Sand, A.

    1974   *Das Gesetz und die Propheten: Untersuchungen zur Theologie des Evangeliums nach Matthäus.* Biblische Untersuchungen 11. Regensburg: Pustet.

Scott, Bernard Brandon

    1985   'The King's Accounting: Matthew 18.23-34'. *JBL* 104: 429-42.

    1985   *The Word of God in Words: Reading and Preaching.* Philadelphia: Fortress.

Schenk, Wolfgang

    1976   'Das Präsens historicum als makrosyntaktische Gliederungssignal im Matthäusevangelium'. *NTS* 22 : 464-75.

Schlatter, A.

    1929   *Der Evangelist Matthäus.* Stuttgart: Calwer.

Schweizer, Eduard

    1970   'Observation of the Law and Charismatic Activity in Matthew. *NTS* 16: 213-30.

    1974   *Matthäus und seine Kirche.* SBS 71. Stuttgart: KBW Verlag.

    1976   *The Good News According to Matthew.* Trans. by D. Green. London: SPCK, 1976.

    1983   'Matthew's Church'. Trans. by Robert C. Morgan. In *The Interpretation of Matthew*, pp. 129-55. Ed. Graham N. Stanton. London: SPCK.

Segovia, Fernando F., ed.

    1985   *Discipleship in the New Testament.* Philadelphia: Fortress.

Senior, Donald

    1976   'The Death of Jesus and the Resurrection of the Holy Ones (Mt. 27.51-53)'. *CBQ* 38: 312-29.

    1983   *What are They Saying about Matthew?* New York: Paulist.

Senior, Donald, and Stuhlmueller, Carroll

    1983   *The Biblical Foundations for Mission.* London: SCM.

    1985   *The Passion of Jesus in the Gospel of Matthew.* Wilmington, Del.: Michael Glazier.

Sheridan, Mark

    1973   'Disciples and Discipleship in Matthew and Luke'. *BThB* 3: 235-55.

Shuler, Philip L.

    1982   *A Genre for the Gospels: The Biographical Character of Matthew.* Philadelphia: Fortress.

Soares Prabhu, G.M.
    1976   *The Formula Quotations in the Infancy Narrative of Matthew*. AnaBib 63. Rome: Biblical Institute Press.
Spencer, Richard A., ed.
    1980   *Orientation by Disorientation: Studies in Literary Criticism and Biblical Literary Criticism*. PTMS 35. Pittsburgh: Pickwick.
Stanton, Graham N.
    1974   *Jesus of Nazareth in New Testament Preaching*. SNTSMS 27 Cambridge: CUP.
    1982   'Salvation Proclaimed: Matthew 11.28-30'. *ExT* 94: 3-9.
    1983   ed. *The Interpretation of Matthew*. London: SPCK.
    1983   'Matthew as a Creative Interpreter of the Sayings of Jesus'. In *Das Evangelium und die Evangelien*, pp. 273-87. Ed. Peter Stuhlmacher. WUNT 28. Tübingen: Mohr.
    1983   'The Origin and Purpose of Matthew's Gospel: Matthean Scholarship from 1945-1980'. In *Aufstieg und Niedergang der römischen Welt*, II, 25, 3. Ed. H. Temporini and W. Haase, pp. 1889-1951. Berlin: Walter de Gruyter.
    1984   'The Gospel of Matthew and Judaism'. *BJRL* 66: 264-84.
Stendhal, Krister
    1962   'Biblical Theology, Contemporary'. In *The Interpreter's Dictionary of the Bible*, Vol. 1, pp. 418-31. Nashville: Abingdon.
    1967   'Matthew' In *Peake's Commentary on the Bible*. Ed. M. Black and H.H. Rowley. London: Nelson.
    1968   *The School of St. Matthew*. 2nd edn. Philadelphia: Fortress.
    1983   'Quis et Unde? An Analysis of Matthew 1-2'. In *The Interpretation of Matthew*, pp. 56-66. Ed. Graham N. Stanton. London: SPCK.
    1984   'The Bible as a Classic and the Bible as Holy Scripture'. *JBL* 103: 3-10.
Stock, Augustine
    1982   *Call to Discipleship A Literary Study of Mark's Gospel*. Good News Studies 1. Wilmington, DEL: Michael Glazier
Strecker, Georg
    1962   *Der Weg der Gerechtigkeit*. FRLANT 82. Göttingen: Vandenhoeck & Ruprecht.
    1983   'The Concept of History in Matthew'. In *The Interpretation of Matthew*, pp. 67-84. Ed. Graham N. Stanton. London: SPCK.
Stroup, George W.
    1984   *The Promise of Narrative Theology*. London: SCM.
Suggs, M.J.
    1970   *Wisdom, Christology and Law in Matthew's Gospel*. Cambridge, MA: Harvard University Press.
Tagawa, Kenzo
    1969-70 'People and Community in the Gospel of Matthew'. *NTS* 16: 149-62.
Talbert, Charles H.
    1977   *What is a Gospel? The Genre of the Canonical Gospels*. Philadelphia: Fortress.

Tannehill, Robert C.
  1975   *The Sword of His Mouth*. Semeia Supplements. Philadelphia:
         Fortress.
  1977   'The Disciples in Mark: The Function of a Narrative Role'. *JR* 57:
         386-405.
  1979   'The Gospel of Mark as Narrative Christology'. *Semeia* 16: 57-95.
  1980   'Tension in Synoptic Sayings and Stories'. *Int* 34: 138-50.
  1986   *The Narrative Unity of Luke-Acts: A Literary Interpretation. Vol.*
         One: The Gospel According to Luke. Philadelphia: Fortress.
Theissen, Gerd
  1983   *Miracle Stories of the Early Christian Tradition*. Trans. by F.
         McDonagh. Edinburgh: T & T Clark.
Thiemann, Roland F.
  1985   *Revelation and Theology: The Gospel as Narrated Promise*. Notre
         Dame, Ind.: University of Notre Dame Press.
Thiselton, Anthony C.
  1977   'The New Hermeneutic'. In *New Testament Interpretation:*
         Essays on Principles and Methods, pp. 308-33. Ed. I. Howard Mar-
         shall. Exeter: Paternoster.
  1980   *The Two Horizons: New Testament Hermeneutics and Philosophi-*
         cal Description with Special Reference to Heidegger, Bultmann,
         Gadamer, and Wittgenstein. Exeter: Paternoster.
Thompson, G.H.P.
  1960   'Called-Proved-Obedient: A Study in the Baptism and Temptation
         Narratives of Matthew and Luke'. *JTS* 11: 1-12.
Thompson, William G.
  1970   *Matthew's Advice to a Divided Community: Mt. 17,22-18,35.*
         AnaBib 44. Rome: Biblical Institute Press.
Toit, A.B. du
  1977   'Analysis of the Structure of Mt 4.23–5.48'. *Neotestamentica* 11: 32-
         47.
Trilling, Wolfgang
  1964   *Das wahre Israel: Studien zur Theologie des Matthäus-Evangeli-*
         ums. SANT 10. 3rd edn. Munich: Kösel-Verlag.
  1969   *The Gospel According to St. Matthew*. NT for Spiritual Reading 1.
         London: Sheed & Ward.
Tuckett, Christopher M.
  1983   *The Revival of the Griesbach Hypothesis: An Analysis and*
         Appraisal. SNTSMS 44. Cambridge: CUP.
  1987   *Reading the New Testament: Methods of Interpretation*. London:
         SPCK.
Tyson, J.B.
  1983   'Conflict as a Literary Theme in the Gospel of Luke'. In *New Syn-*
         optic Studies, pp. 307-27. Ed. W.R. Farmer. Macon, GA: Mercer
         University Press.
Van Segbroeck, Frans
  1972   'Les citations d'accomplissement dans l'Évangile selon Matthieu
         d'après trois ouvrages récents'. In *L'Évangile selon Matthieu:*

Rédaction et Théologie, pp. 107-30. Ed. M. Didier. Gembloux: Duculot.

Van Tilborg, Sjef
  1972   *The Jewish Leaders in Matthew*. Leiden: Brill.

Vorster, W.S.
  1983   'Kerygma/History and the Gospel Genre'. *NTS* 29: 87-95.
  1984   'The Historical Paradigm—Its Possibilities and Limitations'. *Neotestamentica* 18: 104-23.

Waetjen, Herman C.
  1976   'The Genealogy as the Key to the Gospel According to Matthew'. *JBL* 95: 205-30.

Walker, Rolf
  1967   *Die Heilsgeschichte im ersten Evangelium*. FRLANT 91. Göttingen: Vandenhoeck & Ruprecht.

Wilder, Amos N.
  1971   *Early Christian Rhetoric: The Language of the Gospel*. Cambridge, MA: Harvard University Press.

Wink, Walter
  1973   *The Bible in Human Transformation*. Philadelphia: Fortress.

Zumstein, Jean
  1977   *La Condition du croyant dans l'évangile selon Matthieu*. Orbis Biblicus et Orientalis 16. Göttingen: Vandenhoeck & Ruprecht.

INDEX

INDEX OF BIBLICAL REFERENCES

OLD TESTAMENT

NEW TESTAMENT

27.6-8	103	28.16ff.	125, 146
27.6	214	28.16-20	113, 171,
27.8	166, 212		225, 226,
27.9-10	186		246, 256,
27.9ff.	156		258
27.11	201, 241	28.16	158, 183
27.15-25	143	28.17	217, 226,
27.15ff.	123		256, 257
27.15	166, 214	28.18-20	227
27.18	175, 177,	28.19-20	102, 217
	181, 182,	28.19	222, 234
	215	28.20	77, 82,
27.19	157, 252		84, 103,
27.20ff.	156, 184		104, 106,
27.25	103, 157		109, 121,
27.27ff.	102, 241		143, 153,
27.29	201		226, 231,
27.33	179, 180,		258
	214		
27.39	241	*Mark*	
27.40	126, 146,	2.1–3.6	33
	241	4	26
27.41-43	157	4.35-41	21
27.41	242	12.41ff.	153
27.42	241	13	107
27.43	146		
27.46	179, 180,	*Luke*	
	214	1.14	162, 228
27.50	157	4.18-19	220
27.51-53	126	4.21	220
27.54	158	10.2-16	137
27.55-56	183	18.31	220
27.55	158	21.1ff.	153
27.57ff.	158	24	228
27.61	183	24.25ff.	220
27.62ff.	158	24.44ff.	220
27.64	242	24.50-52	228
28	158		
28.1-10	256	*John*	
28.7ff.	158, 183	1.14	228
28.9-10	171	1.16	228
28.9	183	20.31	162, 228
28.11ff.	158	21.24-25	228
28.11-15	103, 177,	21.25	162
	242		
28.15ff.	185	*Acts*	
28.15	158, 166,	1	228
	213	1.1	162

INDEX OF AUTHORS

JOURNAL FOR THE STUDY OF THE NEW TESTAMENT
Supplement Series

DATE DUE

NOV 3 0 '90	DEC 1 2 2002
DEC 15 '91	DEC 1 2 2002 APR 0 9 2004
JAN 1 3 '92	
MAR 1 1 1992	
NOV 9 - 1992	
JUN 1 7 1993	
JUL 2 '95	
APR 1 9 1995	
NOV 2 7 1995	
MAR 1 7 2000 MAY 7 2001	
DEC 2 9 2001	
OCT 1 3 2002	